The Focus on the Family®
Parents' Guide to Teen Health

FOCUS ON THE FAMILY®

PARENTS' GUIDE TO

Teen Health

Raising Physically & Emotionally Healthy Teens

THE FOCUS ON THE FAMILY PHYSICIANS RESOURCE COUNCIL, U.S.A.™

PRIMARY AUTHOR:
Paul C. Reisser, M.D.

MANAGING EDITOR:
Melissa R. Cox

EDITORS:
Vinita Hampton Wright
Lisa A. Jackson

Tyndale House Publishers, Inc.
WHEATON, ILLINOIS

The information contained in this book provides a general overview of many health-related topics. It is not intended to substitute for advice you might receive from your child's physician, whether by telephone or during a direct medical evaluation. Furthermore, health-care practices are continually updated as a result of medical research and advances in technology. You should therefore check with your child's doctor if there is any question about current recommendations for a specific problem. No book can substitute for a direct assessment of your child by a qualified health-care professional.

Visit Tyndale's exciting Web site at www.tyndale.com

Copyright © 1997 by Focus on the Family. All rights reserved. International copyright secured.

Focus on the Family is a registered trademark of Focus on the Family, Colorado Springs, Colorado.

www.family.org

Scripture quotations are taken from the *Holy Bible,* New International Version®. NIV®. Copyright © 1973, 1978, 1984 by International Bible Society. Used by permission of Zondervan Publishing House. All rights reserved.

Photographs copyright © 2001 by Jim Whitmer. All rights reserved.

Edited by Vinita Hampton Wright and Lisa A. Jackson.

Designed by Zandrah Maguigad

Library of Congress Cataloging-in-Publication Data

Reisser, Paul C.
  Parents' guide to teen health / primary author, Paul C. Reisser; editors, Vinita Hampton Wright, Lisa A. Jackson.
    p. ; cm.
  ISBN 0-8423-5413-1
  1. Teenagers. 2. Parenting. 3. Parent and teemager. 4. Adolescent psychology. 5. Teen-agers—Health and hygiene.
  [DNLM: 1: Adolescent Behavior. 2. Adolescent Psychology. 3. Christianity. 4. Parenting. WS 462 R3783p 2001] I. Title: At head of title: Focus on the family. II. Wright, Vinita Hampton, date. III. Jackson, Lisa A. IV. Focus on the Famioly (Organization) V. Title.
HQ796.R39 2001
649¢.125—dc21   2001003510

Printed in the United States

07 06 05 04 03 02 01
 7   6   5   4   3   2   1

Table of Contents

Foreword
by Dr. James Dobson

Under the best of circumstances, raising teenagers is a challenging assignment. As a parent you will at one time or another be called on to don a whole wardrobe of hats, among them teacher, doctor, psychologist, friend, and pharmacist. As you contemplate the challenges ahead, you may feel overwhelmed by the responsibility. How can you nurture healthy self-esteem in your adolescents? How can you teach them to protect themselves from unhealthy ideas, attitudes, habits, and associations? How can you build within them discernment and self-discipline? How can you develop in them, day by day, the values that are so basic to their well-being? And—one of the toughest questions of all—how can you guide them into independence until they themselves are walking with God in wisdom and truth, rather than simply following you?

The most discerning, vigilant, and competent parents ultimately find themselves feeling inadequate to accomplish these important tasks. A parent must have support, guidance, and encouragement—from other parents, from friends and family, from physicians and pastors. And we believe that, ultimately, each child must be entrusted to the care, love, and protection of Jesus Christ. I urge you not to shortchange your teen by underestimating the importance of biblical precepts—either in the values you teach or in the way you conduct your own life. The stakes are simply too high.

Here at Focus on the Family, we recognize that parenting an adolescent involves the care and nurture of the whole person—body, mind, *and* soul. That's why I'm particularly excited to be able to introduce to you this wonderful new offering from Tyndale House Publishers, *The Focus on the Family Parents' Guide to Teen Health*. This comprehensive, well-researched volume offers detailed advice from more than fifty of the country's most highly respected physicians and medical authorities. Some have appeared as guests on the *Focus on the Family* broadcast, and many are members of Focus's prestigious Physicians Resource Council. This book is full of practical, specific guidance on every aspect of raising adolescents—from the early stages of puberty through the young adult years.

And what truly sets this book apart from so many others in the genre is that woven throughout its pages you will find countless helpful hints for instilling in teens the timeless truths of Scripture—and the foundation of faith upon which rests our ultimate hope and salvation.

You yourself may have gotten a rough start in life. You may not have received the nurturing and encouragement you deserved as a teenager. Maybe you've struggled with issues of low self-esteem and feelings of rejection from your own parents. If that's your story, my heart goes out to you. But here's the good news: Starting here, starting now, you *can* do right by your own child. It begins with dedicating yourself and your teen to the care of the only truly perfect parent—the Lord Jesus Christ.

You have been charged by God with a profound and sacred trust: preparing your adolescent to become a godly, independent man or woman. Handle it with care. God bless you!

James Dobson

Acknowledgments

In many ways, the preparation of this book has resembled the process of parenting a child from infancy to adulthood. Our "baby" was born in enthusiastic brainstorming sessions, during which exciting and formidable proposals were set in motion. During the book's infancy, as the first chapters and reference topics were written, we slowly began to appreciate the amount of time, effort, and patience that would be required before our "young adult" would be ready to meet the world.

But there was no turning back. We eventually hit our stride over a period of months as more chapters and topics were written, reviewed, debated, revised, and reviewed again—often as many as nine or ten times over the course of several months. Our "child" grew and matured and received ongoing prayer, loving attention, and correction until another rite of passage arrived: an "adolescence" of sorts, when hundreds of pages of manuscript were presented to Tyndale House Publishers. More questions, suggestions, and insights from Tyndale's team led to further refinements, sometimes after spirited (but inevitably fruitful) discussions.

Finally graduation day has arrived, and our offspring is now vacating the nest and beginning an independent life, one that we pray will enhance and assist your family.

This project is the result of a diligent and cooperative effort of many talented individuals over a period of nearly three years. To all of them we are deeply indebted. While we cannot fully acknowledge the full length and breadth of their contributions, the following is our attempt to give credit where it is most certainly due.

First of all, a standing ovation is due to the members of the Physicians Resource Council review team, who spent endless hours in conference calls and many days in sometimes cramped quarters reviewing literally every letter of the manuscript. We thank you for your dedication, perseverance, patience, professionalism, and commitment.

THE FOCUS ON THE FAMILY
PHYSICIANS RESOURCE COUNCIL REVIEW TEAM
AND CONTRIBUTING EDITORS

Marilyn Maxwell Billingsly, M.D.
INTERNAL MEDICINE/PEDIATRICS—
ST. LOUIS, MISSOURI

Douglas O. W. Eaton, M.D.
*INTERNAL MEDICINE—*ATHENS, ALABAMA

J. Thomas Fitch, M.D.
*PEDIATRICS—*SAN ANTONIO, TEXAS

Patricia O. Francis, M.D.
*PEDIATRICS—*MORAGA, CALIFORNIA

Gaylen M. Kelton, M.D.
*FAMILY MEDICINE—*INDIANAPOLIS, INDIANA

Richard D. Kiovsky, M.D.
*FAMILY MEDICINE—*INDIANAPOLIS, INDIANA

Robert W. Mann, M.D.
*PEDIATRICS—*ARLINGTON, TEXAS

Paul Meier, M.D.
*PSYCHIATRY—*RICHARDSON, TEXAS

Mary Anne Nelson, M.D.
*FAMILY MEDICINE—*CEDAR RAPIDS, IOWA

The remaining members of the Focus on the Family Physicians Resource Council, in both the United States and Canada, also contributed to this project in a variety of ways.

UNITED STATES

John P. Livoni, M.D. (chair)
RADIOLOGY—SACRAMENTO, CALIFORNIA

Peter F. Armstrong, M.D.
ORTHOPEDICS—SALT LAKE CITY, UTAH

Reed Bell, M.D.
PEDIATRICS—GULF BREEZE, FLORIDA

Robb Blackwood, M.D.
FAMILY MEDICINE—CHESAPEAKE, VIRGINIA

Eugene Diamond, M.D.
PEDIATRICS—CHICAGO, ILLINOIS

Thomas E. Elkins, M.D.
OBSTETRICS/GYNECOLOGY—BALTIMORE, MARYLAND

W. David Hager, M.D.
OBSTETRICS/GYNECOLOGY—LEXINGTON, KENTUCKY

Walter Larimore, M.D.
FAMILY MEDICINE—KISSIMMEE, FLORIDA

Alan A. Nelson, M.D.
PSYCHIATRY—REDSTONE, COLORADO

Claudia Nelson, M.D.
PEDIATRICS—REDSTONE, COLORADO

Donald Nelson, M.D.
FAMILY MEDICINE—CEDAR RAPIDS, IOWA

Jeffrey B. Satinover, M.D.
PSYCHIATRY—WESTON, CONNECTICUT

Curtis Stine, M.D.
FAMILY MEDICINE—DENVER, COLORADO

Morton Woolley, M.D.
GENERAL SURGEON—LOS ANGELES, CALIFORNIA

CANADA

Margaret Cottle, M.D. (chair)
PALLIATIVE CARE—VANCOUVER, BRITISH COLUMBIA

Ron Calderisi, M.D.
GENERAL SURGEON—VANCOUVER, BRITISH COLUMBIA

Stephen Genuis, M.D.
OBSTETRICS/GYNECOLOGY—EDMONTON, ALBERTA

Jim Gilbert, M.D.
GENERAL SURGEON—PEMBROKE, ONTARIO

Rosemarie Gilbert, M.D.
FAMILY MEDICINE—PEMBROKE, ONTARIO

Ron Jarvis, M.D.
FAMILY MEDICINE—DUNCAN, BRITISH COLUMBIA

Tim Kelton, M.D.
FAMILY MEDICINE—NORTH YORK, ONTARIO

Peter Nieman, M.D.
PEDIATRICS—CALGARY, ALBERTA

Dickson Vinden, M.D.
FAMILY MEDICINE—CANNINGTON, ONTARIO

Peter Webster, M.D.
RESPIRATORY MEDICINE—TORONTO, ONTARIO

In addition to the members of the Physicians Resource Council, we would like to thank the many contributors who provided research, written material, and reviews of topics in their field of expertise:

Jane Anderson, M.D.
PEDIATRICS—SAN FRANCISCO, CALIFORNIA

Karl Anderson, M.D.
UROLOGY—SAN FRANCISCO, CALIFORNIA

Brian L. Burke Jr., M.D.
PEDIATRICS—GRAND RAPIDS, MICHIGAN

Robin Cottle, M.D.
OPHTHALMOLOGY—VANCOUVER, BRITISH COLUMBIA

Sarah Chandler, M.D.
FAMILY MEDICINE—LUBBOCK, TEXAS

M. C. Culberston Jr., M.D.
PEDIATRIC OTOLARYNGOLOGY—DALLAS, TEXAS

William G. Culver, M.D.
ALLERGY-IMMUNOLOGY—LOVELAND, COLORADO

Joyce Fischer, M.D.
PEDIATRICS—BLUFFTON, INDIANA

Russell Engevik, M.D.
EMERGENCY MEDICINE—JULIAN, CALIFORNIA

Linda Flower, M.D.
FAMILY MEDICINE—TOMBALL, TEXAS

Lawrence P. Frick, M.D.
FAMILY MEDICINE—CHILLICOTHE, OHIO

Stanley Hand, M.D.
OPHTHALMOLOGY—ORLANDO, FLORIDA

John Hartman, M.D.
FAMILY MEDICINE—KISSIMMEE, FLORIDA

Gerald Hough, M.D.
PEDIATRICS—BRANDON, FLORIDA

Duke Johnson, M.D.
FAMILY MEDICINE—TUSTIN, CALIFORNIA

W. Kip Johnson, M.D.
FAMILY MEDICINE—IRVINE, CALIFORNIA

Ronald Jones, M.D.
PEDIATRICS—SPRINGFIELD, MISSOURI

Paul Liu, M.D.
PEDIATRICS—PHOENIX, ARIZONA

Margaret Meeker, M.D.
PEDIATRICS—TRAVERSE CITY, MICHIGAN

Carl Meyer, D.O.
PEDIATRICS—GREENVILLE, PENNSYLVANIA

Michael C. Misko, M.D.
FAMILY MEDICINE—HOLDEN, MISSOURI

D. Brett Mitchell, M.D.
FAMILY MEDICINE—DENISON, TEXAS

John Moyer, M.D.
PEDIATRICS—DENVER, COLORADO

Steve Parnell, M.D.
FAMILY MEDICINE—FAIRMONT, MINNESOTA

Jan Payne, M.D.
PATHOLOGY—ST. PAUL, ALASKA

John C. Rhodes, M.D.
FAMILY MEDICINE—LAS VEGAS, NEVADA

David Sadowitz, M.D.
PEDIATRIC HEMATOLOGY/ONCOLOGY—
CAMINUS, NEW YORK

Bodo Treu, M.D.
FAMILY MEDICINE—OMAHA, NEBRASKA

G. Scott Voorman, M.D.
OTOLARYNGOLOGY—THOUSAND OAKS,
CALIFORNIA

James C. Wilkes, M.D.
PEDIATRICS/PEDIATRIC NEPHROLOGY—
LEXINGTON, KENTUCKY

Franklin D. Wilson, M.D.
ORTHOPEDICS—INDIANAPOLIS, INDIANA

Gentry Yeatman, M.D.
ADOLESCENT MEDICINE—TACOMA,
WASHINGTON

We would like to thank the following individuals for reviewing segments of the completed manuscript for accuracy:

Mary Beth Adam, M.D.
ADOLESCENT MEDICINE—TUSCON, ARIZONA

Stephen Apaliski, M.D.
PEDIATRIC ALLERGY—FORT WORTH, TEXAS

Sarah Blumenschein, M.D.
PEDIATRIC CARDIOLOGY—FORT WORTH, TEXAS

Paul Bowman, M.D.
PEDIATRIC HEMATOLOGY/ONCOLOGY—
FORT WORTH, TEXAS

Preston W. Campbell, M.D.
PEDIATRIC PULMONOLOGY—NASHVILLE,
TENNESSEE

James Cunningham, M.D.
PEDIATRIC PULMONOLOGY—FORT WORTH, TEXAS

Mary Davenport, M.D.
OBSTETRICS/GYNECOLOGY—BERKELEY, CALIFORNIA

Mary A. Eyanson, M.D.
PEDIATRICS—CEDAR RAPIDS, IOWA

David Michael Foulds, M.D.
PEDIATRICS—SAN ANTONIO, TEXAS

Roni Grad, M.D.
PEDIATRIC PULMONOLOGY—SAN ANTONIO, TEXAS

W. Wayne Grant, M.D.
PEDIATRICS—SAN ANTONIO, TEXAS

David Gregory, D.Ph.
PHARMACOLOGY—NASHVILLE, TENNESSEE

Lyn Hunt, M.D.
PEDIATRIC GASTROENTEROLOGY—
FORT WORTH, TEXAS

Vernon L. James, M.D.
DEVELOPMENTAL MEDICINE—
SAN ANTONIO, TEXAS

Cheryl Kissling, R.N.
LACTATION CONSULTANT—CEDAR RAPIDS, IOWA

Mary Kukolich, M.D.
GENETICS—FORT WORTH, TEXAS

Risé L. Lyman, D.D.S.
GENERAL DENTISTRY—SAN ANTONIO, TEXAS

Everett Moody, M.D.
PEDIATRIC OPHTHALMOLOGY—ARLINGTON, TEXAS

Britt Nelson, M.D.
PEDIATRIC INTENSIVE CARE—ARLINGTON, TEXAS

Amil Ortiz, M.D.
NEONATOLOGY—SAN ANTONIO, TEXAS

Steve Phillips, M.D.
PEDIATRIC NEUROLOGY—SACRAMENTO, CALIFORNIA

Judith L. Pugh, M.D.
PEDIATRIC NEPHROLOGY—SAN ANTONIO, TEXAS

S. DuBose Ravenel, M.D.
PEDIATRICS—HIGH POINT, NORTH CAROLINA

Brian Riedel, M.D.
PEDIATRIC GASTROENTEROLOGY—
NASHVILLE, TENNESSEE

James Roach, M.D.
PEDIATRIC ORTHOPEDICS—FORT WORTH, TEXAS

Mark Shelton, M.D.
INFECTIOUS DISEASES—FORT WORTH, TEXAS

Glaze Vaughn, M.D.
PEDIATRIC SURGERY/UROLOGY—
FORT WORTH, TEXAS

Teri Walter
PHYSICAL THERAPY—ARLINGTON, TEXAS

Paul Warren, M.D.
BEHAVIORAL PEDIATRICS—PLANO, TEXAS

Rick Weiser, M.D.
ADOLESCENT MEDICINE—PLEASANTON, CALIFORNIA

Also, this project would not have been possible without the immeasurable support of our loving spouses, Alan Cox and Teri Reisser. Your love, patience, and endurance literally kept us going. This project is not only ours but yours. We appreciate and love you!—Melissa R. Cox, Paul C. Reisser, M.D.

EDITORIAL STAFF
PRIMARY AUTHOR: Paul C. Reisser, M.D.
MANAGING EDITOR: Melissa R. Cox
TYNDALE EDITORS: Vinita Hampton Wright,
Lisa A. Jackson

FOCUS ON THE FAMILY
Bradley G. Beck, M.D., MEDICAL ISSUES ADVISOR
Lianne Belote, ADMINISTRATIVE ASSISTANT
Lisa D. Brock, RESEARCH EDITOR
Bob Chuvala, RESEARCH EDITOR
Kathleen M. Gowler, ADMINISTRATIVE SUPPORT
Karen Sagahon, ADMINISTRATIVE SUPPORT
Keith Wall, RESEARCH EDITOR

SPECIAL THANKS TO:
Glenn Bethany
Kurt Bruner
Charmé Fletcher
Anita Fuglaar
Al Janssen
Mark Maddox
Dean Merrill
Craig Osten
Mike Yorkey
Rolf Zettersten

COVER PHOTOS:
Jim Whitmer

Introduction

Whether you have just realized that your oldest child is growing taller by the minute, and before long will no longer be a child

. . . or you live with a houseful of energetic teenagers who are stretching your parenting skills (and your patience) to new limits

. . . or you are embroiled in a crisis with a teenager: an unexpected pregnancy, drug abuse, a run-in with the law, a runaway

. . . or your high-school, college-bound, or newly independent adult son or daughter is getting ready to leave the nest

. . . or you are a pastor, teacher, coach, or health-care provider who interacts with adolescents on a regular basis, this book is dedicated to enhancing your relationship with the people in your life who are making the transition from childhood to adulthood.

It is our sincere hope that you will find this book to be a useful resource, a source of inspiration, or perhaps even a lifeline during a storm. Its contents are adapted and updated from *The Focus on the Family Complete Book of Baby and Child Care*. Within these pages you will find, among other topics:

- Information about the important physical and emotional developments between childhood and adulthood.
- Strategies for building strong relationships with teenagers and for guiding them toward an adult independence that is physically, emotionally, and spiritually healthy.
- Detailed reviews of some critical areas of risk for teenagers: sexual activity, alcohol and drug abuse, eating disorders, and depression.
- Insights for parents: how to survive and thrive during these critical years in your young adult's life.

We hope that you will find this book interesting enough to read cover to cover, but it can also be used as a resource for topics that are of particular interest or concern to you. As you begin to look through it, please keep the following in mind:

First, while this book covers a number of subjects in some detail, it is not an encyclopedia. Rather, it is intended to serve as a road map to help orient and guide you as you, in turn, orient and guide the teenagers in your life. It doesn't provide cookbook directions for every conceivable situation you might encounter. The basic principles set forth in this book can be used to steer both teenagers and adults in the right direction, but they must be prayerfully molded and adjusted to fit each family's unique circumstances.

Second, the medical information in this book is not a substitute for specific input that you receive from your teenager's physician. While it is important that you consider carefully who will provide health care for your adolescent (see page 54), *when dealing with a medical issue no book can substitute for a direct assessment by a qualified professional.* Furthermore, while we have made diligent efforts to include up-to-date information, in the field of health care the "current wisdom" changes continuously (especially in areas such as immunization guidelines). What was the latest news when this book went to press may be outdated in a matter of months. This is another reason to check with your teenager's doctor if you have any questions about a particular medical situation you might encounter.

Finally, while we have sought to provide information that is both accurate and practical for everyday situations, you will also notice that this book is not "values neutral." Preparing a teenager for independent adulthood involves not only preserving physical and emotional health but instilling moral and spiritual values as well. This involves much more than saying grace at the table or offering foxhole prayers during a family crisis. Our children and teenagers are entrusted to us by God, if only for a season. You will find throughout this book a number of important themes relating to that sacred trust, and they are of the utmost significance. In the final analysis, nothing is more important than "passing the baton," diligently and prayerfully guiding the next generation to experience a vibrant relationship with God and to live in accordance with biblical precepts.

This book has been, and continues to be, a labor of love for the Focus on the Family Physicians Resource Council. Our heartfelt desire is that it will enhance the life of your children, and your life as well, for years to come.

Preparing for Adolescence

ADOLESCENCE: THE PERIOD OF PHYSICAL
AND PSYCHOLOGICAL DEVELOPMENT FROM
THE ONSET OF PUBERTY TO MATURITY.

Between approximately the twelfth and twenty-first birthdays, your child will undergo rapid and intense physical, psychological, and social changes, and at the end of this period she will no longer be a child. Just as you probably approached the "terrible twos" (sometimes called the "first adolescence") with a combination of eager anticipation and a little apprehension, you may now have a similar mix of positive expectation and growing concern as the "real thing" arrives. Without a doubt, adjustments and challenges are ahead for everyone in the family.

Indeed, the years to come may at times feel like a canoe trip down a mountain river. The scenery is constantly changing; the ride is always interesting and often pleasant, but choppy waters, roaring rapids, and an occasional waterfall may await you around the next bend. Your job will be to stabilize the family canoe as much as possible and, by all means, prevent it from turning over before your adolescent reaches the calmer waters of adulthood. Dr. James Dobson has aptly stated that "parenting isn't for cowards," and the coming years may well serve up the greatest tests of your parental fortitude.

It won't be all trials and turbulence. These are highly rewarding years for many families, full of accomplishments, commitments to worthwhile causes, and experiences that aren't possible until children are grown and more mature. You can't expect your two-year-old to appreciate a basketball game, a performance of *Les Miserables*, or a great sermon, but your sixteen-year-old can share these experiences with you and be as interested or enthralled as any adult.

Painting the Big Picture

Many children enter the preteen and teen years unprepared for the gamut of changes and challenges that await them. As a result, a grade-schooler may enter adolescence happy and well adjusted and within a few short years emerge battered, bruised, and thoroughly discouraged—along with the rest of the family. A good deal of this turbulence is potentially preventable if parent and child alike are willing to do some preparation. For the parent, reading this book and others dealing with the teenage years is a good place to start. Talking with family members or friends who have completed the process of rearing adolescents may yield some helpful hints (or cautionary tales). A visit with your church's youth leader may be helpful. But it is of course your child who will be making the transition, and therefore it makes sense for her to have a few huddles with the head coach—that would be you—before the big game begins.

Your school-age child is likely to be much more interested now in what you have to say than she will be later. Once she enters the adolescent years, it may seem as if she has temporarily changed the frequency of her mental tuner so she won't receive your broadcasts. While you may now feel as though you've got her number, in a few years you might hear a busy signal.

Years ago, Apollo astronauts would pass behind the moon as part of their normal flight plan. During those tense minutes, communication between the spacecraft and mission control would be impossible. When they emerged from the dark side of the moon, contact would resume. You may face a dark-side-of-the-moon experience in the coming years, during which a cool head and lots of prayer will be needed while you wait for your child to emerge from the other side. But you may avert or shorten it by walking your child through the trajectory called adolescence before the rocket takes off.

Ideally, you should plan on having a series of conversations with your prepubertal child at age nine or ten for a girl, and perhaps a year or two later for a boy. Some parents plan a special weekend away from home, perhaps in the mountains or at a pleasant hotel, in order to have some undistracted, one-on-one time during which these discussions can take place. If possible, both parents should be involved in this process. If you are a single parent, don't feel that you can't deal with most (if not all) of the topics involved in this preadolescent briefing. If you feel uneasy talking about the physical transition to adulthood with your prepubertal child of the opposite gender, you may want to enlist a trusted friend, a relative, or your youth pastor to help with this particular topic.

Before you embark on this series of discussions, you may want to brush up on information about this upcoming period of your child's life. Another excellent resource is Dr. James Dobson's book and tape series entitled *Preparing for Adolescence*, which is directed specifically toward the child who is about to embark on this voyage toward adulthood. Some parents have found it helpful to listen to the tapes with their children and then discuss them, while others digest the materials on their own and adapt them to their own children's specific needs and personalities. Feel free to mine your own memories for illustrations and recollections about how you felt when you were growing up. If you know any cautionary tales about people who made some unwise decisions, don't hesitate to tell them. Your child will probably remember such stories long after these conversations are over and may even pass them on to her children.

During this preparation, you will want to talk about the following subjects, among others:

The physical changes that will be taking place in the near future. Along with hormonal and sexual developments, there will be rapid growth of bone and muscle, although the timing and rates may vary greatly among children. As a result, an eighth-grade gym class may contain skinny boys with alto voices who are competing and taking showers with peers who are hairy, muscular, and highly intimidating. Remind your child that, whatever his particular timing might be, the transition to adulthood will indeed take place. (How many men with boys' voices has he seen recently?)

The emotional weather forecast. The transition from childhood to adulthood is usually marked by times of intense emotions, especially during the early teen years. When things are going well, she may feel ecstatic. When there is a problem, the world will seem to be coming to an end. Relationships with her peers may swing wildly from love to hate and back again—within the same day.

The valley of the shadow of lack of confidence. Your child needs to know that all who pass through this period feel unsure of themselves. This goes for the most popular, attractive, athletic, intelligent students as well—they *all* desperately crave acceptance and approval. It also holds true for the tough, mean, sarcastic types who make everyone else miserable.

The herd instinct. Because everyone wants desperately to be accepted and avoid ridicule during adolescence, the opinions of peers can carry incredible and sometimes ridiculous weight. Your child must understand the importance of standing her ground, even in the face of intense pressure, when she is being pushed to say or do something she knows to be wrong. The obvious areas to stress are those that might threaten life and health: smoking, drinking, illegal drugs, sex, breaking the law. But a few seemingly less dangerous concessions to peer pressure can also set long-term negative habits in motion. Under the influence of a poorly chosen friend, your child might sample the following:

- Music with antisocial or amoral lyrics
- Films, videos, or Internet sites with violent or pornographic content
- Occultic or death-oriented games
- Obscene, profane, or simply disrespectful language
- Counterproductive attitudes about school, church, and family

Explain to your child that anyone who might pull her in any of these directions simply does not have her best interests in mind. Getting into something that violates the standards you have set at home in order to impress a friend or win someone's approval is like throwing her most prized possession down the toilet.

As will be discussed in the following chapters, you will need to pick your battles in the area of conformity to the crowd. If peer standards call for everyone to wear white socks and sneakers, and anyone who wears dark socks and dress shoes is declared a geek, let her wear the official footwear. Within reason, she shouldn't have to suffer ridicule in areas that do not involve ethical or moral standards.

The process of picking a husband or wife. What kind of person will your child be looking for? You will want to spend some time with this one, stressing the importance of shared faith and values, character, and the ease of making conversation with anyone who may become a marital partner. Good looks and the buzz of romantic chemistry are nice frosting on the cake, but they aren't enough to serve as the foundation for a lifelong journey. Remind your child that you will be praying for that special person, whoever he or she might be. If you haven't done this before, now is a good time to start.

Reassure her that these growing pains will not last forever. Remind her also that, in contrast to the fluctuations of her emotions, the whims of the peer group, and whatever is "hot" and "not" during the coming years, some things will last: your love for her, her place in your family, and above all, the care and involvement of God in her life.

Sex education: meet the faculty
Later in this book we will present some important information and perspectives to communicate with teenagers about their sexuality. But waiting for the arrival of puberty to discuss this subject with your child is like chasing a train which has already left the station. It is important, if at all possible, to lay some important groundwork well ahead of this physiological milestone.

For decades movies and sitcoms have presented a caricature of the sweaty-palmed, birds-and-bees conversation in which Dad stammers through a convoluted description of sex to a preadolescent child—who, it turns out, knows all of the details already. The humor arises from the tension most parents feel about discussing sex with their kids. ("What if we tell him too much?" "Will this rob him of his innocence?" "What if he starts asking about what *we* do?")

What isn't so funny is the reality that too many children learn about sex from everyone *but* their parents. Playground slang and obscenity, a distorted description of intercourse from the tough kid up the street, or worst of all, a look at some pornographic pictures or videos often provide a child's first jarring glimpse of sex. What should be seen as the most beautiful, meaningful, and private communication between a married couple becomes a freakshow curiosity. "Mom and Dad did *that??* More than once?!"

Efforts by public schools to correct misinformation from the street and lack of information from home often leave out a critical ingredient: the moral framework within which the facts about reproduction must be presented. Without an ethical context, sex education becomes little more than basic training in anatomy, physiology, pathology, and contraception.

Many churches have made laudable efforts to teach biblical principles of sexuality to their youth groups. But these important concepts are not always accompanied by accurate medical information or refusal skills. Furthermore, youth group presentations usually begin late in the game (i.e., during the teen years) and rarely involve an ongoing dialogue about this subject.

The best place for a child to learn about sexuality is at home, from those who care most about him. Anyone can teach the basic facts about reproduction in an hour or two (or they can be read in any of several reference books), but you are in the best position to put this information in the proper context and to give it the right perspective over a period of years. There are no cut-and-dried formulas for carrying out this assignment, but keep the following principles in mind:

Giving a child facts about reproduction, including details about intercourse, does not rob him of innocence. Innocence is a function of attitude, not information. A school-aged child who understands the specifics of sex, while seeing it as an act which in the proper context both expresses love and begins new life, retains his innocence. But a child who knows very little about sex can already have a corrupt mindset if he has been exposed to it in a degrading, mocking, or abusive context.

If you feel squeamish or inhibited about broaching this subject with your child, reflect for a moment about your own attitudes. Do you harbor any feelings that sexual activity, even within the context of marriage, is somehow base or something that God really doesn't approve of?

Don't wait to tell your child everything you know about sex during a single, intense marathon session. Doing so risks either waiting until it's too late or dumping more in the child's lap than he can process. Ideally, information should be released gradually, during many conversations over a period of several years.

In many instances, you will be giving information on a need-to-know basis. Your five-year-old is probably going to want to know how the baby inside Aunt Susie is going to get out. But she may not think to ask how the baby got there, and you don't need to broach the subject at that time. On the other hand, if you haven't yet had any discussions about reproduction with your ten-year-old, you will need to take the initiative to start some conversations. She has already heard all sorts of things at the playground and needs to hear from more reputable and mature sources.

What if your child asks you questions you can't answer? Be honest, and then do some research. You gain far more stature in your child's eyes by showing candor than by bluffing. You may not have a detailed knowledge of the intricacies of the menstrual cycle or the developmental stages of puberty, but you're never too old to learn. (You can brush up on some of these topics by reading the sections later in this book, on pages 35-54, regarding adolescent growth and development.)

Sex education: the curriculum
As you ponder the process of communicating to your preteen child about sex, remember that the primary message you need to give him—more important in the long run than the specific facts and figures—is the importance of respect:

- Respect for the body each of us has been given, and for the Creator of that body

- Respect for the wonder of reproduction
- Respect for privacy in sexual matters, not only his own, but for parents', friends', and others'
- Respect for his future and an understanding that sexual activity can have a profound effect on his health and happiness for the rest of his life
- Respect for marriage as the appropriate context for sexual expression

Think in terms of a gradual and relaxed release of information to your child, beginning with the basic naming of body parts and a general understanding of where babies come from during the pre-school years, and progressing to full disclosure of the reproductive process before puberty begins (usually by ten to twelve years in girls and twelve to fourteen years in boys).

Only you can judge the readiness of your child, but in most cases when the Big Question—Why and how does a baby start to grow inside a mother?—needs to be answered, offer a very simple but straightforward explanation. You can talk about how a mother makes a tiny egg inside her body every month, and if there is some sperm from the father to join with the egg at the right time, a baby will begin to grow.

When you get more specific about the process which brings the man's sperm and the woman's egg together, remember to stress context: a man and woman who are married and love each other very much have a special time, just for the two of them, when they get very close to each other—in fact, so close that the man inserts his penis into the woman's vagina. After a while he releases his sperm inside of her. Younger children will usually find this idea rather strange, and you can stress that when the man and woman love each other very much, they feel very good while this is going on.

You will need to supply a name for this activity: "Having sex" is probably the most direct without being vulgar; "making love" is a little vague; and "sexual intercourse" is rather clinical, although children should know that this is the term they'll be hearing later in life. Throughout, however, stress how good sex is—provided it occurs at the right time, with the right person, in the context of a marriage.

Sooner or later, you will also need to talk about situations in which single adults are pregnant or raising children without a partner. Indeed, you may be having these conversations with your children as a single parent. Children will need to know that some people have sex even though they are not married and that a baby may begin to grow inside of a mother as a result. Or they may be married when the baby starts to grow but not married later on.

Whether you will want or need to delve more deeply into the complexities of adult life will depend upon your situation and the age of your child. A young child is going to be more concerned about basic information and his own security with you, whether married or single. A child approaching puberty will probably need more details: What happens when a single woman becomes pregnant? Do they all have their babies? Why do some mothers and fathers split up?

These may be emotional questions to tackle, especially if you have been involved in a divorce or are raising one or more children on your own for whatever reason. But without condemning others or justifying irresponsibility, this can be an appropriate time to talk about the fact that sexual activity should not be taken lightly. You may want to mention that the Designer of human beings laid down some rules about sex for good reason—not to be a killjoy but to maximize our enjoyment of it and to prevent painful consequences. Sex experienced within those boundaries—between one man and one woman, maintained within a marriage relationship to which both are committed for the rest of their lives—is not only right but the safest and most pleasurable.

Preparation for the onset of puberty
As your child approaches puberty, you are going to have to shift gears from talking about sex in general to more specific briefings on his or her own sexuality. Whether you make this a specific discussion or include it as part of a more extensive explanation of what lies ahead during the adolescent years, you will want your child to be ready for the physical changes that are about to take place.

Girls need to know about breast development, new hair growth, and the reproductive cycle. The first menstrual period should be viewed in a positive light, as a passage into adulthood rather than a burden or a "curse of women." Some parents honor the occasion by taking their daughter to dinner at a nice restaurant or presenting a special gift. This event is usually the final stage of pubertal development. If you and your daughter stay in communication about the changes she is experiencing, you can usually anticipate and discuss what she can do if her first period begins when she's away from home.

Similarly, boys should be aware that changes are on the horizon, such as deepening of the voice, enlargement of the genitals, and new hair growth. They should also know about the likelihood that they will have an unexpected emission of seminal fluid during the night (the "wet dream"), and that this is not a sign of disease or moral failure.

Parents will need to discuss with their child the increasing interest in the opposite sex. The boy or girl will also need to be prepared to deal with attention from the opposite sex if and when it occurs. This is an important time to review specific guidelines, and perhaps a little street wisdom, about relationships and physical contact. While reinforcing the importance of saving sex for marriage, what will you say about other kinds of affectionate touching?

Your preadolescent child will most likely wonder if you're going overboard in broaching this subject. "Dad, I'm not going to jump into bed with people, okay? What's the big deal?" But he or she must understand that we are all designed in such a way that physical contact, once started, naturally progresses to increasing intimacy. Indeed, sex is like a car that begins rolling down a hill. At first the hill is nearly flat, but then it becomes progressively steeper. The farther you go, the harder it is to stop. That in itself isn't bad or wrong but simply the way we're made. Since the right time to have sex will be some years away, it will be important to make sure that the car doesn't roll very far before the wedding night. This means that your child will want to have a clear idea what his or her boundaries are and how to maintain them effectively, well before the first socializing with the opposite sex begins.

At some point (probably more than once) during these years, you will need to deal with the subject of **masturbation.** As children approach adolescence, you will have to make a judgment call on what to say about the significance of self-stimulation after puberty arrives. It is extremely likely that masturbation leading to sexual climax will occur at some point, especially for a male. If he is racked with guilt about it and repeatedly vows never to let it happen again, he will probably expend a lot of energy feeling like a moral failure and worrying about his spiritual welfare.

But when masturbation becomes a routine and frequent habit, especially when accompanied by vivid sexual fantasies or, worse, the viewing of pornography, it can be damaging to sexual and emotional health. In essence, a young man may have hundreds of sexual experiences associated with unrealistic or overtly distorted imagery, reinforced with the extreme pleasure of sexual release. At the very least, when he marries, his real-life sexual partner may seem disappointing by comparison, and his physical and emotional bonding with her may be impaired. This problem will be more significant if there have been many actual sexual partners before the wedding night. At worst, he may come in contact with violent or degrading images and associate his own sexual release with them.

Your approach to this issue will need to be both tactful and realistic. *A bottom line worth stressing is that masturbation should not play a major role in your child's life, either as a source of relentless guilt or as a frequent and persistent habit that displaces healthy sexual relations in the future.* If it happens once in a while, it happens. But it should not be pursued as a form of recreation, especially while viewing sexually provocative material, and should never be allowed to occur with other people.

Who should deliver these messages to your growing child? In many families, everyone will feel more comfortable if mothers talk with daughters and fathers with sons. It may be more fruitful in the long run, however, if both parents participate in many of the discussions of sexuality, where mother and father can each offer specific perspectives, and one can pick up the thread if the other draws a blank in a particular area. This also solidifies the notion that sex is a matter for couples who are committed to one another and provides your child with two sources of appropriate information rather than one. In single-parent families in which the child is of the opposite sex from the parent, a trusted friend, relative, or youth pastor may need to fill in some gaps in sensitive areas.

While it may be useful to have both parents involved in discussions of sexuality, it will usually not be wise to talk to more than one child at once. This is especially important when you are dealing with your child's own sexuality rather than with less personal topics. A ten-year-old girl who is learning about very personal changes that will be taking place in her body should not have a wisecracking eight-year-old brother in the room. If necessary, take her to a place where you can ensure privacy before you bring up these subjects.

Understanding the Tasks of Adolescence

Before we move on to explore the length and breadth of changes that unfold during adolescence, we should pause for a moment to consider where all of them are leading. Adult stature and physical characteristics are genetically programmed and will thus develop inevitably with the passage of time, barring some unusual setback. Being informed about these changes can be helpful, but not at all necessary for them to occur.

But there are other critical endpoints in the transition to adulthood which do not always arrive automatically, let alone easily or smoothly. Indeed, reaching them requires work on everyone's part. All too often parents lose track of the sweeping tasks that their teenagers must accomplish, and at times they may even unwittingly interfere with the successful completion of those tasks. Keeping them clearly in mind will help you provide purposeful and optimistic leadership for your adolescent, and will serve as a horizon to orient you as you navigate through any turbulence that might arise in the coming years.

The task of achieving independence from parents

With rare exception, adolescents develop a powerful drive to become independent, to be in charge of their daily affairs and their future. As a result, bucking the limits, challenging authority, and resisting constraints imposed at home and school are pretty much par for the course. Just as in the first adolescence of toddler days, the extent of willfulness and the lack of good judgment can at times be spectacular. And while it may sometimes seem outrageous, some degree of struggling against parental control is a normal and necessary part of growing up.

Your job in helping your adolescent complete this task is to release your grip in a controlled and reasonable manner. You still have the right and responsibility to make house rules. But when you impose (and defend) them, you need to do so calmly and respectfully. "Because I'm the mom, that's why!" may have worked with your two-year-old, but it will rarely be appropriate anymore. Few things exasperate and discourage a teenager more than being treated like an immature child, even if it may seem appropriate (to you) at the time.

Even more important is linking your adolescent's blossoming independence to the realities and responsibilities of adult life. He will need hundreds of age-appropriate reality checks before he leaves your nest, and you are in the best position to provide them.

The task of accepting and respecting one's body
Your adolescent is (or soon will be) in the midst of intense physical changes, especially during the early years of this period. Virtually all systems in the body are involved, but those affected by new surges of hormones will generate the most attention and concern. Three issues will dominate the landscape:

What's happening to me? If your adolescent has not received some advance warning about the changes of puberty, a friendly and factual huddle about this subject will be most reassuring. Even if your teenager already appears quite mature physically, the impact of hormones and rapid growth on emotions, energy, and various parts of the body may not be clear to her—or you. Your input and, if needed, her physician's can calm many concerns.

Do I like this body? Adolescents are keenly interested, at times seemingly obsessed, with body image—both their own and everyone else's. As a result, comparisons with others are always in progress. Whoever holds the winning ticket in the physical sweepstakes—the most attractive features, the knockout figure, the well-sculpted muscles, the athletic prowess—will nearly always reign supreme where teens gather. But even Studley Dooright, the campus megahunk, and Barbie Dahl, the queen of the prom, will be plagued by doubts about their appearance and worthiness.

No matter how well-assembled your teenager might appear to you and others, from her perspective someone will always seem to have a better package. Negative comparisons with that person—sometimes amazingly unrealistic—are likely. And an adolescent with an obvious physical deficit may be cruelly taunted by peers and develop a lifelong preoccupation with appearance. Accepting one's body and taking appropriate care of it are important tasks to be accomplished during this transition to adulthood.

Your job here is a delicate one. Your teenager will need generous doses of reassurance that worth is not dependent on appearance, even when the culture around her says otherwise. You will have to endure the fact that any positive comments you make about looks, temperament, accomplishments, or inherent value may not be met with expressions of thanks. It may appear that what you say doesn't count, but it does—in a big way.

One challenge for parents will be to find the fine line between making constructive suggestions and being a nag. Your adolescent's preoccupation with looks may not necessarily translate into specific actions to improve them or to appear pleasing to adults. In fact, at times the opposite will be true. The current "dress code" in middle school, for example, may decree an extremely casual, semiunkempt look in order to appear "normal." As will be discussed later, within limits, generational differences in clothing and hairstyles may not be worth a family battle.

But sometimes you may need to take the initiative. If he suffers from acne, he'll need your help and some professional input to bring the blemishes under control. If she is clueless about clothes, Mom or a savvy relative may need to help rehabilitate the wardrobe, a project that does not need to be expensive. If weight is a problem, tactful efforts to move the scale in the right direction may improve your adolescent's self-image and general health. These efforts should be positive, stressing healthy foods and activities for everyone in the family, without focusing all the attention on one person. If there is a major problem related to food—whether an unhealthy obsession with thinness or weight that is far above the norm for an adolescent's height—professional help should be sought from a physician, dietitian, counselor, or all of the above.

Will I respect this body? Whether or not they are comfortable with their physical appearance, adolescents must decide how they will care for themselves. Lifestyle and habits established at this age may continue well into adulthood, and it is never too early to establish a healthy respect for the one and only body they will ever occupy. Prudent eating habits can be modeled and encouraged, and you can also point out that exercise isn't merely something to be endured during P.E. class but is also worth pursuing (in moderation) for its own sake. Unfortunately, some teenagers who harbor a mistaken belief that "nothing can happen to me" choose to engage in substance abuse, sexual misadventures, and other risk-taking behaviors that could establish long-standing negative habits or leave permanent physical (not to mention emotional) scars.

Your work in this arena should have begun years ago, and if this took place, your child's concept of respect for his or her body will have roots dating from the preschool years. Even so, reasonable vigilance, good role modeling, and forthright and open conversations about risky behavior will need to be on your agenda until your adolescent has completed the transition to full independence.

The task of establishing healthy peer relationships
The impact of peers on adolescents cannot be underestimated. The right people crossing their path at critical times can reinforce positive values and enhance the entire process of growing up. The wrong individuals can escort them into extremely negative detours or literally suck the life out of them.

Your job is to pray with utter abandon for the friends your adolescent will make over the next several years. Without being too pushy about it, make every effort to make friends with your teenager's friends. If your home is the most teen friendly in the neighborhood, chances are the troops will gather under your roof or in your backyard and respond to your influence in the process.

Because peers can play such a serious role for good or ill in your teen's life, you will need to be forthright and directive about where and with whom her time is spent—especially in the early years. If the drama club, 4-H, Scouts, or athletic teams provide a consistently healthy niche, by all means encourage them. But if a new "friend" who manifests an abundance of toxic language and behavior enters your adolescent's life, don't hesitate to take some defensive measures. This may include insisting that they spend time together only under your roof with an adult on the premises (and no closed bedroom doors). If it becomes apparent that your teenager is being swayed toward destructive habits, however, reasonable measures to keep them separated will be necessary.

If your church has a strong and active youth group, do everything you can to support it and your teen's involvement in it. But if your youth group has gone stale or has become a clique zone, find another one. The program should honor your family's faith and values, of course, but should also accept all comers, build positive identities, and be fun as it promotes spiritual growth.

The task of developing a coherent identity

Whether they are National Merit Scholars or total nonconformists (or both), adolescents are fervently searching for a clear sense of identity. Whatever the guise or getup, the questions they continually ask boil down to these: *"Who cares about me?"* and *"What can I do that has any significance?"*

If the answers are "my God, my family, and my close friends" and "impacting the world in a positive way," your main task—and it usually will be a pleasant one—will be serving as cheerleader and sounding board as your son or daughter finds the best track on which to run.

If the answers are "my friends (and hardly anyone else)" and "having fun (and hardly anything else)," the ultimate outcome could be more unpredictable. Most adolescents with this mind-set eventually grow up and find a productive niche, while some stay in this shallow, meandering rut well into adulthood. Some also drift into drug use or sexual activity in their search for the next diversion—and ultimately pay dearly for it.

For the teenager whose answers are "no one" and "nothing," if different answers are nowhere on the horizon, the consequences may be more serious: depression, acting out, even suicidal behavior.

Obviously, it is important that your child enter adolescence with some clear and positive answers to the questions of caring and significance. During the coming seasons, she will probably ask them often and in many different ways—some of which may catch you way off guard. Even if she has lost her bearings or abandoned common sense, you will still need to communicate that your love and her significance are unshakable. As in earlier years of childhood, you will need to enforce limits and help her make some course corrections until she is on her own. But she must always know that your fundamental love for her will never change, regardless of grades, clothes, a messy room, dented fenders, or more serious issues.

The task of discovering personal gifts, interests, and passions

One of the most important and life-enhancing aspects of adolescence is the process of looking at a variety of activities and interests. If her childhood interests in Scouts and piano lessons don't continue into the teen years, don't count your time spent in those activities as wasted. She may want to explore drama or gymnastics for a while, and they may become her new passions—or she may discover that the piano really is her true love after all. Your encouragement for her to find and develop her strengths and perhaps to overcome what she (and you) might have considered her weaknesses will pay off in many ways. Not only might she find a niche of true excellence and accomplishment, but all of these activities—even the ones that don't pan out as permanent interests—will broaden her fund of knowledge and experience. Furthermore, your support during these efforts will repeatedly affirm her value.

This is also a time during which many young people develop and hone a social conscience. Altruism often peaks during the teen years, and she may find considerable satisfaction in helping others solve problems and in volunteering to serve in worthy causes. Teenagers can be surprisingly empathetic to the suffering of others, and they may go to great lengths of energy and time to lend someone a helping hand. You will obviously want to encourage selfless and sacrificial behavior—at times you may find your own conscience stirred by your adolescent's willingness to love the unlovely.

You should model practical concern for the needs of others and at the same time offer guidance as to the parameters of your teen's involvement. For example, your daughter might want to rescue a friend from an abusive family situation by inviting her to stay at your home. Perhaps you are able to offer a safe haven—certainly an honorable and meaningful action—but you will also need to walk your daughter through some of the realities and details that may not have occurred to her in the rush to help. If you have a particularly generous and tenderhearted teen at home, you will have to pass along a little street wisdom to help prevent her charitable instincts from being soured by encounters with users and abusers who might take advantage of her.

The task of developing a worldview

The adolescent years are a crucial period in an individual's development of a worldview—the basic (and often unspoken) assumptions that govern attitudes, decisions, and actions—and young people often make decisions during their teens that will literally set a course for the rest of their lives. Many make permanent spiritual commitments at church, camp, or other events and continue to mature in their faith as the years pass. But these are also years during which fundamental questions about God and the universe are asked, and parents may find their own beliefs (or lack thereof) held up for inspection.

Many teens feel the need to chart a different spiritual course from their parents during these years, a development that can make parents feel very uneasy. *What if he turns away from God and all we have taught him over the years?* Before you lose too much sleep over this question, remember that your child must eventually make his own decision whether or not to follow God. You can't do it for him. In fact, to some degree an examination of what he has heard as a child is a healthy process, because he must understand eventually how his faith applies to adult situations and problems.

Your primary job will be to keep your *own* relationship with God thriving—which should include meaningful time in prayer for your child(ren) on an ongoing basis. Spiritual vitality that manifests genuine joy, peace, and other positive expressions on a consistent basis will ultimately communicate more to your adolescent than a lot of clever (or convoluted) answers to his questions. In matters of faith (and in other arenas as well), teenagers are particularly responsive to honesty and integrity and turned off with equal fervor by hypocrisy.

If his need to assert his independence from you spills into the spiritual realm, you may need to entrust his growth in this area to other adults (or even peers) who can positively influence his view of God, faith, and the world in general. Youth leaders, teachers, young couples or single adults, or other friends of the family can often "stand in the gap" for you in this area. Do what you can to encourage these contacts and interactions (without being pushy about it) and then leave the results in God's hands.

Understanding the Hearts
and Minds of Teens

For centuries teenagers have routinely challenged and at times exasperated their parents. Public and private turmoil about what to do about the younger generation is not unique to our moment in history, nor are most of the fundamental concerns that a child will encounter during her eventful passage into adulthood. This chapter will deal with many aspects of that important process, along with a number of parenting attitudes and strategies that can help an adolescent navigate through it in a positive and productive way.

When your child was a newborn, coping with short nights of sleep, dirty diapers, and crying spells may have hampered your ability to marvel at the incredible little person before you. When she was a turbocharged and at times defiant toddler, the nonstop effort required to keep her (and your home) safe and sound may not have given you much time to appreciate her rapidly developing abilities. Similarly, when your adolescent experiences normal growing pains and emotional turbulence (and possibly a crisis or two) during the coming years, it may be all too easy to lose sight of a number of very encouraging and gratifying developments.

Yes, there will be a lot of problems to solve, arriving in all shapes and sizes (often when you least expect them). You will need to guide, monitor, and sometimes intervene to keep the cultural wolves a respectable distance from your teenager's door. You may have to put out some fires or even an occasional four-alarm blaze.

Hopefully, through it all you will be able to recognize and appreciate in your adolescent many of the positive attributes that are common in this age-group. (Be sure to praise them for these.) How and when these qualities will be expressed will vary with each individual, but be on the lookout for them:

- Energy and enthusiasm
- Idealism
- Concern for the needs of others—often coupled with a willingness to offer help in ways that adults might find risky or "unrealistic"
- A desire for meaningful relationships
- A sense of humor that can be witty and insightful
- A concern for fairness and justice
- An interest in other cultures and countries
- Development of new skills in athletics, the arts, crafts, the use of tools, writing, and speaking—often with extraordinary achievements
- Curiosity—not only about the *way* things work in the world but *why*
- Willingness to commit to worthwhile causes and to back up that commitment with specific actions
- Ability (and attention span) to appreciate sophisticated music, drama, films, and artwork
- A deep desire for a relationship with God and a willingness to make a lifelong commitment to serve Him

Despite the relatively few years separating one generation from the next, most adults seem to have amnesia about their own adolescence. Parents who have already "been there, done that" may have difficulty recalling how they felt and thought between the ages of twelve and twenty-one. As you read through the stages of adolescent development in the next few pages, try to recall what you were experiencing during those years. Whether your effort brings fond memories, a lot of pain, or merely a sigh of relief that you don't have to go through *that* again, you will connect more smoothly with your teenager(s) if you can remember what it's like to walk a mile in their sneakers.

Since many important differences exist between a twelve-year-old seventh-grader and a college student, it is helpful to divide the adolescent years into three developmental phases:

- Early adolescence—ages twelve through fourteen (middle school)
- Middle adolescence—ages fifteen through seventeen (senior high)
- Late adolescence—ages eighteen through twenty-one (college/vocation)

Each adolescent's life will run on a unique track, of course, and all sorts of variations on the basic themes occur during each phase. Some middle-school students may appear intellectually and emotionally ready for college, while some college students behave as though middle school were still in session. Some thirteen-year-olds are immune to the opinions of their peers, and some twenty-one-year-olds' convictions change with each day's companions. But some familiar trends and behaviors about each of the three phases are generally recognizable.

Issues in Early, Mid, and Late Adolescence

EARLY ADOLESCENCE

Take an informal poll of one hundred adults about what years of their lives they would never want to repeat, and you will probably hear "junior high" or "middle school" most often. All too frequently, a relatively well-adjusted, good-natured twelve-year-old enters the seventh grade and two or three years later emerges emotionally (if not physically) battered and bruised. What turns these years into such a war zone?

First, the tides of puberty are likely to be flowing at full speed. Among other things, these generate much concern and self-consciousness about physical changes that are (or aren't yet) under way. Such worries are intensified by the marked variations in development at this age. Within the same class will be skinny thirteen-year-old boys with squeaky voices standing next to hairy hulks who appear qualified for the defensive line of the high school football team. Similarly, flat-chested girls who have yet to experience their first menstrual cycle are mingling with fully developed counter-parts who could pass for women several years older. The inevitable comparisons and insecurities can become more acute at the end of gym class if many classmates shower together.

Second, wide mood swings and strong emotional responses to the ups and downs of life are the order of the day. Physical and hormonal components contribute to this stormy weather in both sexes, although the biochemistry of the monthly cycle can accentuate the mood swings in girls.

Like the two-year-old, the young adolescent experiences life in extremes. If she gets a friendly smile from a guy she thinks is cute, everything is coming up roses. If she finishes last in the fifty-yard dash, the whole world stinks. Today two girls declare their undying friendship; tomorrow they announce they hate each other. Last summer he campaigned passionately for a new guitar; today it gathers dust in his room.

Emotional reactions to life's twists and turns, even in a stable home environment, can provoke physical responses as well, especially headaches, abdominal pains, and fatigue. While any of these may be caused by the daily strain of growing up, they should be evaluated by a physician if persistent or disruptive. Insomnia, withdrawal from activities that were once enjoyed, irritability, and a marked change in appetite could signal full-blown depression, a more significant problem that should be taken seriously and treated appropriately.

In addition to these physical and emotional upheavals among individual adolescents, bringing many of them together (as occurs every school day) creates a social stew containing large doses of these volatile ingredients:

- An intense need for acceptance by peers.
- An equally intense concern about looking dumb, clumsy, or at all different from the surrounding herd of other early adolescents—who themselves are intensely concerned about looking dumb, clumsy, or at all different from every-one else.
- An ongoing struggle with self-confidence or overt feelings

of inferiority, even among those who are the most attractive and talented (or tough and hostile).

- A surprising—and at times shocking—intolerance for anyone who looks or behaves a little unlike everyone else.
- A limitless capacity for creative (and often obscene) insults, put-downs, and jokes directed at nearly everyone—but especially the one who is different. This is particularly and sometimes painfully obvious in group settings. Kids who can be quite civilized on a one-to-one basis or who pledge their allegiance to virtue and values at their Sunday-night youth group can unleash a torrent of crude slurs during a slumber party or a school-yard basketball game. In some cases, nonstop verbal harassment can escalate to physical confrontations or violence.

Consequently, school represents more than classroom activities and homework for many adolescents. It can be a daily social gauntlet—unpleasant at best, a barbaric ordeal at worst—requiring every ounce of effort and energy just to complete the round-trip back to home base. As a result, if *any* physical symptom is present when the alarm clock goes off—a headache, a minor cold, too little sleep the night before, some menstrual cramping—you may encounter major resistance when you try to pry your middle-schooler out of bed.

While you might expect your young adolescent to come to you for aid and comfort or take cover from the daily shellings at school, the opposite may take place. The budding (or broiling) urge for independence, combined with mood swings, extreme self-consciousness, and intolerance for anything that strikes them as "stupid" or "lame," may begin to drive an alarming wedge into your relationship.

This is the age at which kids may decide that their parents are hopelessly naive, out of touch with reality, or terribly short on intelligence. Your adolescent may avoid sitting with you at church. You may hear criticism of your clothes, musical tastes, and opinions. And don't even think about wearing that slightly weird hat or doing something a little unusual (such as humming your favorite tune a little too loud) in a public place—especially the mall. You may be strongly rebuked for this "embarrassing" display, especially if (heaven forbid) someone she remotely knows might possibly see it. Her concern, of course, will not be for your reputation but hers.

This apparent detachment from you and the family may extend to cutting other moorings to the past. One day your son may suddenly pack up his action figures, shove his baseball cards into a drawer, and insist that you replace the race-car wallpaper that was painstakingly installed in his bedroom just a few years ago. Your daughter's dolls and figurines may suffer a similar fate. Some adolescents also choose this time to abandon cute childhood nicknames in favor of more grown-up-sounding names. Don't be alarmed and certainly don't smirk or ridicule if you are told one day that Suzie wants to be called Susan or that Skipper is now Jonathan. Such sudden announcements that childhood is over may catch you off guard, provoking a lump in the throat or even a few tears. But welcome the transition as best you can. Pack up the toys and memorabilia they don't want, and save them for their own children.

During this period, early adolescents typically form and main-

The Silent Treatment

Anger, you can tolerate. Rebelliousness, you can guide. But your young teenager's silence is something you don't know how to handle. As a parent, your role so far has been to nurture and protect your child in rough situations. But how can you help her if she won't tell you what's going on?

The first step in dealing with a suddenly silent middle schooler is to relax. As difficult as it may be, recognize that your child's withdrawal is probably normal.

As young teens begin to explore their own individuality and independence, the first thing they must do is move away from you emotionally. Even if your son knows you *want* to talk and are willing to listen, sharing a problem with you might make him feel as if he's giving up hard-earned freedom and space. As long as he still talks to you sometimes, this turning from you can be a healthy step toward maturity.

You might notice your child going to friends or other adults for conversation and advice. Again, this is normal, but it's a good idea to pay attention to who she's talking to. Encourage her to confide in God, church youth leaders, or older, more mature Christian friends.

Just because your child talks less doesn't mean the talking has to stop altogether. Let him know you understand some of what he's going through. Talk about the struggles you remember facing when you were his age and how you felt. Ask him to tell you about a struggle or success he's currently experiencing.

tain strong same-sex friendships, even as interest in members of the opposite sex is growing more intense. Infatuations and crushes are to be expected, but intense romances and dating are not good at this age for a number of reasons.

As already mentioned, friends and peers can play a major role in reinforcing or undermining the values that matter to you. You may become frustrated by the fact that a classmate's half-baked opinions seem to matter more than all the common sense you've imparted over the years. But choose wisely if you decide to intervene, because the more you complain about her newfound friends, the more vigorously she may defend them. Some streetwise vigilance, ongoing prayer, and evenhanded but candid conversations about who's hot and who's not on the current friendship list (and why) should be regular agenda items for your busy week.

While the value of your parental stock may seem to be falling by the hour, you may be surprised (and perhaps a little hurt) to see your adolescent form a powerful attachment to another adult. A teacher, choir director, favorite aunt, coach, or youth leader can become the object of intense admiration and attention. This common

continued

You might find that your young teen is more talkative when the two of you are riding in the car or working on a jigsaw puzzle together. When the focus is on something other than himself, your child will be more willing to open up to you.

It's also important to understand that at this stage a child's communication skills are still not fully developed. Research has shown that as a young teenager's mental development progresses, his communication skills drop. It's not until later adolescence that kids gain the ability to fully put their thoughts and feelings into words. It's up to you to show them how to talk and invite them to express what's going on in their lives. During those times when your child does want to talk, don't hurry her. Give her time to think through what she wants to say. Try not to say it for her, unless you're simply reflecting something she's already said ("Are you saying . . .?"). I often suggest parents ask their teens to give them three sentences about what's going on in their lives. This gets the child talking without feeling like she has to say more than she wants to.

Seek God's guidance before you talk with your young teen, asking for insight and help. Then look for ways to help your child develop his communication skills.

While you won't be able to heal all the hurts that your teen is feeling, your presence and availability mean more than you know.

by Karen Dockrey

turn of events can be a blessing if the object of this affection is an ally who shares your values and goals and who moves her in positive directions. But someone with a less constructive agenda can have a significant negative impact.

MIDDLE ADOLESCENCE

For many adolescents and their parents, senior high brings a breath of fresh air after the suffocating social environment of middle school. By now the most significant transitions and transformations of puberty are well under way or completed for nearly everyone. The apprehensive question "What's happening to me?" is replaced by the more reflective "So *that's* what was happening." Physical attributes and attractiveness are still major concerns, but obvious differences in development among members of this age-group are far less common.

Opposite-sex relationships are likely to move beyond crushes and awkward nonconversations into friendships and romances that can displace the same-sex and group camaraderie of the past. The issue of appropriate expressions of physical affection should be candidly broached. If you brought up this topic a couple of years ago, it may well have seemed like a philosophical question. But when real-life relationships are involved, it becomes a very practical one.

While peer influence remains strong, many of the extreme, often ridiculous herd instincts of two or three years ago have begun to

---

The Boy-Girl Thing

Up until now, your child has probably had lots of friends, both boys and girls. But as she reaches the age of nine or ten, she may begin to prefer friends of the same gender and see the opposite sex as, well, different. The same child who climbed trees with the neighborhood boys just last year is now giggling with her girlfriends about who's the cutest guy in the class. You might even wonder, *Is this normal? Is she old enough to like boys?*

The answer to both questions is *yes.* And while your child is not ready to start dating, this is the age where she'll develop the tools she needs to build healthy, loving relationships in the future.

You'll play a major role in helping your child learn to relate to the opposite sex. Start by taking her feelings seriously. Listen to the way your child talks about the opposite sex and encourage her to use respectful language.

Talk about the difference between real love and love that is superficial and self-fade. No longer does everyone need to look, dress, and talk exactly alike to avoid nonstop ridicule. In fact, many adolescents now pride themselves on their tolerance and acceptance of all manner of eccentricities among their cohorts. (This does not necessarily extend to adults, however.)

Teens in this age bracket tend to find at least one group they identify with and that provides friendships, fun, and a sense of identity. Church and service organizations, athletics, performing arts (music, drama, dance, film), academics, and even political/social activism will bring kindred spirits together. Idealism may flourish during these years, and commitments made to God and basic values can be fervent and life-changing. If you share one or more of these interests, you can cement deep and satisfying bonds with your teenager.

For many families, however, these years bring a crescendo of conflict. The urge for independence that provokes detachment and verbal criticism from middle-schoolers can deteriorate into a Grand Canyon–sized rift or all-out war at this age. Now, however, you're not dealing with a foot-stomping two-year-old or a misbehaving grade-school child. He may no longer be intimidated by your size or stern look. In order to demonstrate his separation from your influence, he may undergo extreme alterations of appearance, including weird haircuts and hair colors, body piercing, tattoos,

continued

seeking. Sit down together and look up 1 Corinthians 13:4-6 and Galatians 5:22-23. Point out that true love chooses to be patient, kind, secure, humble, considerate, persistent, good, gentle, self-controlled. As she develops friendships—both male and female—help her look for these character traits in others. As she discovers what makes a good friend, she'll also be learning what makes a good mate.

At this age, kids become almost desperate for information about the opposite sex. Girls often look to teen magazines for answers to their questions, while boys sometimes turn to pornography. Point out that neither resource offers any solid answers or lasting solutions. Instead, provide books and magazines based on scriptural principles.

While it may be hard to believe that your child is already thinking about the opposite sex, don't worry. With your help and guidance, these early signs of maturity can be the beginning of a lifetime of healthy, godly relationships. *by Karen Dockrey* and clothing that looks like it came from another planet. If you have a major blowup over some issue, he may take off for parts unknown. He may have access to transportation (his own or someone else's) and may be able to crash temporarily at a friend's place if things aren't going well at yours.

Furthermore, adolescents at this age are capable of carrying out acts with far more serious consequences. Their quest for self-determination or outright rebellion can be combined and energized by an unspoken belief in their own power and immortality. As a result, risky behavior involving alcohol, drugs, and motor vehicles, as well as other physical feats of daring and stupidity, are more likely now. If the social niche that satisfies longings for identity happens to be a gang, crime and violence may enter the equation. Furthermore, intense sexual drives, sensual imagery in films and music, peer pressure, and increased opportunities for intimacy markedly increase the risk for sexual encounters—often with disastrous results. These can indeed be the times that try parents' souls.

For the vast majority of teens, a rebellious phase will eventually

Dealing with Behavior Meltdown

What do you do when a child declares war on your family, the neighborhood, or the entire civilized world? One teenager who goes off the deep end can, without question, rock a lot of boats in the community. Social workers, doctors, lawyers, police, and clergy may all be in the loop, while Mom and Dad endure an avalanche of pain, frustration, guilt, and expense.

If you find yourself embroiled in a civil war at home or confronted by a teenager who is making some dangerously bad decisions, you need to keep these principles in mind:

Take the bull by the horns. Don't tolerate flagrant disrespect, destruction of your home or other property, criminal activity, or abuse from one of your children. Drastic action may be necessary to keep this type of behavior from tearing your family to shreds. Use your allies including other parents, counselors, clergy, and the police. If more conservative measures aren't working, you may need to consider informing him that he cannot remain under your roof if these acts continue. Living at home would then become a privilege to be earned on your terms, with some critical minimum requirements: no drugs, no booze, no stealing, no sex, and no verbal or physical abuse of anyone in the family.

If he breaks the law and is arrested, depending on the circumstances you may need to choose not to bail him out, as painful as this decision would be. In doing so you end. Only a small percentage will doggedly continue in antisocial and self-destructive paths. Usually a combination of maturing emotions, stabilizing identity, and unpleasant consequences brings an unruly adolescent to his or her senses. As the years pass and the School of Life dishes out hard lessons and reality checks, parents seem to gain intelligence in the eyes of their maturing offspring. In a few decades many of today's rebels will be asking their parents for advice about their own teenagers' uprisings. If you have been tearing your hair out over an adolescent's behavior, don't despair; more likely than not, within a few years you and your grown child will be back on the same team.

LATE ADOLESCENCE

The conclusion of the teen years and the beginning of the twenties often bring stability to a number of areas but also raise new issues. Physical appearance is rarely the ongoing concern that dominated early adolescence, and efforts to improve looks will not only be more common but generally more productive. Direct peer-group

continued

would have but one purpose: allowing him to experience the brunt of his bad decisions and to come to his senses.

Don't live with false guilt. Perhaps you have made mistakes (who hasn't?) in raising your prodigal offspring. But even those who work diligently to "bring up a child in the way he should go" (to quote Solomon in the book of Proverbs) can find themselves in the midst of a parent's nightmare. Each child is an independent being with a free will who decides if he will proceed in the "way he should go" or "depart from it." Even this famous verse is not an ironclad guarantee but a statement of the way things generally happen.

Don't underestimate the depth of your adolescent's emotions. Serious problems are not "just a phase he's going through," and often disruptive behavior on a child's part is the manifestation of real suffering and inner turmoil. By all means seek professional help, and if possible try to engage your adolescent in the process of determining what type of counselor or program would be most appropriate in the current situation. For help, call The New Life Treatment Centers, 1-800-NEW LIFE, or a treatment center near you.

Pray without ceasing, and don't give up. Even if you have to allow him to reap the bitter harvest of his choices, continue praying for his safety and return to sanity. More often than not, even the most die-hard prodigals eventually get tired of the pigsty and trudge home.

manipulation of opinions and actions will be less obvious, although attitudes about the issues of life are not likely to be set in concrete.

Your advice and values will be more readily accepted, acknowledged, or at least tolerated by your older adolescent. By now your offspring will probably be wiser and perhaps sadder as well. While active rebellion is likely to subside as the twenties arrive, some consequences of unwise behavior during the past few years may not go entirely away. Hopefully, however, your teenager will arrive at this final phase without having made any difficult detours, or at least without obtaining any serious or painful scars. But whether the past few years have been smooth sailing or stormy weather, the dawn of independent adult life now looms on the horizon. Your parenting job isn't over until you have escorted your grown child across this threshold into the world of grown-up rights and responsibilities. In a real sense, you will work yourself out of a full-time job.

This process includes a number of transitions that may prove as challenging for you as for your teenager. You must progress

- from parent to caring friend and confidant;
- from gravy train to career guide;
- from being in charge to giving friendly advice—if asked;
- from bailing out and mopping up to allowing some consequences to be suffered.

As in all previous parenting tasks, extremes should be avoided. Give a teenager too much independence too early and he may suffer serious harm on the campus of the School of Hard Knocks. But hold the reins too tight for too long, and you may endure one of these equally painful scenarios:

- A strong-willed young adult who literally tears himself out of your sphere of influence, leaving gaping emotional wounds.
- A compliant "good boy" who never learns how to make his own decisions or earn his own way in the world.
- A rebellious and reckless adolescent/young adult who repeatedly gets into hot water and is always promptly bailed out by concerned and caring parents. Remember that the father of

the Prodigal Son didn't rescue him from the pigpen. The son had to suffer the consequences of his foolishness and then come to his senses by himself.

- The adult child who hangs out at the happy homestead long after his formal education has come to an end and sees no urgency in seeking his own means of support.

There are a number of reasons parents might feel reluctant to release their grown children to stand on their wobbly feet:

- The world seems a lot more treacherous than it was a generation ago. Parents who deeply desire that their children maintain spiritual commitments and ethical standards into adulthood are genuinely concerned about turning them loose into a culture that has lost its moral compass.
- The prolonged educational process required for many careers can keep young adults in a state of dependence on their parents for years. If you're paying those college bills and perhaps offering room and board (or more) during a graduate program, it is difficult not to keep some strings attached along the way.
- The costs of living independently—a place to live, transportation, food, clothing—can be awfully steep, keeping kids in the nest long after they are grown. Young married couples who are struggling to make ends meet may even be tempted (or forced) to move back in with Mom and Dad.
- A child with a significant physical, intellectual, or psychiatric handicap may need parenting well into the twenties or beyond. Even in these difficult situations, however, it is healthy to release as much responsibility and foster as much independence as possible.
- Parents may have invested so much of their lives into their children's formative years that the dawning of adulthood strikes them with apprehension or even dread: "What will we do when they're gone?!"

This difficult task of letting go can be accomplished by keeping the big picture in mind literally from the moment you hear that first cry in the delivery room. Your child is priceless, but she is only on loan to you for a season. Furthermore, while she can't do anything for herself as a newborn, from that time forward you will be in an ongoing process of transferring more responsibilities and decisions to her. Your two-year-old should be feeding herself, your five-year-old tying her own shoes, and your eight-year-old picking out what to wear to school—even though you can do it more neatly, quickly, or skillfully. As the adolescent years pass, your teenager needs to hear repeatedly that you will always love her (whatever paths she chooses) but that your parenting role will be coming to an end much sooner than she realizes.

Your public-service announcements are as important for the strong-willed fifteen-year-old who is stomping her feet and demanding more freedom ("I'm not a child anymore!") as they are for the laid-back eighteen-year-old who needs to know that the free meal ticket won't be issued forever. The responsibilities you transfer will become more complex—driving a car, balancing a checkbook, and (scariest of all) picking a spouse, among many others. But by walking with your adolescent through these processes step-by-step, your final release will seem like a small step rather than a plunge off a cliff.

CHAPTER 3

Bodies in Motion

PHYSICAL CHANGES AND ISSUES IN THE TEEN YEARS

As your child moves through the teen years, physical changes will be the most telling sign of this remarkable transition from child to adult. This chapter will focus on those physical aspects, while emotions, relationships, and other growing pains will be discussed in the chapter to follow. Both chapters will begin with a survey of normal development and then review potential pitfalls, preventive measures, and positive goals for parents and their rapidly growing children. Fasten your seat belt, hold on tight, and enjoy the ride.

Physical Growth and Development

From a physical standpoint, the main event of adolescence is puberty, which serves as the physiological bridge between childhood and adulthood.

Rapid growth and body changes during these years are to a large degree brought about by interactions between several **hormones,** biochemical compounds that are created in one part of the body and sent via the bloodstream to have a specific effect somewhere else. These chemical messages provoke an impressive number and variety of responses throughout the body. All of the hormones and the glands that secrete them are collectively known as the **endocrine system.** Not all hormones, however, are related to reproduction.

Thyroid hormone, for example, plays an important role in the body's metabolic rate. Insulin, secreted by the pancreas, escorts glucose (or blood sugar) into the cells that need and use this basic fuel. Growth hormone, as its name implies, is necessary for the attainment of normal adult height.

Speaking of growth hormone, a major growth spurt is one hallmark of adolescence, usually occurring between the ages of ten and fourteen in girls, and twelve and sixteen in boys. (Perhaps "spurt" isn't the most accurate term for this event, which actually lasts between two and three years.) The rate of growth can vary, but it tends to be the fastest during spring and summer. Weight increases as well, and bones progress through their final stages of maturation. In addition, the percentage of body fat increases in girls and decreases in boys.

Pubertal development in boys

In response to increased levels of the male hormone testosterone, a number of marvelous changes take place as a boy's body grows into that of a man's. Male sexual development usually begins between the ages of ten and thirteen (the average age is eleven), and the process is usually completed in about three years, although it can range anywhere from two to five years. The timing and speed of bodily changes can vary greatly between boys of the same age, and the slow developer may need extra encouragement and continued reassurance that he will eventually reach the goal of manhood. (He can be gently reminded that he probably hasn't seen any men walking around lately with high, squeaky voices.) A boy should be checked by his physician, however, if he begins to show pubertal changes before age nine or has none of these developments underway by age fourteen.

The first physical sign of puberty in boys is enlargement in the size of the testicles and thinning of the scrotum. Hair appears first in the genital area, then on the face, chest, and under the arms. The voice starts to deepen, although it may pass through an awkward phase of breaking, especially when he is excited or nervous.

The testicles begin manufacturing sperm, which are transported through a structure called the **epididymis** (one of which sits adjacent to each testicle) and then onward to the penis through a pair of flexible tubes called the **vas deferens.** The **prostate** begins to produce seminal fluid, which carries sperm out of the body during ejaculation. The newly functioning sexual equipment will at times unexpectedly carry out its functions during the middle of the night in what is called a **nocturnal emission** or "wet dream," a normal event that an uninformed adolescent might find alarming. Along the same lines, boys may be concerned or embarrassed by unexpected erections, which can occur at very inopportune times (for example, just prior to giving a report in front of a class). Neither of these should be interpreted as a sign of impending moral failure. In fact, hopefully you will have briefed your son about these normal events before puberty arrived.

If you are a single mother who feels uncomfortable discussing these matters with your son, consider seeking help from an adult male who not only shares your values but has enough rapport to talk with him about these topics.

Some boys develop a small, button-sized nodule of breast tissue directly under the nipple. This is a common response to changing hormones, although it may cause a minor panic when first discovered ("Is this a tumor?" "Am I going to develop breasts like a woman?"). This area may become a little tender but should return to normal within twelve to eighteen months. If you have any questions, or if breast tissue appears to be increasing in size (a phenomenon known as **gynecomastia**), have it checked by your son's doctor.

Pubertal development in girls
While pubertal development and the reproductive process are relatively straightforward in boys, the changes that take place as a girl progresses to womanhood are in many ways much more complex. (As you will see, they also take quite a bit longer to explain.) Not only does she undergo significant changes in her outward appearance, but inside her body a delicate interplay of hormones eventually leads to a momentous occasion: her first menstrual period (also called **menarche**), announcing her potential to reproduce.

The first visible sign of puberty in girls is the development of **breast buds,** which usually appear about two years before the first menstrual period. Each breast bud is a small, flat, firm buttonlike nodule that develops directly under the areola (the pigmented area that surrounds the nipple). This tissue eventually softens as the breasts enlarge. Occasionally a bud will develop on one side before the other, which might lead to the mistaken impression that a tumor is growing. But the passage of time and (if necessary) a doctor's examination will confirm that this growth is in fact normal.

As the breasts continue to develop, hair begins to grow first in the genital area, then under the arms, and on the legs. The contour of the hips becomes fuller, and the internal reproductive organs grow and mature. Glands within the vagina produce a clear or milky secretion, which may appear several months before the onset of menstrual bleeding. Finally, at the conclusion of an intricate sequence of hormonal events, the first menstrual flow arrives. This typically occurs around twelve years of age, with a range between nine and sixteen.

As with boys, girls who begin this process earlier or later than average will need some information and reassurance. In general, a girl should be checked by her physician if she develops breast buds before age eight or has her first period before age nine. At the opposite end of the spectrum, the absence of pubertal changes by thirteen or menstrual periods by sixteen should trigger a medical evaluation.

For many adolescents (and their parents), the menstrual cycle is a complex mystery or even a source of some anxiety. While this event may not be a routine topic of conversation over Sunday dinner, you might want to refresh your memory or learn about it for the first time well before the first stirrings of puberty in your offspring. Your daughter(s) at some point will have questions and concerns about the monthly flow: What is normal and what isn't? How often should this occur? What if there's a lot, very little, or none at all? What about cramping?

While the menstrual flow will be the focus of your adolescent's attention, it is only a single event in an elaborate process that prepares her physically each month for the possibility of bearing a child. It is therefore both practical and wise for you and your daughter(s) to understand the basics of a woman's reproductive cycle.

Furthermore, in the course of learning how to treat the women in his life with care and respect, a boy also should learn basic information about the female reproductive cycle. How and when he gains this information, however, will depend both on timing and his maturity level. In order to protect boundaries of modesty (and prevent potential embarrassment), be careful about what is said and who is listening when discussing what is going on inside the body of your teenager. Generic comments ("When a woman is having her menstrual period . . .") are more appropriate than naming names ("When Jessica is having her menstrual period . . ."). When in doubt, conversations about such matters with adolescents, who are likely to be extremely self-conscious, will feel safer if carried out in private or at least with boys and girls separately.

A single father who feels out of his element discussing the female reproductive cycle with his adolescent daughter may want to request help from a woman who is mature, is comfortable communicating this information to adolescents, and holds similar values regarding sexuality.

The Menstrual Cycle

In case your memory is a little fuzzy from health-education or childbirth classes, the following section is a primer on the menstrual cycle. If your adolescent is ready and interested, she or he may read along.

What goes on during the menstrual cycle?

Under normal circumstances, each month a woman's body performs a three-act play entitled *Preparing for a Baby*. What you are about to read is a summary of the essential characters and plot. (As with many other aspects of human physiology, there are thousands of other details that will not be spelled out here and thousands more yet to be discovered. The design of this process is indeed exquisite.)

The main characters in the play are:

- The **hypothalamus:** a multifaceted structure at the base of the brain that regulates basic bodily functions such as temperature and appetite. It also serves as the prime mover in the reproductive cycle.

- The **pituitary:** a small, punching-bag-shaped structure that appears to dangle from the brain directly below the hypothalamus. It has been called the "master gland" because it gives orders to many other organs. But it also takes important cues from the hypothalamus.
- The **ovaries:** a matched pair of organs in the female pelvis that serve two critical functions—releasing one or more eggs (or ova) each month and secreting the hormones **estrogen** and **progesterone.** At birth the ovaries contain about 2 million eggs, a woman's lifetime supply. During childhood, the vast majority of these gradually disappear, and by the time she reaches puberty only about 300,000 will be left. During her reproductive years, she will release between three hundred and five hundred eggs; the rest will die and disappear.
- The **uterus:** a pear-shaped organ consisting primarily of muscle, containing a cavity where a baby grows during pregnancy. This cavity is lined with delicate tissue called **endometrium,** which changes remarkably in response to estrogen and progesterone produced by the ovaries. The uterus, also called the womb, is located at the top of the vagina and positioned in the middle of the pelvis between the bladder and the rectum.
- The **fallopian tubes:** a pair of tubes, about four to five inches long, attached to the upper corners of the uterus and extending toward each ovary. Their job is to serve as a meeting place for egg and sperm and then to transport a fertilized egg to the uterus.

Act I: Preparing an egg for launch (the follicular phase). The hypothalamus begins a reproductive cycle by sending a message called **gonadotrophin releasing hormone** to the pituitary gland just a short distance away. The message says, in effect, "Send out the hormone that prepares an egg to be released by the ovary." The pituitary responds by secreting **follicle stimulating hormone** (or FSH) into the bloodstream. Each egg within an ovary is covered with a thin sheet of cells, and the term **follicle** (which literally means "little bag") refers to the entire package of egg and cells together. Under the influence of FSH, eight or ten follicles begin to grow and "ripen." Usually only one becomes dominant and progresses to full maturity.

This follicular phase of the cycle lasts about two weeks, during which the dominant follicle fills with fluid and enlarges to about three-quarters of an inch. The egg contained within it will soon be released from the ovary. At the same time, this follicle secretes increasing amounts of estrogen, which (among other things) stimulates the lining of the uterus to proliferate and thicken. This is the first stage of preparation of the uterus for the arrival of a fertilized egg.

Act II: The egg is released (ovulation). As in Act I, this part of the story also begins in the hypothalamus. In response to rising levels of estrogen, the hypothalamus signals the pituitary to release a brief but intense surge of **luteinizing hormone** (or LH) into the bloodstream. This hormone sets off a chain reaction in the ovary. The dominant follicle enlarges, its outer wall becomes thin, and finally it ruptures, releasing egg and fluid. This mini-eruption called **ovulation** takes only a few minutes and occurs approximately thirty-eight hours after the peak of the LH surge. Sometimes a tiny amount of blood oozes from the ovary as well. This may irritate the lining of the abdomen, producing a discomfort known as **mittelschmerz** (German for "middle pain," because it occurs about halfway through the cycle).

Act III: The voyage of the egg and the preparation of the uterus (the luteal phase). The egg is not left to its own devices once it is set free from the ovary. At the end of each fallopian tube are structures called **fimbria** (Latin for "fingers"), whose delicate tentacles move over the area of the ovary. As soon as ovulation takes place, the fimbria gently escort the egg into the tube, where it begins a journey toward the uterus. The cells that line the fallopian tube have microscopic hairlike projections called **cilia,** which move in a synchronized pattern that sets up a one-way current through the tube. If sperm are present in the outer portion of the tube, and one of them is successful in penetrating the egg, fertilization takes place and a new life begins. The fertilized egg will incubate in the tube for about three days, developing into a multicelled embryo, before arriving at the cavity of the uterus, where it floats for about three more days before implanting. On about the seventh day it "rests," so to speak, implanting in the cavity of the uterus. If the egg is not fertilized, it will live only twelve to twenty-four hours and then disintegrate or pass through the tube and uterus into the vagina. (Since sperm live for forty-eight to seventy-two hours, there are three or four days in each cycle during which intercourse could lead to conception.)

Meanwhile, much activity takes place in the ovary after ovulation. The newly vacated follicle has another job to do: preparing the uterus to accept and nourish a fertilized egg should one arrive. The follicle turns into a gland called the **corpus luteum** (literally, "yellow body" because cells lining the inside of the follicle develop a yellowish color), which secretes estrogen and, more important, progesterone. This hormone, which dominates this luteal phase of the cycle, promotes growth and maturation of the uterine lining. This layer of tissue eventually doubles in thickness and becomes stocked with nutrients. Progesterone not only prepares the uterine "nursery" for a new arrival but also relaxes the muscles of the uterus, decreasing the chance of contractions that might accidentally expel its guest. Progesterone also temporarily stops the preparation of any other eggs within the ovaries.

If the newly formed embryo successfully implants and continues its growth within the uterus, it secretes a hormone called **human chorionic gonadotrophin** (or HCG), which sends an important message to the corpus luteum: "Keep the hormones flowing!" The corpus luteum obliges and for nine or ten weeks continues to provide the hormone support that allows the uterus to nourish the baby growing inside. After ten weeks, the **placenta** (the complex organ that connects the baby to the inner lining of the uterus) takes over the job of manufacturing progesterone, and the corpus luteum retires from active duty.

If there is no fertilization, no pregnancy, and no HCG, the corpus luteum degenerates. Progesterone and estrogen levels fall, resulting in spasm of the blood vessels that supply the lining of the uterus. Deprived of the nutrients it needs to survive, the lining dies and passes from the uterus, along with blood and mucus, in what is called the menstrual flow (also referred to as the period or **menses**).

While the menstrual period might seem to be the end of the story, the first day of flow is actually counted as day one of a woman's reproductive cycle. For while the flow is taking place, the three-act play is starting over again as a new set of follicles begins to ripen in the ovaries. This "circle of life" will thus normally continue month after month throughout the reproductive years until menopause unless interrupted by pregnancy, a surgical procedure such as a hysterectomy, or a medical condition that interferes with this cycle.

What is normal during menstrual periods?

The words *menstrual* and *menses* are derived from the Latin word for "month," which refers to the approximate frequency of this event. A typical cycle lasts from twenty-seven to thirty-five days, although for some women normal menses occur as frequently as every twenty-one days or as infrequently as every forty-five days. Most of the variability arises during the first (follicular) phase leading up to ovulation. Assuming that a pregnancy does not begin, the luteal phase (from ovulation to menses) is nearly always fourteen days, with little variation.

During the first year or two after her first menstrual period, an adolescent's cycles may be irregular because of **anovulatory cycles,** in which an egg is not released. If ovulation does not take place, the cycle will remain stuck in the first (follicular) phase. Estrogen will continue to stimulate the lining of the uterus until some of it becomes so thick that it outgrows its blood supply. The shedding of this tissue resembles a menstrual period, but it is unpredictable and usually occurs with very little cramping. When ovulation finally takes place, the lining of the uterus will mature and then be shed all at once if a pregnancy has not started.

After her first menstrual period, several months may pass before a girl's endocrine system matures to the point of producing regular ovulation. During this time it is not unusual for her to skip two or three months between cycles. Since cramping doesn't normally occur unless ovulation has taken place, menstrual pains may not be noticed for months (or even one or two years) after the first cycle.

Menstrual flow normally lasts three to six days, although very short (one-day) or longer (seven- or eight-day) periods may be normal for some women. One to three ounces of blood are usually lost during each cycle, although more or less than this amount may be a regular occurrence without any ill effects.

Virtually all normal activities can be continued during a menstrual period. Bathing or showering is not only safe but advisable in order to minimize any unpleasant odor. Feminine hygiene sprays and deodorant pads may irritate delicate tissue, and douching is unnecessary and should be avoided. Any persistent drainage that is discolored, itchy, painful, or foul-smelling should be evaluated by a physician.

What can go wrong with menstrual periods?

Menstrual cramps (also called **dysmenorrhea**) most often are a by-product of the normal breakdown of the lining of the uterus (endometrium) at the end of a cycle. Chemicals called **prostaglandins** are released into the bloodstream by the endometrium, often with unpleasant effects. The most obvious response is a series of contractions of the muscles of the uterus, which may actually be as forceful as contractions during labor. During a strong contraction, blood may be inhibited from circulating through all of the uterine muscle and, like any other muscle temporarily deprived of oxygen, it will sound off with genuine pain. Prostaglandins may affect other parts of the body during a menstrual period, causing diarrhea, nausea, headaches, and difficulty with concentration. One bit of good news in connection with menstrual cramps is that they do not predict what level of pain a woman will feel later in life during childbirth. In other words, a teenager with severe menstrual cramps is not necessarily going to have equally severe labor pains.

Menstrual cramps can be relieved in a variety of ways:

- Heating pads or warm baths are often helpful, for reasons that are unclear. (These may increase blood flow within the pelvis, improving the supply of oxygen to uterine muscle.)
- Exercise and good general physical condition are often help-

ful in reducing cramps. Walking is a good exercise during this (or, for that matter, any) time of the month.

- Specific prostaglandin-inhibiting medications work well for many adolescents and older women alike. These were formulated to reduce the pain and inflammation of arthritis but were found to also have a significant effect on menstrual cramps. Several are available without prescription: ibuprofen (Advil, Motrin, Nuprin, and other brands), naproxen (Aleve), and ketoprofen (Orudis KT and others). These anti-inflammatory drugs should be taken with food to decrease the chance of irritating the stomach. They are most effective if they are taken at the first sign of cramping and then continued on a regular basis (rather than "here and there" in response to pain) until the cramps stop. Your daughter's physician may recommend one of these medications (sometimes with a dosage schedule different from what is written on the package) or prescribe one of several anti-inflammatory medications. Individual responses vary. If one type doesn't work well, another may seem like a miracle.
- Other pain-relief medications that may be helpful include:
  (a) Acetaminophen (Tylenol and others), which does not inhibit prostaglandins but can be quite effective nonetheless. Some women have found that alternating medications is helpful—for example, starting with ibuprofen, using acetaminophen for the next dose a few hours later, then switching back, and so on.
  (b) Midol, which combines acetaminophen with the antihistamine pyrilamine (which may be mildly sedating). Depending on the particular formulation, Midol may include ibuprofen or a mild diuretic (to decrease fluid retention).
  (c) Stronger pain relievers may be prescribed by a physician if the discomfort of menstrual cramps cannot be controlled by other measures.

If menstrual cramps are disruptive and unresponsive to home remedies and nonprescription medications, it is important that they be evaluated medically. Abnormalities of the cervix (the opening of the uterus) or the uterus itself or a syndrome called **endometriosis** (in which tissue that normally lines the uterus grows in other parts of the body, usually in the pelvis) can on rare occasions be the cause of significant menstrual pain in an adolescent. If the medical examination is normal, the physician may suggest one or both of the following prescription medications:

- **Diuretics** decrease fluid retention but do not directly relieve cramps; however, discomfort may be less annoying if any

Pads or Tampons?

From the very first to the final reproductive cycle, either tampons or external pads may be used to absorb menstrual flow. Each has its specific advantages and disadvantages.

External pads may be more comfortable for a young adolescent who feels uneasy about inserting a foreign object into her vagina. However, pads may cause heat and moisture to be retained around the external genital area (especially in hot or humid climates) and increase the likelihood of local irritation or infection.

Tampons allow more freedom of activity (especially for vigorous exercise or swimming) and less chance of contributing to external irritation. Some parents may worry about tampons causing damage inside or at the opening of the vagina. However, inserting a tampon does not tear the hymen (the ring of soft tissue just inside the labia at the entrance to the vagina), although difficulty inserting tampons may be the first indication of an abnormality of this structure. Very rarely, small vaginal ulcerations may result from improper tampon insertion. Occasionally a tampon may disappear into the vagina and cannot be located by the wearer. This is not a dangerous situation, although if left behind for more than a day or two, a stray tampon can generate a powerful odor and discharge. A doctor or nurse practitioner can retrieve it without much difficulty.

Of more concern is the association of tampon use with **toxic shock syndrome (TSS),** a condition caused by a toxin produced by the bacterium *Staphylococcus aureus.* A number of cases in the early 1980s occurred in connection with a particular type of tampon that appeared to foster the growth of staphylococci in the vagina and irritate the vaginal lining. This tampon was taken off the market, but subsequent evidence has indicated that a primary risk factor for the development of TSS is the *amount of time a tampon is left in the vagina.*

Most of the symptoms of this problem are nonspecific: fever, chills, vomiting, diarrhea, sore throat, and faintness (caused by a drop in blood pressure). A more specific sign is a sunburnlike rash on the palms and soles. Toxic shock syndrome is treated in the hospital fluid retention is relieved (see Premenstrual Syndrome later in this chapter).

- **Birth control pills** (oral contraceptives) may be helpful in reducing or eliminating significant cramps that are not adequately controlled by other means. In fact, for many adolescents this may be the only type of medication that is helpful in reducing severe cramps that regularly interfere with normal activity. Each four-week cycle of pills provides three weeks of estrogen and progesterone in a specified amount. This prevents the LH surge and ovulation and also usually results in less proliferation of the lining of the uterus than

continued

with large doses of antibiotics as well as fluids given intravenously to maintain blood pressure. The development of flulike symptoms and light-headedness—feeling faint or actually passing out, especially associated with standing up or other changes in position—may be very significant if they occur during a menstrual period. These symptoms should be evaluated by a physician *as soon as possible.*

Fortunately TSS is rare. (Some staphylococcal infections are associated with TSS and may have no involvement with tampon use; thus they can occur in men and women, for example, a postoperative wound infection.) Most physicians feel that tampons are safe for both adolescents and older women, although fifteen- to nineteen-year-olds are at the most risk for developing toxic shock syndrome from tampon use. Simple precautions can markedly reduce this risk:

- First, and most important, don't leave a tampon in place for more than six hours.
- Follow the manufacturer's instructions closely.
- Insert (and remove) a tampon carefully.
- Store tampons in a clean, dry place.
- Wash hands thoroughly before inserting or removing tampons.
- Use tampons with the least absorbency necessary to control the flow. Tampons are now graded for absorbency as follows:
  (a) Junior
  (b) Regular
  (c) Super
  (d) Super plus (not recommended for use by adolescents)
  Less absorbent tampons are smaller and less likely to irritate the lining of the vagina. If a tampon is difficult to remove, a smaller size should be used.
- Consider alternating tampons and pads during the same menstrual period. (For example, use tampons during the day, pads at night.)

occurs during a normal cycle. During the fourth week, no hormones are present in the pills, so during this time the lining is shed as in a normal cycle. However, the smaller amount of tissue involved usually generates less cramping.

A decision to use birth control pills should not be made casually. A medical evaluation to rule out other causes of pain may be necessary. Nausea, headaches, bloating, and/or worsening of acne are unpleasant side effects experienced by some users. The pills must be taken consistently each day to be effective.

In addition, the use of birth control pills may raise parental concern: Could taking them for menstrual cramps (or any other therapeutic purpose) indirectly lower your adolescent's resistance to sexual activity? If you don't know the answer to this question, now is the time for candid conversation about sexuality. It would be unfortunate to withhold a treatment that might reduce debilitating pain because of a parent's vague mistrust of an adolescent who is actually fervently committed to remaining abstinent. Furthermore, the decision to postpone sex until marriage should be built on a strong, multilayered foundation. If the absence of contraceptives is the only reason she is avoiding intercourse, she needs to hear and understand many more reasons.

Irregular menstrual periods may be a cause for concern if they are

- too rare, occurring every three or four months after more than a year has passed since the first period;
- too frequent, with bleeding or spotting occurring throughout the month;
- too long, lasting more than seven or eight consecutive days;
- too heavy, soaking through more than six to eight pads/ tampons per day.

For any of these problems, a medical evaluation is usually indicated to discover the underlying cause. In many instances the diagnosis will be anovulatory cycles resulting from an immature endocrine system. But other physical or even emotional events can also interfere with the complex interaction of hormones that brings about the monthly cycle. These include:

- *Medical disorders.* These could include malfunctions of the endocrine system (including pituitary, adrenal, or thyroid glands) or abnormalities of the ovaries, uterus, or vagina.
- *Significant changes in weight.* Obese adolescents can generate enough estrogen in their fat cells to impact the lining of the uterus. At the opposite extreme, stringent diets or the severe reduction in food intake seen in anorexia will effectively shut down the menstrual cycle.
- *Extreme levels of exercise.* Female athletes with demanding training programs may have infrequent periods or may stop their cycles altogether.
- *Stress.* Stormy emotional weather is no stranger to the adolescent years, and personal upheavals can cause a teenager to miss one or more periods.
- *Pregnancy.* In some cases an absence of menstrual cycles could indicate that a pregnancy has begun.

It is important that extremes in menstrual flow (whether too much or too little) be evaluated. Not only may the underlying cause have great significance, but the menstrual irregularity could have damaging consequences of its own. For example:

- Very frequent or heavy bleeding may outstrip an adolescent's ability to replenish red blood cells, leading to iron deficiency **anemia.** Often there is an inadequate amount of iron in the diet to keep up with what is being lost each month. Anemia can cause ongoing fatigue, poor concentration in school, light-headedness, or even fainting episodes.
- Absence of menstrual periods related to a continual failure to ovulate may result in months or years of nonstop estrogen stimulation of the uterus. Without the maturing effect of progesterone, the lining of the uterus may be at increased risk for precancerous abnormalities.
- Adolescents who stop their cycles because of weight loss or intense physical training (or both) may suffer an irreversible

loss of bone density, known as **osteoporosis.** Normally a problem faced by women much later in life (typically well after menopause), osteoporosis can lead to disabling fractures of the spine, hips, wrists, and other bones.

It is impossible to state a single course of action that will resolve all the various forms of menstrual irregularity. However, if there appears to be no underlying disturbance that needs specific treatment and the problem is determined to be irregular ovulation, a doctor may recommend hormonal treatment to regulate the cycle. This may take the form of progesterone, which can be given at a defined time each month to bring on a menstrual period. Or birth control pills may be recommended to restore some order by overriding a woman's own cycle and establishing one that is more predictable. As mentioned earlier, the decision to use this type of medication in an adolescent must be made with particular care and discernment.

PMS and PMDD. As many as 75 to 90 percent of women experience some degree of discomfort that may occur for a day or two prior to menstruation, or may extend over the entire two-week period following ovulation. Mild physical or emotional distress during this time, sometimes called "premenstrual tension," is very common. But 20 to 40 percent of women experience symptoms severe enough to disrupt normal activities. This is commonly called *premenstrual syndrome,* or *PMS.*

A specific cause for PMS has not been identified, but the effects are all too familiar for many women, including adolescents. Physical symptoms can include bloating and fullness in the abdomen, fluid retention (with tightness of rings and shoes), headaches, breast tenderness, backache, fatigue, and dizziness. More dramatic are the emotional symptoms: irritability, anxiety, depression, poor concentration, insomnia, difficulty making decisions, and unusual food cravings. These can occur in various combinations and levels of severity.

The most striking feature is usually the instability and intensity of negative emotions, which can send other family members running for cover. Some teenagers and older women feel like Dr. Jekyll and Ms. Hyde—calm and rational for the first two weeks of the cycle and out of control for the second two weeks, with dramatic improvement once the menstrual flow is under way. Between 3 and 5 percent of women have premenstrual emotional storms severe enough to cause significant disturbances at home, school, and work, a condition specifically designated in recent years as *premenstrual dysphoric disorder,* or *PMDD.*

A few decades ago PMS was considered primarily a psychological event, an "adjustment reaction" to reproductive issues or life in general. This is no longer the case. PMS should be taken as seriously as any other physical issue. While no quick-fix remedies or lifetime cures exist for PMS, a number of measures can help your adolescent (and others at home) reduce its impact:

- *Make sure the emotional and physical symptoms are, in fact, PMS.* Adolescent emotions are often intense and variable, and other life issues (involving school, friends, etc.) may be at the heart of the problem. If there is any question, symptoms can be charted on a calendar, along with menstrual periods, for two or three months. You should see an improvement for at least a week following menses. Symptoms that continue well after a period is over or throughout the cycle involve something other than (or in addition to) PMS, including depression (see chapter 9).

- *Keep the lines of communication open and plan ahead.* A teenager whose cycle is well established will be able to predict when the more troublesome days are coming. This may give others at home a little advance "storm warning," and they will be able to respond with an extra measure of TLC or at least a little slack. This is particularly important if more than one person at home has difficulty with PMS, since the collision of two unstable moods can be quite unpleasant. If your daughter is currently irritable because of the time of the month and a change for the better is likely in the immediate future, you would be wise to postpone any conversations about emotionally charged issues for a few days if possible. It is important to acknowledge the reality of PMS symptoms without allowing them to become a blanket excuse for blatant disrespect, acting out, or abandonment of all responsibilities.

• *Encourage sensible eating, exercise, and sleep patterns.* Frequent, smaller meals and avoidance of overtly sugary foods may help keep blood glucose levels (and mood) a little more stable. Avoiding salt can reduce fluid retention. Caffeine may increase irritability, so decaffeinated drinks (and medications) are more appropriate. All-around physical conditioning through the entire month can improve general well-being and help her navigate more smoothly to the end of a cycle. Inadequate sleep will aggravate many, if not most, physical and emotional symptoms.

In addition, a variety of remedies, nutritional supplements, and medications have been recommended at one time or another for this problem. Some have a more consistent track record (and better scientific support) than others, and your adolescent should consider getting advice from her physician before trying any of these. Ultimately the bottom line for any PMS treatment will be an honest assessment of the effectiveness, safety, and side effects for the individual taking it.

• *Nonprescription medications* such as acetaminophen, ibuprofen, or naproxen to reduce aches and pains may be of some help. Remember that anti-inflammatory medications (such as ibuprofen or naproxen) should be taken with food to avoid nausea or irritation of the stomach, which would obviously be undesirable.

• *Calcium* (1,200 milligrams per day) and *magnesium* (200 milligrams per day) supplementation have both been shown to reduce symptoms of PMS (especially physical discomforts) by 40 to 50 percent. Improvements may not be noticed, however, until two or three cycles have passed while taking supplementation.

• *Vitamin E* supplementation (usually at 400 international units per day) has shown mixed results in research studies on PMS.

• *Vitamin B_6*, which has long been advocated as a remedy for

PMS symptoms, has performed poorly in controlled studies and probably has limited usefulness at best. If numbness or tingling of the hands or feet occur while taking this vitamin, it should be discontinued. Megadoses of any vitamin or mineral that exceed RDAs (recommended daily allowances) are not recommended for this condition.

- A number of *herbal preparations,* such as evening primrose oil, have been advocated for one or more symptoms of PMS, but research studies investigating such claims have yielded mixed results. While the scientific jury is out, keep in mind that the Food and Drug Administration (FDA) does not certify herbal remedies for safety and effectiveness.

- *Prescription medications* that are most widely used for PMS fall into three basic categories. Obviously, the use of any of these will require evaluation and follow-up by a physician.

  (a) *Diuretics.* For many women, much of the discomfort from PMS arises from bloating and fluid retention, so the use of a mild diuretic (or "water pill") to maintain normal fluid levels during the second half of each cycle can be effective.

  (b) *Antidepressants.* Many PMS symptoms, and certainly those of PMDD, essentially duplicate those seen in depression. It now appears that a fundamental physiological problem in PMS/PMDD involves changes in the levels of biological messengers in the brain known as neurotransmitters (especially serotonin). New research has demonstrated significant reduction in both emotional and physical premenstrual distress with antidepressants known as *selective serotonin reuptake inhibitors* (or *SSRIs*), such as fluoxetine (Prozac or Sarafem), sertraline (Zoloft), paroxetine (Paxil), and venlafaxine (Effexor). These drugs are safe and not habit-forming, but individual responses and side effects vary considerably. Often doses lower than needed to treat depression are effective in reducing PMS/PMDD symptoms.

  (c) *Hormonal manipulations* (such as oral contraceptives) have been utilized with variable success, although they are not commonly prescribed for adolescents with PMS.

Women who take supplemental progesterone during the second half of the menstrual cycle may report marked improvement, a worsening of symptoms (especially depression), or no effect at all. Hormonal preparations should be utilized in adolescents only after thoughtful consideration of the pros and cons by patient, parent, and physician.

Medical Exams and Evaluations during Adolescence

During the next few years, your teenager will probably need medical input on a number of occasions. Screening exams for sports, camp, and general health assessment will need to be done. Injuries arising from sports or other vigorous activities may need attention. Problems related to menstruation may require medical evaluation and intervention. In addition, a variety of symptoms and emotional concerns may arise during these years.

Adolescent health-care guidelines recommend yearly visits to the doctor for assessment, screening, and guidance, even if there have been evaluations during the year for other medical problems. Quick exams for camp or sports, especially those done assembly-line style on large groups of adolescents, should not substitute for more comprehensive physicals by your regular health-care provider. If there are special health problems, more frequent exams may be necessary. Most doctors will talk with parent and teen together during the visit, but part of the time will be spent without the parent present. This is usually done in order to increase the likelihood that the doctor is receiving accurate information, with an assumption that many teenagers might feel uncomfortable answering sensitive questions in front of their parents. It is customary during this time alone for a physician to assure the young patient of the confidentiality of their conversation. *It is therefore extremely important that you consider carefully who is going to provide health care for your adolescent.*

In an ideal situation, you will be dealing with someone

- who is medically competent;
- whom your teenager trusts and can talk with comfortably;
- who knows you and your family;
- whom *you* trust, and who shares your basic values.

The last qualification is particularly significant because of the near certainty that your teenager will eventually be in a one-on-one situation with the physician. Your son or daughter may feel more comfortable discussing sensitive topics with a doctor than with you, even if you have an extremely close and honest relationship. You will want to be certain that the advice and counsel given behind closed doors, especially regarding sexual behavior, will not contradict or undermine principles you have been teaching at home. During these critical years, everyone needs to be on the same team.

Although adolescents usually have an interest in discussing a variety of topics with their doctors, they may feel embarrassed to broach certain subjects. The physician should have the interest (and time) to ask some probing questions and then offer sound input based on the response. (There is no guarantee, of course, that a teenager will tell "the whole truth and nothing but," even when confidentiality is assured.) Along with questions about past history and any current symptoms, specific topics that are usually on the physician's agenda (if not on the patient's) include:

- Growth and development. Younger adolescents are particularly concerned about whether they are normal, especially if pubertal changes are taking place earlier or later than in their peers.
- Physical safety, including the use of seat belts, bicycle or motorcycle helmets, and appropriate sports equipment
- Current dietary practices. Are they healthy, erratic, or extreme in any way?
- Vaccination history
- Exercise and sleep. Is there enough of each?
- Tobacco use
- Alcohol and drug use
- Sexual activity
- Relationships at home and school
- The emotional weather. Are there any signs of depression?
- Sexual or other physical abuse. A physician who is attentive to an adolescent's physical well-being and demeanor may be the first to detect signs of abuse. By law the physician is

required to report any concerns about abuse to the appropriate local social-service or law-enforcement agency.

In addition to the usual elements of a medical exam (height and weight, ears, throat, neck, chest, heart, abdomen), a few other areas are important:

- Blood pressure. While not common in adolescents, **hypertension** (elevated blood pressure) must be evaluated further if it is detected.
- The spine. Special attention is given to **scoliosis,** a sideways curvature of the spine. There are specific guidelines regarding the degree of curvature that help determine whether treatment is needed, and if so, what methods might be appropriate.
- The groin area should be checked for **hernias** (primarily in boys).
- The testes should be checked for appropriate development and for any masses. Testicular cancer is unique for its prevalence among young men, and teenagers should get in the habit of a brief monthly self-check for unusual growths in this area.
- The breasts in both sexes.

When should a girl receive her first internal pelvic exam? Most medical authorities recommend that this be done

- if there is a symptom or concern about disease: vaginal discharge, pelvic pain, or other symptoms in this area normally cannot be diagnosed by history alone;
- if a girl has become sexually active;
- if she is going to be married in the near future;
- if she is in her late teens or early twenties, even when there are no specific concerns;
- if she is going to start on birth control pills.

Needless to say, no adolescent (or any older woman) is excited about having a pelvic exam, especially if there is discomfort in this area to start with. It is important that whoever does the exam explain step-by-step what is going to happen and then talk her through it while it is being done. She should be reassured that it is normal to feel nervous and awkward and that while the exam is not particularly comfortable, it shouldn't be extremely painful either. Both patient and parent should understand that a pelvic exam does not terminate a girl's virginity. Sexual morality is not violated by a medical procedure whose purpose is to help assess, diagnose, and treat a physical problem.

A young girl should feel free to tell her physician when and where it hurts and know that the exam will be modified if she is having a lot of pain. Many teenagers feel more comfortable if the exam is done by a physician they know and trust, regardless of gender, while others specifically prefer that it be done by a female health-care provider. In either case, the examiner should be accompanied by a female attendant.

Normally during a pelvic exam, the external genitals are briefly inspected, and then a speculum (the "duckbill" instrument) is gently inserted. A narrow speculum should be available for younger patients, and this should pass through the **hymen** (the ring of soft tissue just inside the labia at the entrance to the vagina) without tearing it. The vaginal walls will be checked, and a **Pap smear** is normally done. During a Pap smear, some cells are gently obtained from the cervix and then transferred to a slide. The cells are examined microscopically for evidence that might indicate that a sexually transmitted infection, a cancer, or a precancerous condition is present. Tests for specific sexually transmitted infections may also be done.

Then the examiner will insert one or two fingers into the vagina while the other hand gently presses on the lower abdomen. Much information can be obtained from this simple maneuver, including the size of the uterus and ovaries and the location and intensity of any tenderness. A rectal examination may also be done at this time. This involves the gentle inserting of one finger into the anal opening, with or without another finger present in the vagina. Depending upon the clincal situation, important information may be obtained during this examination. Needless to say, gloves are worn by the examiner during the entire pelvic/rectal examination.

Some additional tests may be done during a basic physical exam. These could include:

- Vision and hearing screening
- Urinalysis
- Blood tests, especially:
  (a) a blood count to check for anemia (especially in girls)
  (b) cholesterol and other circulating fat molecules (called lipids) if there is history of elevated cholesterol or heart attack before age fifty-five in one or more family members
- A screening test for tuberculosis may be put on the arm. A temporary local reaction (redness and a firm bump at the injection site) within two or three days indicates a past exposure to tuberculosis. If this occurs, further evaluation will be necessary to determine the appropriate course of action.

Immunization updates often given during the adolescent years:

- A **tetanus and diphtheria (Td) booster** should be given ten years following the last injection, which in most cases will have been at four or five years of age. Thus Td is typically given at a fourteen- or fifteen-year-old checkup, unless an injury prior to this age required an earlier booster. Remind your adolescent that this is normally repeated every ten years for the rest of his life. A booster may be given after five years if he sustains a wound that results from a puncture, crush injury, burn, or frostbite, or one that is contaminated with dirt, feces, or saliva. In addition, some physicians give a tetanus booster if five years have elapsed since the last one and the adolescent is going on a wilderness expedition or to a foreign country where vaccine might not be available.
- **Measles/mumps/rubella (MMR) vaccine** should be given if your child has had only one injection thus far. It is unwise to count on a single immunization during infancy to protect against these infections throughout adolescence and adulthood. (Many colleges now require proof of two doses of MMR prior to entrance.)

- **Hepatitis B vaccine** should be given if the series has not been completed already. Parents who are aware that this infection is transmitted primarily through sexual contact and intravenous drug use may feel it is unnecessary to subject their son or daughter to a three-dose vaccine. ("My kid won't do those things—why does he need these shots?") But a significant proportion of hepatitis B cases occur among people who are not involved in any risky behavior and who have no clear-cut exposure history. Since this infection can potentially be lethal or cause significant chronic illness, the vaccine is a good investment.

- If your adolescent has never had **chicken pox (varicella)** and has not been previously immunized against it, vaccination against this virus would be advisable, especially because infections in teenagers and adults tend to be more severe than in younger children. Prior to the thirteenth birthday, only one dose of varicella vaccine is needed, while after age thirteen two doses should be given four to eight weeks apart. Varicella vaccine may be given at the same time as an MMR and/or Td injection. However, if varicella and MMR are not given simultaneously, an interval of at least a month should separate the two.

- If your teen is planning to travel extensively, especially to rural or impoverished areas of foreign countries, you may want to have him vaccinated against **hepatitis A,** which is transmitted through contaminated food and water. Because the vaccine is very safe, and because thousands of cases of hepatitis A occur every year within the United States, many physicians recommend routine immunization against this virus, even for those who are not planning to travel. The hepatitis A vaccine provides long-term, specific, and effective immunity. While a single dose of the vaccine should provide adequate protection, a booster dose is recommended six to eighteen months following the initial immunization.

- The **influenza** virus makes an annual appearance in most communities during the winter, provoking fever, aches, and coughing that are often more intense than a garden-variety upper respiratory infection. While most adolescents recover from influenza after a few days of rest, fluids, and acetaminophen for their aches and pains, those with significant medical problems such as heart disease, diabetes, or chronic respiratory disturbances (especially asthma) may suffer severe complications. These individuals normally are given influenza vaccine each year in the fall. Because new strains of this virus appear annually, a new vaccine must be prepared each year.

• **Meningococcus** is a type of bacteria which can cause a severe form of meningitis, or inflammation of the membranes which cover the brain and spinal cord. While uncommon, meningococcal meningitis can be a devastating illness. Because some strains of the meningococcus are highly contagious, and because people who live in close quarters are at a slightly higher risk of becoming infected than the general population, many colleges and universities are now suggesting that students who live in dormitories (especially freshmen) receive vaccination against this bacteria. Check with your teenager's physician and/or her college's student health service regarding additional information and availability of this vaccine.

Check with the doctor's office if you have any questions about the advisability of these immunizations. This is particularly important if your adolescent has a significant medical problem, especially one that affects the function of the immune system (for example, leukemia, HIV infection, pregnancy, or a cancer under treatment with chemotherapy). In addition, be sure to inquire about precautions or potential side effects of any vaccine that he or she might be given.

Acne

Pimples, pustules, and the occasionally more serious cysts and scars of acne occur primarily during the teen years, when a child's self-consciousness is very often at an all-time high. Nearly 80 percent of adolescents experience acne to some degree. Girls tend to be affected at an earlier age, but acne occurs in boys more frequently and with greater severity. While in most cases acne clears up on its own eventually, it should be treated and not ignored, because some of the physical and emotional scars it leaves can last many years.

Acne originates in areas of the skin where there are large numbers of rudimentary hairs combined with large **sebaceous glands,** so named because they secrete a thick, oily material called **sebum.** The majority of these glands are present on the face, chest, upper back, and shoulders.

CAUSES The hormonal surges of puberty stimulate the production of sebum, which normally passes uneventfully to the surface of the skin. Sometimes, however, the channels leading from sebaceous glands to the skin become blocked by dead cells. Sebum then accumulates into a visible bump commonly known as a pimple or **whitehead.** If the enlarging mass of sebum pushes outward to the skin surface, oxidation—not dirt—darkens the fatty materials, forming a **blackhead.**

Bacteria on the skin surface gain access to the buildup of sebum and multiply, releasing chemical by-products that not only irritate the skin but also attract white blood cells. The resulting inflammatory reaction produces more prominent irritated bumps called **pustules** or the larger (and more damaging) **acne cysts,** which in severe cases can leave disfiguring scars.

FACTORS THAT WORSEN ACNE Why some teenagers develop a major acne problem while others are spared is not always clear, but a number of factors are known to aggravate acne:

- Tight-fitting clothing or headgear. Wet suits, helmets, headbands, and bras that rub skin may provoke changes in the skin area directly below them.
- Picking or scratching pimples and pustules.
- Hot, humid environments that cause heavy perspiration. Sunlight, however, can help some cases of acne, but beware of excessive sun exposure and the risk of burning.

- Some girls have a flare-up of acne before their menstrual periods, in response to hormonal fluctuations, when the outlet of the sebaceous gland becomes more obstructed.
- Medications, including **isoniazid** (used to treat tuberculosis), **phenytoin** (Dilantin, used to control epilepsy), and **steroids** (whether forms prescribed by a physician or **androgens** used inappropriately by athletes to build muscles) may worsen acne. Some birth control pills improve it, while others will aggravate it.
- Oils and dyes in cosmetics and hair sprays can plug the sebaceous glands, so water-based products are better for people who are prone to acne. *Note: The impact of these factors on any given teenager's skin will vary a great deal.*

EFFECT OF DIRT AND DIET   Acne is not caused by dirt on the skin, and aggressive scrubbing (especially with abrasive materials) can actually make it worse. A mild, unscented soap should be used daily to remove oils from the skin surface.

The role of diet in acne has been more of a legend than reality. Despite persistent beliefs that greasy or sweet foods turn directly into pimples, dietary changes in fact have not been proven to cause or cure acne in the general population. However, anyone who

---

Health Problems, Hypochondria, or Cries for Help?

You may at times become frustrated by ongoing physical complaints from your adolescent, especially those that sound very compelling in the morning and seem to evaporate by midafternoon or weekends. How do you know whether to offer TLC and bed rest or to escort him out to the bus stop despite his complaints? The answer isn't always easy. More than once you may struggle with guilt after discovering he *was* sick after you overruled his protests and sent him to school. On other occasions, you may be compassionate in the morning then feel like you've been had when he takes off on his bike at the end of the day.

If symptoms are frequent, ask your health-care provider to help sort things out. To get the most out of this consultation, spend time before the visit talking over the problem with your teenager, listing the problems (fatigue, headaches) and their characteristics (how often, how long, what helps, what makes it worse).

While you're at it, try to get a feel for the social weather at school, in the neighborhood, or at church. Questions with no obvious right or wrong answer ("Who do you like to hang around with?" or "What's your least favorite class?") may open the window to

notices a consistent relationship between a particular food and acne should consider avoiding that food.

TREATMENT Medications commonly used for acne treatment include the following:

- **Benzoyl peroxide** kills the skin bacteria that cause inflammation and helps open the ducts through which sebum passes to the skin surface. It is available without a prescription in 2.5, 5, and 10 percent strengths in several forms. Liquids and creams are better for dry skin, while gel forms are more helpful for oily skin. Benzoyl peroxide can be applied once or twice daily after washing the affected area with mild soap and water. It will improve the majority of acne cases if used consistently. If using benzoyl peroxide for one or two months doesn't help, a doctor should be consulted. A family physician or pediatrician can manage most cases of acne, but for more severe outbreaks, a dermatologist may be needed.

- Topical retinoids are derivatives of vitamin A that slow the accumulation of cells which obstruct the flow of sebum to the skin. **Tretinoin** (Retin-A in various forms and strengths) has been available for many years and is extremely effective in

continued

some current events and possibly tip you off about pressures that might be contributing to the symptoms.

Ultimately, your teen's doctor will need to ask questions, including, perhaps, a little gentle probing into the issues of the patient's daily life. If the medical evaluation uncovers a specific diagnosis, be sure that both you and your adolescent understand what should be done about it—including the parameters for going to school versus staying home. If the problem doesn't appear to be an ongoing physical illness, all of you together should develop a game plan for dealing with mornings when he doesn't feel well and agree on the ground rules for school attendance.

If you do indeed uncover personal issues that are contributing to physical symptoms, don't back away from working toward solutions. Whether it's a hard-nosed teacher, local bullies, an acute absence of friendships, or some other emotion-jarring problem, your teenager needs to know that you're on his team and that you weren't born yesterday. Making progress in one or more of these areas will usually go a long way toward shortening his symptom list.

unplugging pores and even causing **comedones** (blackheads) to be expelled from the skin. This can be alarming at first, because the new appearance of comedones on the surface will suggest that the medication is making the acne worse. But

Healthy Sleep During the Adolescent Years

The teen years are often fast-paced and packed with activities. School, sports, socializing, part-time jobs, church, and youth group functions all conspire to overload teens' schedules. Add to this active lifestyle the physical changes that occur during adolescence, and it's not hard to understand how teenagers might become shortchanged on sleep. Sleep is sometimes described as food for the mind. Without enough of it we are more prone to negative moods and are less able to control our emotions. Likewise, sleep deprivation diminishes our capacity for processing information and reacting accordingly.

Inadequate sleep can impair a student's academic performance. One survey found that 60 percent of children under the age of eighteen complained of being drowsy in school within the previous year, with 15 percent reporting that they have fallen asleep during the school day.[1] School drowsiness is correlated with lower grade performance.[2]

Drowsiness can lead to tragic results when one is behind the wheel. Fatigue, lapses in attention, and delayed response time associated with sleepiness are associated with more than 100,000 automobile crashes each year, resulting in over 1,500 deaths and 71,000 additional injuries. Young drivers (under age twenty-five) are involved in more than half of these crashes.[3]

Just how much sleep does your adolescent need? While each person is different, some research indicates that the average teen needs at least 8.5 to 9.25 hours of sleep each night. Only 15 percent of adolescents get that much, and one in four teens routinely acquire 6.5 hours of sleep or less. Physical changes during adolescence have curious effects on sleep and sleepiness. For many teens, daytime drowsiness increases even when they manage to get an optimal amount of sleep.[4] Likewise, sleep patterns appear to be shifted later in the day, so that the typical high school student's natural time for falling asleep moves back to 11:00 P.M. or later.[5]

Even though your teen might find himself needing more sleep, finding it isn't always easy. Here are some tips from the National Sleep Foundation that can help young people obtain the rest they need:

- Establish regular times for going to bed and getting up. If you depart from your normal schedule (such as on weekends), avoid delaying bedtime by more than an hour and waking more than two hours later than your regular schedule. If you are sleepy during the day, you may benefit from taking a nap in the early afternoon, if possible, or after school. Try not to take naps much later in the day, however, since they may interfere with sleeping at night.
- Find out how much sleep you actually need in order to feel refreshed and ready to start the day. Even if you get the recommended amount of sleep, you could still

this effect is only temporary. Tretinoin typically causes some redness and peeling of the skin. *Skin treated with tretinoin sunburns more easily, so avoiding the sun or using a strong sunscreen is important.* The combination of tretinoin applied

---

continued

awaken feeling tired. If this happens repeatedly, you may have to adjust your sleep routine (for example, by going to bed earlier).

- Get into bright light as soon as possible in the morning and avoid it in the evening. Light signals the brain that it's time to be awake.
- Know your body's rhythm, and try to adjust your schedule so that you are engaged in activities that are best suited to your level of alertness. For example, avoid scheduling lecture classes—or activities which require mental alertness for safety, such as driving—during times when you tend to be sleepy.
- Stay away from caffeine in the afternoon, as it may interfere with your nighttime sleeping pattern.
- Relax before going to bed. Avoid intense studying, exercise, computer games, or other activities that stimulate the brain.

Here are some things parents can do to help their teenagers get the proper amount of rest:

- Educate yourself about the sleep needs of adolescents. Many parents automatically interpret an increased need for sleep as laziness. Don't berate a teen for sleeping in on Saturday mornings.
- Look for signs of sleep deprivation in your teen and talk with her about her level of sleepiness and sleep habits. Don't allow your child to drive if she is drowsy or sleep deprived.
- Encourage your adolescent to take ownership of his own sleep schedule. Keeping a sleep diary for seven to fourteen consecutive days can help pinpoint areas of the daily routine that need attention.
- At the end of summer vacation, help teens adjust their sleep routine to fit their school schedule. Altering sleep schedules drastically is not likely to work since the body's internal clock is rather resistant to such changes. Instead, by going to bed fifteen minutes earlier than usual for a week at a time, individuals can usually shift their sleep schedules successfully. If conservative measures are not working, you may wish to consult your adolescent's physician or a sleep-disorder professional.
- Be a good example. Examine your own habits. Do you regularly burn the candle at both ends and then fight drowsiness much of the time? If so, make whatever changes might be necessary to model healthy sleeping patterns you'd like your teen to imitate.

at bedtime (thirty minutes after washing and drying the face) and benzoyl peroxide every morning should control 80 to 85 percent of acne in adolescents. Adapalene (Differin) has been available since 1997 and for some may be less irritating than tretinoin. Tazarotene (Tazorac) gel is another newer product which is similar in action to tretinoin.

- Antibiotics applied topically or taken orally sometimes help by reducing the population of bacteria on the skin. Oral forms of **tetracycline** or **erythromycin** are particularly helpful when inflammation is intense. Tetracycline and similar drugs cannot be given to pregnant women or children under twelve because these drugs discolor the teeth of a developing fetus or a child.

- **Isotretinoin** (Accutane), an extremely potent derivative of vitamin A which is taken by mouth rather than applied to the skin, is used in the most severe cases of acne. Isotretinoin acts essentially like an enhanced version of tretinoin, and 90 percent of even the worst cases of acne will respond to treatment over a four- to five-month period. This drug has a number of potential side effects, including dry skin, itching, and changes in liver function. Most important, it can cause significant deformities in a developing fetus if taken during pregnancy. Any woman who plans to take isotretinoin must consider this fact very carefully. Some physicians will not prescribe isotretinoin to an adolescent or adult female unless she agrees to take oral contraceptives.

- **Azelaic acid** (Azelex) is a newer topical medication that is unrelated to the others listed above. Derived from cereal grains, it inhibits skin bacteria, decreases the sebum that blocks pores, and reduces inflammation. It is applied twice daily to skin that has just been washed and should be continued for four weeks before deciding whether or not it is helpful.

Whatever approach is taken, it is important to remember that (1) treatment can only control acne, not cure it. For most people, this problem will fade away before adulthood. (2) Once treatment is started, it might be several weeks before there is a visible change.

For the teenager who is agonizing over the latest crop of facial bumps, this news may bring little comfort. Parents (and a physician, when appropriate) will need to be empathetic and supportive. Sometimes support will involve a gentle reminder to be consistent with treatment.

Physical Fitness and Sports

Your teenager may have seemed like a perpetual-motion machine during his toddler and preschool years, and perhaps you looked forward to when he might slow down a little. Now you may be facing a very different problem. Many preteens and adolescents shift gears into a sedentary lifestyle, especially if you allow TV and video games to encroach on time once spent outdoors. Studies of physical fitness in children and teens over the past two decades have shown a gradual decline in strength and endurance with a concurrent rise in percentage of body fat.

For better or worse, habits developed early in life are likely to continue for decades into the future. The benefits of maintaining regular exercise throughout life include a reduced risk of coronary artery disease and other medical problems, improved energy and sense of well-being, and better stress management. Your adolescent isn't going to be motivated by concerns over heart attacks and diabetes that may occur forty years from now. But he may be interested in activities, sports, and games that involve muscle motion, especially if they are part of your family's way of life. Exercise and fitness need to be modeled, not just talked about.

Family members can exercise together in countless ways. The most basic is a twenty-five to thirty-minute walk four or more times a week, an activity that many adults choose for fitness. While adolescents may enjoy being part of a brisk family stroll, especially on a balmy summer evening, over the long haul they are more likely to prefer more vigorous and/or competitive pursuits. Bicycling, swimming, roller-skating or in-line skating, and skiing can offer excellent conditioning, provided that appropriate safety precautions are taken. And these activities can be enjoyed for many years.

Many adolescents participate in organized team sports programs such as basketball, baseball/softball, football, and soccer. Others become active in individual competitive sports such as swimming, gymnastics, or skating. In some families, teens become involved in archery, bowling, sailing, or horseback riding. There are few athletic or physical skills that adolescents cannot begin to learn during these years, with these cautions:

- Take stock of your adolescent's physical and emotional readiness to compete in a particular sport. Consider delaying participation in collision sports, such as football or hockey, if your adolescent's physical development is delayed compared to his peers. Collision sports such as football or hockey should be postponed until age fourteen unless they are specifically noncontact forms of these games.
- Because of its potential for causing damage to the brain, boxing should be avoided completely.
- Exercise discernment if your teenager wants to join a martial-arts program. Martial-arts classes are more popular than ever, and they can help build confidence as well as skills in self-protection. But some guidelines are in order. Make sure that the emphasis is on building balance, coordination, and restraint, not on thrashing an opponent. Check out the safety guidelines in the classes. For example, breaking boards should not be part of the curriculum before the age of twelve because of the risk of damage to bones, tendons, and ligaments in the hands and feet. Also watch out for any religious or mystical component that might be incompatible with your faith.
- In order to achieve a competitive edge, some adolescent athletes—especially those involved in strength-driven sports such as weight lifting—mistakenly conclude that they should take **anabolic steroids,** drugs which can increase muscle bulk. (These are very different from **corticosteriods** prescribed by physicians for conditions such as asthma.) The use of such drugs is universally opposed by medical organizations because of their numerous side effects and

potential hazards. Ironically, in men these can include breast enlargement (called **gynecomastia**) and in women, increased body hair, acne, deepening of the voice, and baldness. Anabolic steroids can also raise blood pressure and cholesterol, increase the risk of forming blood clots which might lead to a stroke or heart attack, provoke a variety of emotional disturbances, and stop bone growth prematurely, leading to a reduction of adult height. Because taking anabolic steroids to enhance performance is incompatible with fair competition, collegiate, Olympic, and other sports programs prohibit their use and penalize those caught doing so. Parents should beware of cultivating or condoning a "win at all costs" mindset among athletes or their coaches, which may increase the risk for adolescent steroid abuse.

When Is It Okay to Quit?

Your daughter begged you to let her begin gymnastics classes, but now her muscles are sore, and it's clear that it is hard work—much harder than she thought it would be. Furthermore, she's not as good as the other girls, and more than a couple of times she's landed with a painful thud on the mat. She's had enough, but you've spent ninety-five dollars for a class that will continue for another six weeks. Do you let her bail out or make her continue to the bitter end—perhaps quoting the adage that "winners never quit and quitters never win"?

The answer will depend on your adolescent and her track record. If she has a habit of making enthusiastic false starts and rarely bringing any project to completion, she will probably benefit from the experience of struggling to complete the course she started. This reality therapy will be especially important if you have funded the classes after she promised to finish them. In this case, being true to her word is the issue rather than the classes themselves.

When the activity in question is something that other family members enjoy together, such as skiing or skating, some positive encouragement to struggle through the learning process in order to enjoy a lifelong payoff would be appropriate.

If she has been consistently involved in other long-term activities but is clearly miserable in this one, you may want to let her quietly retire. Make sure the problem isn't a mismatch with the wrong coach, or a mistaken entry into a group that is too advanced. At times a change of venue, trainer, or team can make a significant difference. However, if the activity proves to be a dead end, don't berate her for it. Allowing her to maintain her dignity will accomplish far more than any trophy on the family shelf.

Participation in sports and competition can have many benefits: developing strength and coordination, acquiring self-discipline, learning cooperation and sportsmanship, and building friendships. But these activities also have the potential to cause physical injury; generate considerable stress or permanent emotional scars; and nourish a host of negative attitudes, including elitism, hostility, and an obsession with winning. To maintain balance and build positive experiences through sports, revisit the following questions on a regular basis:

- Is your teenager really interested in this activity? You may have loved football, but he may prefer swimming.
- Is your adolescent physically and emotionally ready to practice and compete in the sport?
- Is the proper protective equipment available and used at all times?
- Do the coaches and trainers enjoy working with this age group, including those who are the least skilled? Are they focused on the right attitudes and values (see below), or do they appear driven to win at all costs? Are they competent?
- Do you have the resources and time to support your teenager through the tryouts, practices, and events?
- How heavily is your adolescent's—or your own—self-concept dependent on his success? Does the emotional weather at your home rise and fall with the fortunes of his team or his ranking at the last swim meet?
- Are positive values being taught and modeled by all concerned? Is unsportsmanlike conduct tolerated? Are parents who watch the events behaving themselves?
- *Are we having fun yet?* The vast majority of young contenders will not become professional athletes or Olympic contenders, so the experiences of sports and competition should be enjoyed, not endured. If the sport becomes a thorn in your teenager's side or constantly drains her of energy and joy, reconsider goals and priorities.

CHAPTER 4

Parental Survival Skills

Without a doubt, the adolescent years are a crucial and eventful period—not only for your child but for you as well. Working through it successfully requires wisdom, finesse, attention to detail, and above all, prayer. Prayer is particularly important because you cannot predict the future or know for certain how your children will respond to the challenges and opportunities that cross their paths.

It is inevitable that we will make mistakes. We will miss important signals from our children about their desires and needs and overreact to others based on *our* desires and needs. We may at times become too distracted, tired, overcommitted, or swamped with other responsibilities to do much more than attempt to put out fires. For the single parent raising one or more teenagers, every aspect of this job may seem overwhelming.

With all that is on the line at this critical time, we dare not float through these years without coming before God every day, seeking His wisdom in the face of our inadequacies. With that important perspective in mind, here are some basic principles that can serve as guideposts for your teen-rearing efforts. The exact paths that you and your family travel will be uniquely your own.

Know thyself.
Among the things you most want for your adolescent in the coming months and years are good health, success in school,

meaningful friendships, a positive impact in the community, spiritual vitality, and a loving spouse. Your teenager probably would agree with most of these, at least in principle. But when it comes to the details and the means of accomplishing these goals, you can count on differences of opinion and plenty of them. Furthermore, it is likely that your basic assumptions about what matters in life and what doesn't will be challenged, sometimes vigorously, during the process of rearing a teenager. How you react will probably be driven by your own needs and desires as much as by any consideration of what's best for your child.

The familiar phrase "Know thyself" is no empty cliché when you are parenting adolescents. As one or more of your children approach the teen years, you need to take stock of a few important issues of your own:

Where are you looking for fulfillment and contentment? Do these rise or fall with your adolescent's appearance, grades, social life, performance in sports, or other accomplishments? If things don't go well in one of these areas, how much will this rock your boat and why? Are you more concerned about his well-being and future or your own? Has your sense of significance been built upon the rock of a solid relationship with your Creator or on the shifting sand of your teenager's performance or opinion of you?

The answers will affect whether you can accept and appreciate your teenager on a day-to-day basis, warts and all, or whether there will always be another hurdle he must clear to earn your favor. It is not your teenager's responsibility to enhance your image in the community, duplicate your successes, atone for your failures, or provide you with vicarious pleasures.

Equally important, your feet will need to be firmly planted on solid emotional ground if and when your adolescent enters a phase of annoying negativity. If you begin to sense that your viewpoints or your company is at the moment no longer valued, you will need the internal strength to ward off pangs of rejection or a flush of resentment. Recognizing that this is a common adolescent phase will help, of course. You may find some comfort in the following wry observation:

When I was a boy of fourteen, my father was so ignorant
I could hardly stand to have the old man around. But when
I got to be twenty-one, I was astonished at how much the
old man had learned in seven years.   —MARK TWAIN

Above all, knowing that your worth doesn't hinge on the ebb
and flow of teenage opinion will help you avoid angry reactions
(which can create a much more serious rift in your relationship),
while allowing you to deal forthrightly with any disrespectful behavior or comments.

Does your life have any margin? Is your calendar jammed? Are you
physically, emotionally, and financially spent most of the time? Do
you have any spare time or energy to deal with a problem at school
or an adolescent crisis (there will be plenty of them) or simply to
get to your teenager's performance in the school play?

Many parents arrive at midlife neck deep in responsibilities and
commitments—just as their kids are entering and passing through
adolescence. The burden doesn't suddenly arrive on the doorstep
one day, of course. It gradually accrues over the years as the career
track accelerates, monthly expenses (and debt) mount, and volunteer positions at church and in the community expand. At the
same time, parents may find themselves taking care of *their* parents, whose health or faculties may be failing. All of these cares and
concerns can be so overwhelming that a teenager's anxiety about a
weekend date or an overdue homework assignment may seem
trivial.

Retreating from a marginless, stressful, chronically tiring lifestyle requires a number of conscious decisions, and perhaps some
sacrifices, from everyone at home. But it also is a powerful act of
love, especially when it allows for more time and energy to be spent
on building relationships within the family. *Years from now, your
grown children will not care nearly as much about your accomplishments, career track, or net worth as they will about the quality of relationship they had with you while growing up.*

Are you invested too heavily in your growing children? Are they the
intellectual and emotional center of your life? Will there be a

gaping hole in your life when the last young adult leaves the nest? Many parents—especially moms who have poured themselves without reservation into their children's lives—underestimate how emotional the process of letting go will be. Feelings of abandonment and depression may arrive unexpectedly as the last child departs. In some situations, one or both parents become inappropriately embroiled in the details of a grown child's life.

While your children must be a priority in your life, remember that two of you became a family before you had any babies, and that basic unit will continue after they are grown and gone. Maintaining your marriage, lifelong learning, and worthwhile projects are as important for parents as for kids.

Are you nurturing your marriage? As you approach your child(ren)'s adolescent years, are you still on the same team as your spouse? Do you build one another up in front of the kids, or do you unleash verbal attacks for all to witness?

An intact, stable marriage in which affection and mutual respect are openly demonstrated is a valuable asset for raising teenagers. Adolescents learn volumes about relationships from watching interactions at home. When the teen weather is stormy, a united parental front will be very important in restoring calm and maintaining limits. There will be many occasions when one parent can help quiet a conflict between a teenager and the other parent— not by contradicting his or her mate but by supporting and reaffirming him or her. If either partner believes that your marriage needs a tune-up, by all means set aside whatever time is necessary to work with a counselor or pastor.

Are you thinking about walking out on your marriage? Do you think that this would be a good time to escape and start over, now that the kids are older and can "handle it better"?

Think again. With all the physical, emotional, and developmental changes of adolescence in full swing, losing a parent to divorce at this time is a major blow. No matter how skillfully you may offer reassurances that "things will be okay—in fact, probably better" or pledge your undying love and interest in your child's life, with very rare exceptions a divorce will create a profound sense of loss and insecurity. All hands are needed on deck during these important years. If your marriage is in a preterminal condition, find a good counselor, roll up your sleeves, and get to work repairing it.

If you are bringing up one or more adolescents as a single parent, are you maintaining a healthy balance between love and limits? Are you overcompensating for the demands on your time, any lack of resources, or perhaps guilt over your marital situation by being too permissive or overly strict? Do you have a relative or good friend you can call upon to lend a hand when conflicts arise?

Rearing teenagers is a major undertaking for two parents and a far tougher assignment if you are on your own. Without the balance provided by another adult, you may find yourself drifting toward one or another extreme in your parenting style. You may need to be particularly careful about becoming so emotionally attached to your child that he or she becomes a surrogate spouse. This state of affairs is unhealthy for both of you.

If at all possible, enlist another mature person (such as a relative or perhaps a member of a support group) to spend time with your teenager. Someone who knows you and your child(ren) well can be particularly helpful in providing another vantage point if you reach an impasse with an adolescent.

Are you modeling behavior that you don't want your teen to imitate? If you are a smoker, don't be surprised if your daughter becomes one also. If you use alcohol on a regular basis, especially as a means to blow off steam or "party hearty," your son may very well follow in your footsteps. If you believe that adolescent sex is no big deal as long as everyone is "protected" or if you carry on sexual relationships outside marriage, don't expect your teenager to remain sexually abstinent.

The adage about actions speaking louder than words is the gospel truth with teenagers. If you're going to talk the talk about health and morals, be prepared to walk the walk as well.

Show genuine interest and respect.
Adolescents despise being treated like little kids. They hate being talked down to. They bristle when orders are dished out and there's

no room for discussion. They shut down if they try to express a heartfelt thought and no one listens or someone ridicules it. More often than not, their tempers flare and feelings are hurt because of the *way* something is said—disrespectfully—rather than because of the actual issue.

In other words, they are just like adults.

Even though your teenager may be light-years away from grown-up maturity and responsibilities, you will build strong bonds and smooth your path over the next few years by talking to her as you would to another adult you respect. This, like anything else in life that is worthwhile, takes time and energy. Specific ways to build and maintain a relationship with your teenager include the following:

Take her out for a meal, one-on-one, on a regular basis. Ask questions about what she's interested in and listen carefully to what she says.

Take advantage of common interests. Does she love to ski? Take some time off work and head for the nearest mountain that has snow and ski trails on it. Is he an avid movie- or theatergoer? Go with him and talk about what you've seen. Is he crazy about baseball? Take him out to a ball game and be sure to show up to watch if he's on a team. Does she enjoy chess, Scrabble, or other games? Become a willing (but not too aggressive) opponent.

The Importance of Opposite-Gender Relationships

In many families fathers have more interests in common with sons and mothers with daughters. But the importance of nurturing father-daughter and mother-son relationships cannot be overstated.

The tendency in father-son and mother-daughter relationships is for the parent to compare (with some anxiety) the progress of the child to memories of his or her own adolescence. Thoughts such as *He's not doing as well as I was at this age* or *I don't want her to make the same mistakes I did while growing up* can cloud your appreciation of your teenager's uniqueness and your enjoyment of his or her company. Since Dad was never a girl and Mom never a boy, these ongoing comparisons and concerns aren't as likely in opposite-gender relationships.

For a girl, Dad is usually *the* man in her life for many years. How he treats her will affect her relationships with men throughout her teenage and adult years. She will be looking to him for affection, respect, and affirmation of her femininity and will usually

Ask your teen's opinions about things going on in the world, your community, and your family. If she says something that isn't exactly well informed, don't jump in and "straighten her out." You can gently guide her in the right direction during the natural flow of conversation without making her feel like an idiot after opening up about her views.

When she wants to talk, put down the paper, turn off the TV, look her in the eyes, and pay attention.

Find things to praise—even when there's always much more that you might criticize—and do it often.

If you commit a genuine offense—whether a stray comment that is sarcastic or hurtful, an action that causes your teenager genuine embarrassment or pain, or some other error in judgment—have the courage to apologize. If there has been an argument and both you and your adolescent have said things you later regret, you may need to be the first one to admit that you were wrong. You will not lose face by doing so, but instead you will gain great respect (although you may not hear about it until a few years have passed).

At unexpected times, express satisfaction or outright joy that she is your daughter or he is your son. If you have trouble with this, ask yourself why. It could be that you are breaking new ground here,

continued

expect the same type of treatment from the males in her life later on. If she has lived with neglect, criticism, and abuse, she may spend years enduring the same from men who are basically perpetually self-centered, irresponsible, and predatory. But if she has been treated with courtesy and respect, she isn't likely to tolerate men who treat her otherwise.

For a variety of reasons, mothers and daughters may butt heads more often during the adolescent years than at other times in their lives. A father's input can help de-escalate conflicts and build Mom's image in the mind of his frustrated daughter.

Mothers can also have a unique relationship with their sons who are nearly grown. While Dad can and should instill standards for behavior with members of the opposite sex, Mom can usually better serve as an adviser regarding matters of the heart. If a son is struggling with a relationship that is tying his emotions in knots, a woman's perspective can offer both insight and comfort.

modeling unconditional acceptance that wasn't explicitly stated when you were growing up.

Know who (besides you) and what is influencing your teenager. While you as the parent have the primary assignment in shaping your adolescent's journey to adulthood, many other people, institutions, and social forces will have supporting roles. But not all of them will have your teenager's best interests at heart.

Two generations ago the general drift of our culture encouraged basic virtues: honesty, responsibility, sobriety, and the expression of sex within marriage, among others. If a teenager used drugs, was promiscuous, or openly defied authority, he was considered a juvenile delinquent. Today that is no longer the case. Even a casual look at the music, videos, and films geared to adolescents is a harrowing experience. Themes of casual or predatory sex, drug use, violence, death, and despair are not only commercially successful but readily accessible in virtually any home via cable, video rentals, or the Internet. And even public-service and educational messages created for teenagers in the interest of health and safety assume that premarital sex (hetero or otherwise) is the norm, and that condoms should be present and accounted for in every wallet or purse.

These voices, and those of many peers and even educators, sing a lethal siren song every day of the week: "No standards or values are absolute. Anything goes. You are the center of your moral universe."

Unless your family lives in an extremely isolated area, it is virtually impossible to keep these harmful messages and influences away from your adolescent. In fact, a child who is kept in a social vacuum for eighteen years and then suddenly leaves for college, the job market, or the military won't know what hit him when he gets a taste of what's out on the street. You can and should, therefore, keep your eyes open and be prepared to talk about whomever and whatever you think might be having a negative impact on your teenager's mind and emotions. Specifically, you should note:

Friends. The importance of peers has already been described, especially for early and middle adolescents. As much as you can, get to know and even make friends with your teenager's friends. Listen to what they have to say. An adolescent who likes and respects you will be less likely to encourage your own teenager to disregard your opinions. You may help smooth out a conflict between him and his parents. You might even learn a thing or two about your own child. As you get to know your teen's friends, you can also pray for them.

If you can't connect and it appears that one or more friends are pulling your teenager in directions that are destructive or dangerous, you may have to take the social bull by the horns. Calmly, rationally, and carefully present your concerns. Very often your teenager may be relieved to have a reason to disengage from one or more relationships. In a *worst-case* scenario, you may have to insist that one or more friends are off-limits, which will probably generate a fair amount of protest. Obviously you can't patrol the corridors at school, but you need to make it clear that freedom and privileges will be seriously restricted if she refuses to cooperate. Keep in mind that this plan of action should be reserved for situations in which your child's health and welfare are clearly on the line and not for isolating your teenager from friends whom you find merely annoying.

Music. With a few exceptions, contemporary music plays a prominent and intense role in the life and thought processes of adolescents; this has been true for generations. Today, however, this is not particularly good news.

Over the years most parents have complained about the music their kids enjoyed. During the 1950s and early 1960s, the content of most popular music focused on teen romance, the joys of surfing, and an occasional novelty item such as the "Purple People Eater" or "Alley Oop." Obviously, these songs were hardly masterpieces, and many of them celebrated unrealistic or even silly notions about love and relationships. However, their shortcomings pale in comparison to the malignant cultural tide that rolled in during the late 1960s, when drugs and rebellion began to be celebrated more openly.

The realms of heavy metal and rap teem with obscenity, violence (including rape), sexual anarchy, death, and despair. In bygone days rebellion was at least supposed to be fun. Now it's glum at best and murderous at worst. Slick and hyperkinetic videos that accompany rock hits often add a visual punch to the audio assault.

Depending on your teenager's musical tastes, at some point you may need to square off against the rock juggernaut. There is simply no way that relentlessly negative and destructive lyrics can pound into anyone's mind without making an impact. The issue, by the way, is *content*, not style. Some music that is grating to your ears may actually contain lyrics that challenge the listener to a better lifestyle or tell a cautionary tale.

If you hear something that turns you off throbbing through the walls or headphones, call for a joint listening session. Get the liner notes if possible (and a magnifying glass to read them), then review the CD, cassette, or video together with your teenager. Talk about what the lyrics are saying and how she feels when she listens to them. (You may hear, by the way, an argument that "I just like the beat and the music. I don't listen to the words." Don't buy it. More often than not she can recite lyrics.)

You'll need courage to separate your adolescent from music that is toxic, an open mind to endure the stuff that isn't, and wisdom to know the difference. You should also be prepared to suggest alternatives. For families with Christian commitments, there is a thriving world of contemporary music available in a breadth of styles—including pop, rock, rap, metal, and alternative—that specifically (if noisily) promotes positive values. In addition, a little research will uncover secular music that, while not including overtly biblical phrases or themes, combines high-quality musicianship with family-friendly themes.

Movies, TV, videos, and other electronic media. In the mid-1950s, no television had more than twelve channels, the content of movies was constrained by a code of strictly enforced values, the top ten songs on the radio dealt with "moons and Junes," and the most provocative game in the toy store was Monopoly. Today scorching language, gut-wrenching violence, casual nudity, mind-boggling sexual acts, and general disrespect for life and traditional values are readily accessible to anyone, including children and teenagers. Words and images that are inappropriate for kids of all ages (not to mention their parents) can flood a home that does not take deliberate steps to stem the tide.

And while you may be careful about the types of things you allow your family to see, neighbors up the street may be careless about the images flickering on their TV screen or who is in the room to see them. To make matters worse, school-age children and teenagers alike are intensely curious about "adult" matters and consider it a badge of honor to have had a look at something you've declared off-limits. And while violent or sexually explicit sights and sounds create profoundly strong and disturbing memories, repeated exposure has a desensitizing effect that can seriously warp attitudes and erode respect for the human body—and life itself. Unless you cut your family off from civilization altogether, you will need to be perpetually vigilant about the material your son or daughter sees and hears and be prepared to deal with whatever leaks past your defenses.

Your options in dealing with this problem include:

- A simple but rather austere approach: no TV, movies, videos, video games, or Internet. If everyone will go with this flow and you can provide plenty of other forms of stimulation (such as reading, music, games played between human beings, and good old-fashioned, interesting conversation), you may bring up the smartest and most literate kids in town. But if you take too rigid an approach, including strict social restrictions to maintain your rules, sooner or later rebellion is inevitable. It is likely that your preteen or teenager will secretly seek and find some rotting forbidden fruit and ingest it without your knowledge or input.
- At the other extreme, a hang-loose, anything-goes mentality abdicates important responsibilities. Don't become so intimidated by the swarm of media mosquitoes that you shrug your shoulders and take down your protective netting.
- Somewhere in between lies a limited-access approach, which demands time and energy but is potentially rewarding. In this case, the various media are regarded as neutral tools through which either positive or negative material may flow.

Specific standards must be set for your family as well as for individual members based on age and maturity. Viewing is planned and limited, both in time and content. Previewing and choosing material that kids may watch is an important part of the process. Most worthwhile are the opportunities to discuss what has just been seen and to teach some critical thinking. What take-home lessons were depicted? What positive values were portrayed? If negative material was present, what was wrong with it?

Even if you succeed in limiting your family's diet of movies, TV programs, videotapes, and electronic games to material that is wholesome and nourishing, you will still have to deal with too much of a good thing. School-age children and adolescents (not to mention their parents) can easily become TV addicts, and there are good reasons to limit the hours they spend each day staring at the electronic cyclops:

- TV watching is mentally passive. The images, sounds, and ideas generated by the programmers (including blatant sales pitches) are actively pouring into your teenager's mind, while thinking, reasoning, imagining, or creating—and homework—come to a screeching halt.
- TV watching is physically passive. Young viewers who sit for hours are not moving muscles in any meaningful way. Obesity and poor physical fitness are common among avid TV users.
- TV watching can become the centerpiece of family life. Group staring can replace talking, working, playing, eating, or praying together.

To prevent the tube from becoming the center of gravity in your family, set specific ground rules for everyone:

- Preplan how much, when (after homework and other responsibilities are done), and what will be viewed.
- Invest in a VCR and blank videocassette tapes. If something particularly worthwhile is going to be broadcast at an inopportune time, tape it for viewing later. Videocassette record-

ers (and now DVD players as well), when used prudently, can give you more options. Material can be recorded, rented, purchased, or even borrowed from the library, allowing you more control over content and scheduling.

- Think twice before installing a TV in your teenager's room. You'll lose control of the viewing activity, and your child will be isolated from the normal flow of family life.

- Think carefully before subscribing to a cable or satellite service that includes access to unedited films. You'll not only be more likely to waste hours watching something obnoxious that just happens to be on, but your teenager will also find it all too easy to tune in to objectionable material when you aren't around.

TV won't be the only potential media hazard in your adolescent's path during the next few years. You will need to be vigilant in a number of other areas as well:

- Conflicts may arise when "everyone" has seen a certain R-rated film and he wants to go too (at the ripe old age of fourteen), or watch it on videocassette. You will need to set and maintain your own family's standards, but at some point you may want to introduce him to more grown-up subject matter under your supervision. Do some homework and read the write-ups (especially in family-oriented magazines). Sometimes an otherwise excellent film receives an R rating for a brief spurt of bad language or for one or two quick sequences that can be bypassed using the fast-forward button on the remote control. Likewise, a film bearing the milder PG or PG-13 rating may actually be loaded with obnoxious and offensive material. Whatever you and your teenager see, talk about tone and content. Is this film or program selling a viewpoint, and if so, what is it? If something struck you as offensive, why? Was there a positive message involved? What was it? Before he's finally living on his own, he's going to need to learn discernment. Otherwise, while you may succeed in keeping every scrap of offensive material off his mental radar screen while he's in high

school, he's eventually going to be exposed to it later on—
but without your preparation or guidance.

- Video games (whether played on home computers or on
game systems that connect to the family TV set) are enormously popular with adolescents and can consume vast
amounts of their time and money. If you have video-game
equipment of any kind at home, set specific time limits that
can be spent playing with them. Also be careful about the
types of games your teenager buys, borrows, rents, or plays
at the local arcade. While many are good, clean fun, some
consist of nonstop fighting, and a few contain vivid images
of carnage or overtly antisocial themes.

- You must supervise your adolescent's use of computer on-
line services as carefully, if not more so, as his film, video,
or TV viewing. *Don't leave him alone in his room for hours
on end playing with a computer and a modem.* You might
be pleased to think that your budding genius is becoming
proficient with modern communications technology, but he
could be tapping into extraordinarily explicit and perverse
sexual material, antisocial and violent text and images, and
chat rooms where the on-line conversations get very raunchy
and inappropriate. (By the way, Internet filtering—using
either software or a filtered Internet service provider—can
help teens avoid sites they shouldn't be visiting. Unfortunately, no filter poses an impassable roadblock to a resource-
ful adolescent bent on viewing pornography, although
filtering provides at least a "speed bump" at which a person
must slow down before proceeding.) *Make it clear that your
teenager should not give her name, address, phone number, or
any other personal information to someone on-line or agree to
go somewhere to meet any new "friends" she might have spoken
with by modem.* (Sexual predators and other criminals have
discovered on-line services to be fertile ground for finding
unsuspecting targets.)

Literature and nonliterature, including pornography. While you
want to encourage reading as an alternative to TV watching, pay at-

tention to the material your adolescent brings home from the library or bookstore. Much of what lands on current best-seller lists is truly pulp fiction, laced with vivid scenes of horror, violence, and sex that are far more explicit than the contents of most R-rated films. Even the so-called romance novels, whose covers are emblazoned with bare-chested hulks looming over bodice-busting sirens, generally contain an abundance of vivid and immoral sexual material. If your teenager is engrossed in a steady diet of books focused on bloodletting, body counts, and bawdy situations, offer some alternatives of better content and quality. (By the way, what books are on your nightstand?)

A more dangerous influence, one that encompasses a variety of media including books, magazines, and videos, is pornography. Twenty years ago someone who wanted to see a dirty movie had to travel across town and sneak into a seedy theater where no one would recognize him. Since then, an explosion of new technologies has given pornography access to nearly every home. Most cable services offer not only unedited feature films on various "premium" channels but also specific channels whose programming consists entirely of sexual material. Nearly every video store has a back room full of hard-core stuff on cassette and DVD, available for three or four dollars per night. Most major hotel chains offer pay-per-view movies in every room—including a selection of idiotic "adult" films. Now the Internet has become a lawless Dodge City in which extraordinarily harsh and perverse material can be viewed and captured by any adolescent with a computer and a modem. And all of this doesn't include *Playboy, Penthouse,* and the other spin-offs that have cluttered newsstands and bookshops for decades.

Unlike the general run of films and TV, there is no gray zone for pornography. This is not harmless recreation, especially for an adolescent, and certainly not an appropriate source of information about human sexuality, for a number of reasons:

- Pornography paints a distorted picture of human sexuality as nonstop, careless, and meaningless copulation.
- Pornography degrades women, depicting them as brainless

sex toys. Some of it sells the rape myth—that women who say no to a man's sexual advances really mean yes and actually enjoy being raped.

- Pornography is highly addictive for some adolescents (and adults). Consumption of this material might continue into adulthood as a compulsion, contaminating relationships and interfering with a healthy sexual experience during marriage.
- Pornography is progressive for many who become addicted to it. Once someone has seen all the genital gymnastics that a man and woman can do, the search for new excitement may lead to viewing grotesque behavior, sexual violence, and even murder. A few cross the line of sights and sounds to actual participation and criminal behavior.

As your child approaches the teen years, talk about pornography and explain why this material is destructive. Needless to say, there shouldn't be any lurking in your own bedroom. If you as an adult have difficulty staying away from pornography, you should seek counseling from someone who is experienced with this problem.

Nevertheless, it is likely that your teen will stumble upon soft-core material, and perhaps something worse, at some point in his teen years. But what if you are looking through his closet or turning his mattress and stumble onto some sleazy material? Your best approach is neither to ignore it nor to fly off the handle and preach at him for two hours. Instead, plop the magazine (or whatever) in plain view in his room so he knows you found it or casually bring it out when you're ready to talk to him (one-on-one) about your discovery.

Most likely he *knows* that it isn't good to look at it and has dealt with a strong mixture of interest and guilt already, so a low-key approach will be quite effective. (A little humor might even relieve the tension: "Say, this is pretty interesting stuff here! Mom and I were thinking about getting a subscription!") Let him know that *you* know that curiosity about female anatomy is normal at his age, but remind him that this type of material is inappropriate, exploits women, can be as addictive as a drug, and (by the way) is very offensive. Make it clear that you don't want any more of it in your home and give him the honor of dumping it into the trash. It is impossible to know for sure whether he will refrain from looking at pornography somewhere else, of course, but keep your lines of communication open.

If you find material that includes more ominous themes such as homosexuality, violence, or child pornography, you will need to go a step further and get him involved in counseling with a qualified individual who shares your basic views on sexuality.

School and its curriculum. It goes without saying that your teenager's schoolwork should include the basics: reading, writing, math, history, and so forth. In general, it's reasonable to assume that your local schools are staffed by men and women who take their job seriously and have their students' best interests at heart.

But what if a particular teacher seems to have it in for your son or daughter, or a class appears to be pushing a political or social agenda that disagrees with yours? What if the family-life or sex-education unit is contradicting everything you have been teaching at home? And, more important, what if your adolescent is subjected to ridicule for expressing a contrary point of view?

Once again, a calm but purposeful approach is in order. You shouldn't abandon your teenager to fend completely for herself. But you should avoid charging into any situation at school with righteous indignation and verbal guns blazing.

First, get all the facts. Find out what "My teacher doesn't like me!" really means. What exactly was said? Is there a pattern? Can you get some written material from the class to look at? Is it possible that your teenager is primarily at fault because of disrespectful or inattentive behavior? It may help to talk to someone else in the same class to get confirmation that a problem really does exist.

You may be able to coach your adolescent through the situation by suggesting ways to de-escalate a conflict (including apologizing, if necessary). If the problem involves a clash of viewpoints, it may in fact be character building for her to deal with differences of opinion in an open forum. In this case you may choose to help her review the facts to bolster her viewpoint or find someone who can provide the input she needs. Remember—it won't hurt her to think through and defend what she believes.

Think carefully before you demand or choose to have her opt out of a controversial activity. This may seem a noble gesture on your part, but it might generate a lot of unnecessary ridicule from peers. For example, if someone gives a skewed presentation on sexual behavior (stressing condom use over abstinence), it may be appropriate for her to hear it—and then have an open discussion and review at home afterwards. This may also be a starting point for you to influence the future curriculum in a more positive direction. On the other hand, if you have advance warning that extremely offensive material is going to be used, exercise the opt-out choice—and then work diligently to change what happens next year.

If it looks as though the situation is out of hand (for example, your teenager is obviously upset, developing physical symptoms, or doesn't want to go to school because of the pressure) or the deck is stacked (points and grades in the class appear to depend on agreement with a teacher's ideology), you'll need to enter the arena.

Schedule an appointment with the teacher to get his or her perspective on the situation. Ask an open question: "Teresa seems to be having some problems in your class. I wonder what we can do to smooth things out?" If you begin with "Why are you picking on my daughter?" or "You're out of line, and I'm taking this all the way to the school board!" there won't be any discussion at all.

Perhaps you haven't gotten the whole story. Maybe some even-handed give-and-take on controversial issues has been encouraged, and your teenager didn't present her views very well. If so, building bridges rather than lighting fires would be a better course of action.

If, however, it is clear that certain beliefs and viewpoints aren't welcome or are subject to ridicule in the class, and friendly persuasion isn't making any headway, you may have to pursue your teenager's right to a hassle-free education. A meeting of other like-minded parents with the teacher in question, a conference with the principal, and if necessary, a transfer to another class may be appropriate. Your bottom line should not be a tirade that "this school is leading our youth down the road to ruin," but rather the simple notion that school should be a neutral ground for mastering basic material, not pushing a specific social or political agenda.

You can't spend all your time and energy trying to fend off potentially negative influences in your adolescent's life. Aside from your own input, you will also want to identify several allies who can encourage your teenager to move in positive directions. These might include:

- A relative (aunt, uncle, cousin, grandparent, or even a much older sibling) who shares your values. Someone older than your teenager but younger than you may connect well and not seem so "old-fashioned."
- A teacher, coach, youth pastor, or other person in an authority role who also deals effectively and constructively with areas that adolescents care about.
- A physician, nurse, or counselor who has professional expertise and supports your value system. Someone with stature and authority can have a major impact on your teenager, especially if he or she has known her for a number of years. Since health exams—and potentially sensitive discussions— will be on the agenda during the next few years, find out if the physician or nurse practitioner who may be involved is committed to the standards that you promote within your family.
- A positive peer group. Even one friend who shares your adolescent's values can help her resist a negative tide of peer pressure. A thriving church group can take her well beyond merely holding her ground and involve her in making a positive impact among her peers and in your community.
- The parent of one of your teenager's friends. Someone who doesn't have an emotional stake in your adolescent but shares your views on morals and behavior may be able to serve as a positive sounding board for topics that your teenager doesn't feel comfortable discussing with you.
- Films, videos, or music with positive, affirming, or redemptive messages.

You should make every effort, without being too pushy or manipulative, to connect your adolescent with any and all of these resources. But remember, if your efforts are too blatant, your teenager may resist merely because it isn't her idea.

Take on the tough topics: sex and substances.

If parenting an adolescent required only providing guidance through growing pains, schoolwork, mood swings, and preparations for independence, the assignment would still be challenging. But unfortunately we live in an unsettled day and age, a time when various unhealthy choices are often more accessible to teenagers than ever before.

Indeed, the next several miles of your adolescent's highway of life contain several potential road hazards, including premarital sexual activity and its consequences, alcohol, tobacco, and drug use. In many places, no guardrails exist, and steep cliffs await those who swerve a short distance off course. To make matters worse, seductive billboards along the way proclaim that veering toward those cliffs is exciting and pleasurable and that everyone else is doing it.

Like it or not, you don't have the luxury of sending your adolescent off on a journey into adulthood without warning him about destructive detours and deadly cliffs. He should be hearing some of the same advisories from responsible adults at school, church, or within your family, but you can't count on them to do this job for you. You may need to muster enough courage to tell him about poor decisions that turned out to be costly in your own life. At some point, you may have to help him navigate back from a bumpy side road or even pull him out of a ditch.

We all hope that your adolescent will, like many others, avoid these hazards and their consequences. In order to encourage healthy choices and offer effective help when it's needed, you would be wise to be well informed about these important topics. They are discussed in detail in two chapters later in this book, which we encourage you to read carefully:

- "A Parent's Guide to Teen Sexuality," beginning on page 145
- "Tobacco, Alcohol, and Drug Abuse—Resisting the Epidemic," beginning on page 189

While knowledge of these topics is very important, it will be of little value if not utilized in ways that will help mold attitudes and decisions. Finding the best approaches to talking with your adolescent(s) about sensitive subjects requires forethought and patience. The following ideas can help you lay the groundwork for this task:

It's easier to talk about sensitive or difficult subjects if you have good rapport with your child about the easier ones. Time spent building relationships during the preteen years usually pays major dividends later on.

Parents often worry that if they discuss certain topics (especially sex) in any detail, it will "give the kids ideas." Here's a late news flash: The kids already have plenty of ideas, and now they need to hear your viewpoint about them. However, they probably won't ask you, so you need to take the initiative.

Warnings about behaviors that threaten life and limb will be more effective if they aren't diluted by nagging about less serious matters. Accentuate the positive, and what you say about the negative will carry more weight.

Don't expect to communicate your values in a few marathon sessions. Brief but potent teachable moments crop up regularly throughout childhood and adolescence. Seizing these opportunities requires spending enough time with a child to allow them to take place.

It's easier for an adolescent to stay away from the dangerous detours if the main highway is clearly marked, well lit, attractive, and enjoyable. Encourage and support healthy goals, commitments, friends, and activities—all of which are strong deterrents to destructive behaviors.

Your actions will reinforce (or invalidate) your words. The misguided commandment "Do what I say, not what I do" has never worked and never will. However, this doesn't mean that mistakes, miscalculations, and reckless behavior in your past invalidate what you say today. Some parents worry that they can't legitimately warn their kids not to do what they did as teenagers. Heartfelt confessions, cautionary tales, and lessons learned at the University of Hard Knocks can have a profound impact on young listeners. As long as you're not setting a hypocritical double standard ("It's okay for me but not for you"), don't be afraid to share what you've learned the hard way.

Don't shift into "lecture gear" very often, if at all. Your teenager's desire for independence and his heartfelt need to be treated like an adult (even if his behavior suggests otherwise) will cause eyes to glaze and attention to drift if you launch into a six-point sermon on the evils of _____. If you feel strongly about these issues (and you should), say what's on your heart without beating them into the ground.

One way to communicate your view indirectly but effectively is through cassette tapes. You might bring one or more taped messages on a car trip and play them at an appropriate time, perhaps mentioning that they're interesting but not necessarily announcing that you want your adolescent to pay close attention. It helps, of course, if the speaker is engrossing and your teenager isn't plugged into his own portable tape player.

Don't give up if your efforts to broach tough topics aren't greeted with enthusiasm. Even when your tone is open and inviting, you may find that a lively conversation is harder to start than a campfire on a cold, windy night. Your thoughts may be expressed honestly, tactfully, and eloquently, but you still may not get rapt attention from your intended audience. Be patient, don't express frustration, and don't be afraid to try again later. If your spouse has any helpful suggestions about improving your delivery of the messages you care about, listen carefully and act appropriately.

While you state your principles about sex, drugs, and other important matters with consistency, conviction, and clarity, your adolescent also must understand that he can come to you when he has a problem. If your teenager is convinced that "Mom and Dad will kill me if they find out about _____," you will be the last to find out about _____. But if he knows you are a source of strength and help when trouble comes, you will be able to help him contain the damage if he makes an unwise decision. And indirectly, you may show him the attributes of God, his ultimate refuge and strength.

Teach and release responsibilities.

The importance of escorting your adolescent into the realm of adult independence and responsibilities has already been discussed at length. With rare exception she will be very eager to have as much of the first and as little of the second as possible. Ideally, she should be experiencing similar amounts of each. Keep in mind that this includes an introduction to many of the mundane tasks you take for granted every week.

Does she want her own car? If you help her obtain one, she needs to be involved in the whole package. What does the registration cost? What about the insurance? How about maintenance? The use of an automobile should rarely be unconditional. Reasonable school performance, trustworthiness, and probably some contribution to expenses (perhaps the insurance, the upkeep, or even saving up for a percentage of the whole purchase) should be part of the bargain. If she gets a ticket, she's going to have to pay for it. Let her look over the registration bill every year as well. This isn't much fun, but she'll have to do it eventually when she's out of your nest.

Another useful reality check is escorting your teenager on a guided tour of your monthly bills. Let her see what you pay for mortgage, taxes, utilities, and the other things she takes for granted every month. Better yet, let her fill out the checks and the register with you during a bill-paying session. She'll learn about a few significant nuts and bolts of everyday life and save you some time as well. Help her open her own checking account and show her how to balance it every month.

It also should go without saying that everyone at home should have specified duties in maintaining household cleanliness and order. Be sure to hand out age-appropriate housekeeping assignments (which may be daily, weekly, or both), with the understanding that the children should do their chores automatically without requiring nonstop nagging and reminders. If you hear whining about this being an imposition, slave labor, etc., remind the complainer that this is merely the way civilized, responsible grown-ups live.

If your adolescent's behavior causes any harm or damage,

whether accidental or otherwise, make sure she participates in the restitution and repairs. If you automatically bail her out of every consequence, you will succeed only in perpetuating childish irresponsibility. Indeed, one of the most significant parting gifts you can provide for a grown child is a practical, working knowledge of consequences. Adulthood often involves asking sober questions about a future course of action: "If I do _____, what is likely to happen? What things might go wrong with my plans? What do I need to do to prepare for the possibilities?"

When she has a red-hot idea for an activity or a project, enjoy her enthusiasm but also coach her through the potential problems she may not have thought about. You can do this, by the way, without raining on all of her parades. At times she may think you're a party pooper for bringing up the negatives, but reassure her that you're only doing so because she's almost an adult—and that's what adults do.

Go to bat when necessary.
While you want your adolescent to become increasingly self-reliant as the years pass, there will be times when a problem simply overwhelms him. If it looks like he's going down for the count, don't sit on the sidelines.

School problems have already been mentioned as an area where you may have to take part in the conflict. A more common situation in which he may need help is in dealing with harassment, especially in middle school. The social swamp at this age breeds amazing verbal and physical abuse, and your young adolescent may not be up for the battle—especially if he displays any vulnerability. Always ask about hassles from other kids if he repeatedly looks distressed, depressed, haggard, or literally beat up. A little persistence may be needed to get to the core of the problem (and the name of the perpetrator) because kids in this age-group desperately fear ridicule or reprisals.

The solution to harassment, by the way, is not preparing your son for a fistfight after school. Instead, swift and decisive (but nonviolent) action from one or more adults normally is quite effective. Most schools are ready and willing to put the heat on anyone who is causing this sort of problem—but they will need names. If this doesn't work, consider arranging a meeting with the perpetrator and if possible one or both of his parents in a school official's office. Look him in the eye and make it abundantly clear that even one further episode will bring disastrous consequences and that you expect his parents to cooperate.

If the problem involves risks of extreme violence or gang activity, you will need to seek advice from law-enforcement as well as school officials. In a worst-case scenario, a change of school (or home schooling) may be necessary to bring your adolescent through this situation in one piece. *Do whatever it takes (within the bounds of the law) to protect his safety and self-respect.*

A less dangerous (but still very painful) situation that may require your strong arm around a slumped shoulder is loneliness or repeated rejection by peers. If your adolescent can't seem to make or keep any friends, don't shrug and tell her that she'll get over it. She may not. Try to find out what's going wrong and help her make whatever changes are necessary to alter this course.

If she needs to work on grooming, lend a hand (or find someone who can). If you overhear her talking to others in a way that is an obvious turnoff, coach her on conversational skills. Encourage her to invite a friend over for an evening or a special outing. Work with her to find a niche in the community where healthy friendships can develop. And if all else fails, go out of your way to be her best friend until other candidates cross her path.

There will be times when you won't be able to be all things for your adolescent, and other supportive adults in your child's life may need to lend support. Single adults, church youth workers, neighbors, and relatives can fill in a number of gaps and provide a rich, meaningful influence for years to come. Try to keep your son or daughter in contact with different types of people who might have a positive impact. (You might invite them to be guests around your dinner table, for example.)

Keep them busy, within reason.
Without jamming her schedule to the gills, encourage worthwhile activities—a job, church-related projects, sports, or performing

arts, for example—to add structure to the hours that aren't involved in education. As long as she's not overcommitted and exhausted, these can make her life more well-rounded, add to her social network, and (usually) reduce the risk of her getting into trouble.

Stay on your knees.

This section on parental survival skills began with this admonition, and it is worth briefly repeating. You are not omniscient, omnipotent, or omnipresent. (That is, you can't know everything, do everything, or be everywhere.) But your adolescent's Creator is. Talking to Him regularly about your young adult in the making will therefore help you maintain your perspective, sanity, and strength. These times of prayer can also be opportunities to acknowledge and thank God for the incredible growth and changes that you are witnessing as your child approaches adulthood.

CHAPTER 5

Encouraging Spiritual Growth and Building Character

Spiritual Growth

It is a sad fact that some children who have been taken regularly to Sunday school and church will grow up to ignore God and reject the values their parents taught (or *thought* they had taught) at home. To their utter dismay, Mom and Dad learn too late that this training just didn't "take," and they wonder what went wrong.

The Old Testament story of Eli is an example. The devoted priest failed to influence the behavior of his own boys; both sons became profane and evil young men. Samuel—one of the greatest men in the Bible—witnessed Eli's parental mistakes and yet proceeded to lose his children too! The message the Bible communicates is loud and clear: Devotion to God is not inherited. God does not guarantee that our children will follow Him simply because we do. The reason, of course, is that every child must eventually decide *on his or her own* whether to follow, ignore, or reject God. If parents could lock in a child's commitment to God—if it were in fact impossible for the child to say no—then the child's love for God would not be love at all but the meaningless response of a preprogrammed machine.

Nevertheless, the fact that parents cannot preordain their child's faith does not mean that they shouldn't attempt to encourage it in a healthy way and to pray daily for his spiritual growth. Parents are admonished in the book of Proverbs to "train a child in the way he should go"—which means, among other things, that parents need some specific ideas about what that "way" should be.

It is appropriate and desirable for a child to be exposed to a carefully conceived, systematic program of religious training, one that continues through the adolescent years. Yet many parents approach this project in a haphazard manner. A great place to begin is with the *Focus on the Family Parents' Guide to the Spiritual Mentoring of Teens,* a comprehensive overview of spiritual development in teens.

If a son or daughter is to be encouraged toward spiritual awareness and maturity, it is important to have a clear idea of what specific goals are to be pursued. Below is a checklist for parents, a set of targets that apply to both childhood and adulthood. These scriptural concepts provide the foundation upon which all future doctrine and faith will rest. They should be taught deliberately and affirmed to adolescents in a manner appropriate for their age.

Concept I: Loving God

> *One of the teachers of the law came and heard them debating. Noticing that Jesus had given them a good answer, he asked him, "Of all the commandments, which is the most important?"*
>
> *"The most important one," answered Jesus, "is this: 'Hear, O Israel, the Lord our God, the Lord is one. Love the Lord your God with all your heart and with all your soul and with all your mind and with all your strength.'"*   —MARK 12:28-30

- Is your teenager learning of God's love through the love, tenderness, and mercy of his parents?
- Is he learning to talk about the Lord Jesus and include Him in his thoughts and plans as part of his everyday experience?
- Is he learning to turn to God for help whenever he is frightened, anxious, or lonely?
- Is he learning to read the Bible?
- Is he learning to pray?
- Is he learning the meaning of faith and trust?
- Does he understand that God loved him so much that He sent His Son to die for him?
- Is he learning that loving and serving God is the ultimate source of joy and freedom in life?

Concept II: Loving others

"The second is this: 'Love your neighbor as yourself.' There is no commandment greater than these." —MARK 12:31

- Is she learning to understand and empathize with others?
- Is she learning not to be selfish and demanding?
- Is she learning to share?
- Is she learning not to gossip and criticize others?
- Is she learning to serve others?

Concept III: Following God's rules

Fear God and keep his commandments, for this is the whole duty of man. —ECCLESIASTES 12:13

In addition to loving God and loving neighbors:

- Is he learning to honor God's name and not to misuse it?
- Is he learning that one day of the week—the Sabbath—is to be set apart from normal activities and dedicated to God?
- Is he learning to honor and respect his parents?
- Is he learning to value human life at all ages—from conception to advanced age—without regard to appearance, race, physical condition, or mental capacity?
- Is he learning to respect the gift of sex and the importance of preserving sexual experiences for marriage?
- Is he learning to respect the possessions of others: neither stealing nor borrowing without permission and making restitution if he damages another person's property?
- Is he learning to be truthful and honest?
- Is he learning the ultimate insignificance of material goods?

Concept IV: Following God's direction

Teach me to do your will, for you are my God. —PSALM 143:10

- Is she learning that her primary purpose on earth is to serve the Lord?
- Is she learning to obey her parents as preparation for later obedience to God?
- Is she learning a healthy appreciation for God's justice as well as His love?

- Is she learning that there are people in many types of benevolent authority roles—teachers, coaches, police, youth leaders—to whom she must submit?
- Is she learning the meaning of sin and its inevitable consequences?

Concept V: Acquiring self-control

But the fruit of the Spirit is love, joy, peace, patience, kindness, goodness, faithfulness, gentleness and self-control.

—GALATIANS 5:22-23

- Is he learning to control his impulses?
- Is he learning to take proper care of the body that God has given him?
- Is he learning to work and carry responsibility?
- Is he learning to tolerate minor frustration?
- Is he learning to memorize and quote Scripture?
- Is he learning to give a portion of his allowance (and other money) to God?

Concept VI: Acquiring an appropriate self-concept

For everyone who exalts himself will be humbled, and he who humbles himself will be exalted.   —LUKE 14:11

- Is she learning a sense of appreciation?
- Is she learning to thank God for the good things in life?
- Is she learning to forgive and forget?
- Is she learning the vast difference between self-worth and egotistical pride?
- Is she learning to bow in reverence before the God of the universe?

Developing Positive Character Traits

The development of positive, stable character traits should flow directly from spiritual growth. If a person's religious activities—Sunday school, Bible reading, prayer, and so on—are not accompanied by virtuous behavior, then his or her faith is shallow, false, or self-deluding.

*What good is it, my brothers, if a man claims to have faith but
has no deeds? Can such faith save him? Suppose a brother or sister
is without clothes and daily food. If one of you says to him, "Go,
I wish you well; keep warm and well fed," but does nothing about
his physical needs, what good is it? In the same way, faith by
itself, if it is not accompanied by action, is dead.* —JAMES 2:14-17

Similarly, attempts to train an adolescent to be virtuous will have
only limited success if he lacks a clear understanding of God's love
and justice or if he does not demonstrate personal repentance and
submission to God's leadership.

Spiritual maturity and character will not develop during ran-
dom lectures crammed into a few minutes every month. Parents
need to plan ahead, focusing on the values they intend to instill.
They must also take advantage of unscheduled "teachable moments," when a situation naturally lends itself to a discussion about
positive (or negative) behavior. However this important task is carried out, the following are some important character traits, listed
alphabetically, on which to focus.

Courage is frequently portrayed in movies as the primary require-
ment for heroes and heroines embroiled in daring exploits. But adolescents need to understand that courage is also important for
everyday life, both now and in the future. Indeed, one who learns
courage as a teenager is more likely to be secure as an adult. Courage encompasses several elements:

- Daring to attempt difficult but worthy projects.
- Saying *no* to the pressure of the crowd.
- Remaining true to convictions, even when they are unpopu-
  lar or inconvenient.
- Being outgoing and friendly, even when it's uncomfortable.

Courage can also apply to more highly stressful situations:

- Applying resources in creative ways when faced with overwhelming odds.
- Following difficult instructions in the face of danger.

- Confronting an opponent in an honorable way, confident that what is morally right will ultimately succeed.

Determination can help your child avoid becoming a pessimist. This trait helps a child:

- Realize that present struggles are essential for future achievement.
- Break down a seemingly impossible task by concentrating on achievable goals.
- Expend whatever energy is necessary to complete a project.
- Reject any distraction that will hinder the completion of a task.
- Prepare to handle hardships that lie ahead, whether the task is spiritual, physical, emotional, or relational.

Fidelity and chastity are rarely taught within our culture (by movies, television programs, popular music, etc.) and not as often by educators, coaches, or even church leaders as they were a generation ago. Therefore it is important that your adolescents hear clearly from you about the benefits of reserving sexual activity for marriage. They also need to grasp the serious potential consequences of sexual immorality: sexually transmitted infections, infertility, crisis pregnancies, and a broken heart.

Honesty is not always rewarded in our culture, but it is a bedrock virtue. Without it, all of your child's most important relationships will be compromised and unstable. Teenagers should be taught that truthfulness is critical when dealing with:

- Family members, friends, and acquaintances
- School
- Organizations, including future employers
- Governmental agencies
- God

Dishonesty must be discouraged in all its forms, whether it be outright lying to another individual, misrepresenting to an employer what one has (or hasn't) done, cheating on a test, plagiarizing, or doctoring an income tax return.

Humility arises from an honest assessment of one's own strengths and weaknesses, such that boasting is not necessary to gain acceptance or to feel contentment. Humility also involves submission to duly constituted authority, obedience to the law, and fairness in work and play. Most important, humility will keep your teenager on his knees in prayer.

Kindness and friendliness should be presented to an adolescent as admirable and far superior to being "tough." Adolescents need to be taught that it is usually better to understand than to confront, and that gentleness—especially toward those who are younger or weaker—is in fact a sign of strength. *Do not allow your teenager to become a bully.*

Love in many ways encompasses and surpasses other virtues, as stated by the apostle Paul nearly two thousand years ago:

> *Love is patient, love is kind. It does not envy, it does not boast, it is not proud. It is not rude, it is not self-seeking, it is not easily angered, it keeps no record of wrongs. Love does not delight in evil but rejoices with the truth. It always protects, always trusts, always hopes, always perseveres.* —1 CORINTHIANS 13:4-7

Adolescents should be taught—and shown—how to love their friends, neighbors, and even adversaries.

Loyalty and dependability are traits needed for success in many arenas of life. A person who is flighty and cannot honor a commitment is unlikely to find true happiness or success. Your teenagers need to learn the importance of loyalty to family, employer, country, church, school, and other organizations and institutions to which they will eventually make commitments. If an adolescent learns to be reliable and stand by his word, he will be trusted and see opportunities open before him throughout life.

Orderliness and cleanliness may or may not be "next to godliness," but they can increase a person's chances of success in many areas of life. While no one has ever died of dirty-room syndrome, a teenager who can learn to keep his possessions organized and in order will eventually be able to use his resources to their greatest efficiency. Personal cleanliness and good grooming speak of self-respect and project an important message to others: I care enough about those around me to try to appear basically pleasant.

Respect is a critical commodity in human relationships, whether within families, organizations, or entire nations. It encompasses basic courtesy, politeness, and manners toward others. It has largely been lost in our culture, and it desperately needs to be regained. When a person loses respect for life, property, parents, elders, nature, and for the beliefs and rights of others, a self-serving and destructive attitude will take its place.

Self-discipline and moderation are rare but valuable traits in a culture that claims that you can—and should—have it all. Teenagers need to understand that, even if it is possible for them to do so, it is not necessary or wise to "have it all." Exercising self-discipline over physical, emotional, and financial desires can prevent illness, debt, and burnout later in life. Adolescents should be taught the importance of the following:

- Controlling personal appetites
- Knowing the limits of body and mind
- Balancing work and recreation
- Avoiding the dangers of extreme, unbalanced viewpoints
- Engaging the brain before putting the tongue in gear

Unselfishness and sensitivity are universally appreciated and respected. A child who is more concerned about others than himself will be seen as mature beyond his years and can benefit himself and others.

How Do I Encourage Spiritual Growth and Development?

The answer hinges on the little word *time*. These traits mature over many years of *time* as parents leave enough *time* in their busy lives to spend enough *time* with their children to talk about these subjects many, many *times*.

With enough time, you can encourage spiritual growth and character development in the following ways:

- *Be your teenager's primary role model.* Let him see the values you care about enacted every day in front of him. "Do as I say, not as I do" is a recipe for moral failure.
- *When you have done or said something that was mistaken, inappropriate, or just plain wrong, admit it.* Have the courage to apologize for what went wrong, and then explain why it was wrong. You will gain great respect from your teens for doing so, and they won't forget what you say in these moments.
- *Read or tell stories that illustrate the values you care about.* The Bible is full of them. So is other literature, including dozens of passages that have been compiled by William J. Bennett in anthologies such as *The Book of Virtues, The Moral Compass,* and *The Children's Book of Virtues*.
- *Seize the teachable moment.* When a situation arises in which a moral example (good or bad) is before you, talk to your adolescent about it. *This should not be limited to times during which you are correcting misbehavior.* It might occur, for example, while watching a video, a ball game, an erratic driver on the freeway, or someone acting out in public.
- *Praise your adolescent—in front of others, whenever possible—when he does what is right.* When correcting him or administering disciplinary measures, do so in private.
- *Pray specifically for your teenager's spiritual and character development.*

CHAPTER 6

Conflict within the Family

Conflict between parents and their children is inevitable. The toddler's foot-stomping negativity, the preschooler's refusal to pick up his toys, the school child's disinterest in homework and chores, and the adolescent's adamant declarations of independence from parental restrictions are but a few variations on this universal theme. But conflicts within families are not limited to differences of opinion (or pitched battles) between parents and children. Parents normally disagree with one another about any number of concerns, even in the most harmonious marriages. Furthermore, if they have more than one child, strife between offspring is so common that it has achieved a well-worn title: sibling rivalry. Thus for any family the question isn't so much *whether* discord will arise, but *how to manage it* in a way that will build up rather than tear down relationships.

Conflict between generations

By the time your child has become an adolescent, you will have already experienced innumerable disagreements with him on a host of subjects, both trivial and profound. The vast majority of these boil down to two primary scenarios:

- He is doing something (verbally or physically) that you disapprove of, for any number of reasons, or he is failing to do something that you want him to do.
- He wants something—whether material goods, other resources, or some measure of independence—that you are unwilling or unable to give him.

Obviously the topics and character of conflicts between parent and toddler will be grossly different from those between parent and teenager. With a teenager there are many more potential sources of contention—there wasn't any homework in preschool to argue about, for example. Vocabulary, physical stature, and volatile emotions can dramatically raise the temperature of a discussion, sometimes within seconds. Some issues that have been stewing for several years may suddenly erupt with surprising ferocity during adolescence. In many arenas the stakes of a conflict will be a lot higher during the teen years than they were during childhood. A rebellious five-year-old may refuse to get in the bathtub or throw one of his toys across the room. A rebellious fifteen-year-old may experiment with sex or drugs, with permanent (or even lethal) repercussions. All of these factors may shake the confidence of parents whose oldest child is approaching the twelfth or thirteenth birthday. They can also unleash an unexpected teenage storm which can cause even highly experienced parents to run for cover, hopefully to seek the advice of trusted books and counselors.

Whether your child-rearing experiences have been smooth sailing or continual turbulence since he left the newborn nursery—and whether or not you have been conscious and deliberate about the process—you have been involved in an ongoing process of training and discipline for a number of years. The patterns that you have established (or lack thereof) will play a critical role in the management of conflicts with your adolescent. A review of the entire gamut of training and discipline is beyond the scope of this book.[1] But the key principles are universal for all ages, and they are worth reviewing, pondering, and carefully implementing within the unique circumstances of your own home.

Basic Principles of Discipline and Training: Balancing Love and Limits

> *Discipline*: Training and instruction that is intended to produce a specific pattern of behavior, character development, and moral or mental improvement. (From the Latin *discipulus*: "pupil," derived from *discere*: "to learn.")

Mention the word *discipline* in connection with rearing children and teenagers, and images of various forms of punishment frequently come to mind. *But discipline actually encompasses the entire process of shaping and molding attitudes and behaviors over the years that a child is entrusted to your care, from infancy through adolescence.* This project is deserving of your diligence, fervor, humility, and prayer. In general, it involves an overall mindset rather than a cookbook full of behavioral recipes ("If he does this, you should do that"). Discipline for an adolescent can include a variety of techniques and approaches that vary depending upon the adolescent's age and temperament. And what brings about a desired result with one may prove to be a dismal flop with a sibling. While you definitely will want to have an overall plan in mind, you will have to improvise along the way.

The subject of training and discipline raises a lot of questions, concerns and even some controversy. For example:

How do I sort out all of the input and advice I get, including the impact of my own upbringing? Your approach to discipline will be significantly influenced by your own experiences as a child or adolescent. You may even overcompensate for extremes in the past that have affected you. If you were treated harshly as a child, for example, you may tend toward being permissive, and vice versa. You will also receive plenty of advice (some more worthwhile than others) from relatives and friends, books and magazines, sermons, radio and TV programs, child-rearing classes, and your child's physician. You will have to choose wisely from these resources, separate the wheat from the chaff, and try to avoid a becoming a "Method of the Month Club" parent.

Am I too rigid or too lenient? If you don't worry about this question once in a while, you may be at risk for extreme or unhealthy discipline patterns.

Why is it so difficult? And why does my teenager keep challenging me? Sometimes (or perhaps most of the time) bringing up adolescents seems at best loaded with uncertainty, at worst a perpetual uphill struggle. Why? Because each teen is a unique creation, a person with a mind, spirit, and will of his own. Children are not built like cars or computers; they do not arrive with instruction manuals that guarantee that *B* will happen if you do *A*. While many of their behaviors are predictable in general terms, they are not robots who will automatically yield to your direction.

Extremes in Discipline: What Not to Do

No mother or father disciplines with absolute perfection, and like every other parent in the world, you will make mistakes. You may say or do something that you later regret, or you may neglect one or more worthwhile aspects of the training process. But parenting involves a long learning curve, and children brought up in an environment where it is clear that they are deeply loved will be resilient in the face of numerous parental errors. Nevertheless, stay away from patterns of missteps and omissions that could have a lasting negative impact on adolescents. If any of the following have taken root in your home, remember that it's never too late to make midcourse corrections.

Physical abuse. Punching, slapping, whipping, burning, and other horrors inflicted upon children and teenagers are *not* discipline. They are abuse and have no place in raising a son or daughter. They do not serve to benefit the teenager in any way; they do serve as unhealthy ways for a parent to vent anger. These behaviors indicate a basic defect in the parent's communication skills, the parent's lack of respect for the adolescent's body and emotions, and a gross misunderstanding of a parent's responsibilities. If this type of violence has occurred in your home, seek counseling immediately to prevent further damage. Such help is especially important if you received this sort of treatment as a child, because abusive patterns may continue through generations unless someone has the courage to break the cycle.

Verbal thrashing. Even if you don't throw sticks and stones or break any bones, your words can hurt your teenager. Harsh, degrading, insulting language—"You are so stupid," "I'm disgusted with you," "You jerk," and other insults that can't be printed here—burns its way into the memory and emotions. While physical abuse scars the body, verbal abuse scars the mind and heart, and neither is a proper exercise of parental authority. It is important to seek counseling to rein in these verbal beatings and stop the abuse.

Authoritarianism. This rigid micromanagement of adolescent behavior stresses pure obedience without any understanding or internalization of principles. There may be times when you need to declare, "Because I'm the mom, that's why!" But demanding knee-jerk submission in every detail of life will wear thin as the years pass. You can probably impose this regime on your children when they are younger, but as they reach adolescence, their rebellion will be a virtual certainty—and probably will be spectacular.

Management by yelling and screaming. Some parents arrive at the mistaken conclusion that their children will respond to them only when they raise their voices in anger. This idea usually develops over time through many repetitions of a scenario in which a parent's direction is ignored by a young child—and nothing is done about it. When this pattern is fully developed, a child will have learned to gauge very accurately when Mom or Dad is likely to take action.

Typically, after five or six requests or orders have been ignored, the parent's voice becomes more forceful, words are clipped, and the child's middle name is used: "John Patrick Smith, you get into that tub NOW!" The child has calculated that something unpleasant is likely to occur at this point and heads for the bathroom. The parent comes to believe that anger got the desired results, and he or she may then resort to it more frequently. But in fact, it wasn't the anger but *action* (or the likelihood of it) that got the child moving to comply.

Eventually, if action doesn't always follow the angry words, a child may learn to ignore even the most intense outbursts. By the time he becomes a teenager, he may routinely tune out one or both of his parents as if they were mere background noise. This not only dilutes the effectiveness of all other communication within the family but also engenders a disrespectful attitude between generations. In a worst-case scenario, parent and teen alike are habitually shouting at one another.

Idle threats. Many parents attach threats of dire consequences to the orders they give a child or adolescent: "You'd better not _____, *or else!*" But if the adolescent repeatedly disobeys and *"or else"* never happens, she will learn that a lot of what Mom or Dad says is just hot air. This may escalate to some form of home terrorism; a frustrated parent whose warnings aren't taken seriously may increase the verbal artillery to abusive levels or become enraged to the point of finally making good on some extravagant threat. As with "management by yelling," it is action and consequences early in the game, and not threats alone, that motivate children to follow directions.

Laissez-faire parenting: little or no adult input or involvement. This occurs when one or both parents are too busy, overwhelmed, tired, or indifferent to set and enforce consistent limits. A teenager who is left more or less to his own devices will probably not be very relaxed and happy, but rather quite unsettled, because the boundaries that provide security are missing. Even though most adolescents vigorously push and shove against limits, they will become surprisingly anxious if few or none are present.

Nonstop bribery. Rewards have a definite place in training children and adolescents, but parents should not haggle or make deals over every direction they give—especially those that are not negotiable. A teenager should not become used to the idea that virtue is only worthwhile if there's a prize attached. Moral values eventually need to be internalized, not merely bought and sold.

"Democratic" parenting. One of the great cultural follies of our times is the belief (often expressed with humanitarian fervor) that parents and children should have equal say in all matters and that a mother or father has no right to exert any parental authority over a child or teenager. A variation on this theme occurs when a parent is unwilling or unable to override an adolescent's drives and desires, usually out of fear of rejection, an unwillingness to deal with conflict, or the mistaken notion that anything that causes an adolescent to become upset is terribly harmful.

But conflict is inevitable in any long-term human relationship, including the one between parent and child. Misguided attempts to keep a teenager from experiencing any unhappiness by routinely giving in to her every desire will ensure that she is miserable and unpleasant. Respect for her identity and feelings is important, and during the adolescent years there will need to be a gradual relinquishing of parental control in preparation for adult independence and responsibilities. But someone needs to be in charge while she is growing up.

Overt permissiveness. This is a more extreme and naive version of democratic parenting. Some parents tolerate a great deal of disrespectful and destructive behavior in their teenagers based on the assumption that they are "getting it out of their system." Unpleasant surprises await those who adopt this approach, as years of unrestrained willfulness bear toxic fruit.

Six Basic Principles of Discipline
1. Balance love and limits.
Balance expressions of love—physical affection, kind words, comfort, help—with appropriate boundaries and consequences. Children and adolescents cannot survive without experiencing consistent and unconditional love. From the first day of life through her journey into adulthood, your child must know that your love is rock solid, the foundation from which she can safely and confidently explore her world. From the moment she was born through the day you release her to live on her own, she needs to hear, see, and experience—in hundreds of different ways—a crucial message that summarizes the essence of unconditional love:

> You are loved, you are important, and you always will be,
> no mater what happens. I care enough about you to provide
> for you, stand with you, coach you, correct you, and even
> die for you if necessary. My commitment to you is not based
> on what you do or don't do, how you look, whether your
> body is perfect or handicapped, or how you perform in
> school or sports. It is based on the fact that I am your parent
> and you are my child, a priceless gift that God has loaned to
> me for a season. Eventually I will release you to live your

own life, but while you are growing up, I consider caring for you an assignment of utmost importance.

Adolescents also need boundaries and ground rules. Expressing love and enforcing limits are not contradictory but intimately related. Allowing a teenager to have her way without any restraint is not an expression of love. At the other extreme, harsh, rigid, or authoritarian treatment of teens, even if it produces apparent model citizens, isn't an appropriate exercise of limit setting.

2. Parents must assume leadership in the home.
For a variety of reasons—whether the nonstop attention required to rear younger children, fatigue, distractions, or an overabundance of commitments—it is possible for parents of adolescents to find themselves struggling simply to maintain order and manage the demands of daily life. After a few or several years, teenagers or even younger children may set the family's agenda and even drift into a general disrespect or disregard for their parents' authority. This is an unhealthy state of affairs for three reasons:

- Children and adolescents lack the wisdom, knowledge, experience, and capabilities to train and nurture themselves.
- Teenagers will not gain the skills and responsibility to live independently as adults without ongoing direction from parents who require that the teenagers learn and do things that don't come naturally.
- Children (of all ages) want to know and will ask in a variety of ways, "Who's in charge here?"

Establishing your authority does not mean that you need to be mean-spirited, harsh, or dictatorial. Instead, you are preparing your adolescent for the reality that *everyone* at various times of life must submit to someone else. Eventually a teenager's respect must encompass teachers, coaches, law enforcement officers, employers, and so on. Ultimately, she must also learn to recognize God's authority over her life—and understand that this authority is motivated by love and a boundless desire for her well-being. Whether you realize it or not, your adolescent's concept of God will be affected to a significant degree by her experiences with you during her years at home.

3. *Distinguish among normal behavior, irresponsibility, and willful defiance—all of which need your guidance and correction but in different ways.*

- Throughout your preteen and teenager's years at home, you will have to deal with numerous episodes of irresponsibility—leaving your saw out in the rain, losing her new gloves, forgetting his lunch, not feeding the cat, leaving fast-food wrappers strewn all over the living room.

  These actions need correction, but they usually do not represent a direct challenge to your authority. A steady diet of rewards, consequences, and lots of patience will gradually introduce your child to responsible behavior, and ultimately to mature adult citizenship, over a period of several years.

- On specific occasions (with some teenagers, on a regular basis), however, the issue will be willful defiance. *This takes place when your adolescent (1) knows and clearly understands what you want (or don't want) to happen, (2) is capable of doing what you want, and (3) refuses to do so.*

  Whether passive or "in your face," the adolescent's defiance is asking several questions: Do Mom and Dad really mean business? What's going to happen if I don't do what they want? Are they tough enough to make me? Who's really in charge here?

  When confronted with such a situation, act clearly and decisively, meeting the challenge head-on. Your specific response to this situation will depend to some degree on the age of your adolescent and the way in which the defiance is manifested. Appropriate measures for a twelve-year-old may be ineffective or even counterproductive for a high school senior. But you must not back away from meeting the challenge, dealing with it decisively but also as calmly as possible. The ultimate objective is not merely to bring about compliance on your adolescent's part but a change of attitude as well. Not only must your adolescent not have his way but his attitude about what he has done must be turned around as well. When the conflict is over, you should be on the same team once again.

At times it may be difficult to tell whether your teenager is being defiant or irresponsible. Did he hear you? Did he understand clearly what you wanted? Can he actually accomplish it? Failing to get straight A's is not defiance. But refusing to shut off the TV and sit down with the books after being told to do so probably is. When dealing with willful defiance, attitude is the central issue. As Dr. James Dobson has noted in a memorable adage, "If he's looking for a fight, don't disappoint him." This doesn't refer to having a literal brawl with your adolescent, of course, but rather to a consistent posture of standing your ground when your authority has been clearly challenged.

4. Accept the fact that conflict between parent and child is inevitable.

Whether dealing with a full-blown showdown or managing a series of minor irritations, it is impossible to avoid conflict with your preteen or teenager at some point. Effective, loving parenting is characterized not by the absence of conflict but by the resolution of conflicts in ways that maintain both your leadership and your teenager's dignity.

5. Love and concern for your adolescent's best interests must be your final guide.

The effort required to provide good discipline and training is a continuous expression of love, and that love may take you in some unexpected directions. It may lead you to allow a teenager to suffer some consequences for his irresponsibility, even when you might easily bail him out. If he repeatedly forgets to take his lunch to school, letting him feel hunger for a couple of hours (rather than running the wayward sack over to the school office every day) will change his behavior far more than reminding him sixteen times over the breakfast table. You may both hurt while the consequence is playing out, but the final outcome—a learning experience with long-term benefits—will serve his best interests.

On the other hand, love may also lead you to overlook the specifics of a teenager's transgression based on his intent. If he makes a mess in the kitchen while trying to cook dinner for you, the motive of the heart should overshadow whatever has been strewn all over the counter and floor. (He can, of course, be asked cheerfully to participate in the cleanup effort—another learning experience.)

Love will also cause you to examine your own motives as you deal with different situations. Are you responding harshly to a teenager's offhanded comment because you're tired or overwhelmed? Are you giving in to unreasonable demands or ignoring disrespectful remarks because you were the victim of excessive punishment as a child and don't want to overreact? If you're upset over her messy room, are you concerned about her attitude toward her possessions or what your relatives will think if they see it? If you feel that your motives are unclear and your actions unpredictable, spend some time with an older parent whose child-rearing results you respect, or meet with your pastor or a counselor to discuss what has been taking place.

6. Stay on your knees.
If you think you've got parenting wired because your firstborn has sailed through adolescence with hardly a ripple of turbulence, cheer up. You will probably be blessed with a tornado when his younger sibling enters the seventh grade, and whatever seemed to work with Number One will prove to be a complete flop with Number Two. Similarly, if you've read books (including this one) and feel you've got the discipline situation figured out and reduced to a fine-tuned formula, brace yourself—something thoroughly humbling will probably cross your path in the near future. There is only one Parent who completely understands all sons and daughters on the face of the earth, and seeking His wisdom on a daily basis should be a priority for all who train and nurture adolescents.

Conflict with Adolescents: Basic Guidelines and Ground Rules

Even the teenager who is compliant and agreeable will lock horns with you eventually—or become expert at quieter ways to demonstrate her opinions. When you are challenged on a rule at your home or you see or hear your teenager doing something you don't like, you'll need to heed these principles:

To quote the apostle Paul, "Do not exasperate your children" (Ephesians 6:4). If you choose to comment, nag, or nudge about *everything* she does that isn't up to your standards, be prepared for several years of misery. Yes, she needs your guidance. The choices she makes now can have significant consequences, and she still has lots of room for improvement. But if she hears about her deficits constantly, she will become frustrated and eventually hostile. And guess who she *won't* want to talk to if there's a *real* problem. If all the nitpicky stuff arouses nonstop criticism at home, she can only imagine what will happen in response to a major mistake.

Think through your rules. Ask yourself regularly, "Why am I making this rule?" Does it truly have an impact on your adolescent's well-being? Or does it merely reflect the way things were done when you were growing up?

Don't be afraid to negotiate in some areas. If your teenager respectfully suggests an alternative to a rule or restriction you've imposed, listen carefully. If it's reasonable, seriously consider letting the decision go her way. You will gain some major points and demonstrate that you are truly listening rather than reacting.

Pick your battles carefully. Some things that bother you may not be worth a major conflict with your teenager. Think carefully before starting a war over the following:

- A mess in his or her own room (unless the health department pays a visit). Remember: dirty-room syndrome is a self-limited and nonfatal illness.
- Length of hair
- Earrings (for either gender)
- Style of music
- Sound level of music
- Choice of everyday clothing
- Fast food

- Sleeping in when there's not a specific need to arise for school or work
- How, when, and where homework is done—as long as it is getting done

On the other hand, there are a number of areas (some related to the list above) in which you will need to state your case and hold your ground, or at least have some family summit conferences to resolve your differences:

- A mess that is not confined to his or her room. Everyone who is old enough to walk and understand plain English needs to pick up his or her own clothes, trash, dishes, soft drink cans, and other debris. If you are constantly gathering up your teenager's (or one or more friends') stuff from every room, it's time for retraining. Let everyone (including your spouse, if needed) know that you have resigned from unpaid janitorial duties. Furthermore, after one or two reminders, valuables will be confiscated for an unspecified period, and trash may end up in the owner's bed. You can declare your intentions humorously, of course, but be sure to follow through.
- Extreme alterations of hair. A heart-to-heart talk is in order if your adolescent plans to adopt a totally bizarre hairstyle (such as giant green spikes) that will blatantly announce to the world, "I don't care what anybody thinks of me!" Important issues of acceptance and rejection lie below the surface of outlaw or alien appearances and deserve thoughtful exploration rather than ridicule.
- Body piercing. Aggressive body piercing (nose, tongue, navel, etc.) should be discouraged, perhaps with a reminder about respecting and valuing one's body as well as a check on the current status of peer pressure. In addition, if an infection arises from any of this hardware, removing it can be quite uncomfortable.
- Tattoos. Despite a rising acceptance of "body art" in many circles, your adolescent needs to know that it is extremely unwise to do *anything* with permanent physical consequences when his life is in a state of flux. This is particularly

important if he seems intent on embedding negative or offensive images in his skin. It will cost him a lot of money and discomfort if he wants them removed later on, which is likely. He should also be aware that infections such as hepatitis B or HIV can be spread by contaminated tattoo needles. A makeshift "tattoo parlor" in a friend's garage should be avoided. Tell him that he can have all the tattoos he wants—after he is eighteen and living on his own. By then his interest in body alterations may well have passed.

- Content of music, as was discussed earlier in this chapter.
- Sound level of music. If your adolescent's music is keeping everyone at home (or the entire neighborhood) awake at night, or if you can hear it across the room—when he's wearing headphones—you will need to insist that the volume come down. Ongoing exposure to extremely loud noise can cause permanent hearing loss.
- Choice of everyday clothing. If garments contain images or words that are violent or offensive, they don't belong on your adolescent. You will also need to veto female attire that is blatantly sexually provocative.
- Extremes in food choices—either excessive or limited in variety or amount. Obesity in adolescence is not only a social issue but may set in motion lifelong health problems. Anorexia and bulimia are obsessions with food that can have very serious consequences as well. In a nutshell, being extremely overweight tends to create medical trouble later in life; anorexia can literally be lethal in a few months. Both deserve focused attention and help from your health-care provider. Anorexia may require psychiatric hospitalization because it can be very difficult to treat.
- Toxic friends, as was discussed in chapter 4.
- Tobacco, alcohol, and street drug use, as is discussed in chapter 8.
- Sexual activity—see chapter 7.
- Disappearing. In any home it is a common courtesy—and may be critically important in an emergency—for family members who live under the same roof to be notified of each

other's whereabouts. Your teenager needs to understand that this doesn't mean you're treating him like a child. It is childish and irresponsible to take off for hours at a time—especially at night—without keeping the home front posted. If he's going to be at a friend's house for the evening, it's not unreasonable for you to get a name and number. If he's going to go somewhere else, you need to know the destination.

As he progresses through high school, let him know that you intend to give him more latitude about the time he is expected home, if he is trustworthy in this area. Remind him that this expectation applies to everyone in your home, parents included.

• Disrespectful comments and actions. Much has been said earlier about treating your adolescent with respect. The same should be expected of his behavior toward you. This does not mean that he isn't allowed to disagree with you or even become angry. In fact, there may be times when he is quite upset with you and perhaps for good reason. He needs to know that you are willing to hear his point of view on any thing, even if he is angry, as long as he says it respectfully.

Occasionally a comment uttered in the heat of battle, a roll of the eyes, or a door that closes a little too hard will strike you as inappropriate. It may not have been deliberate, but you need to let him know how it came across and suggest other ways for him to make his case.

If you are definitely on the receiving end of sarcastic or even abusive language—or you hear it being dished out to your spouse—you need to bring the conversation to an immediate halt. Explain as calmly as possible that the issue now is no longer whatever you were talking about but the unacceptable way in which the ideas are being expressed. You may get a blank stare, and you may need to spell out what you found objectionable. If there is an appropriate retraction, you can proceed—and you will have provided an object lesson for your adolescent in how to handle issues later in life.

If your teenager will not back away from comments that

are out of line or the problem escalates, more drastic action will be necessary (see sidebar below).

Do go to the mat when necessary. There will be issues regarding health, safety, moral principles, and attitude that will require you to state your case and hold your ground. You must still be friendly. You can discuss the reasons and suggest alternatives. You can remind your teenager that her total independence is not too many years away, but that for now you're still in charge in a few key areas. You must reinforce your love for her and treat her with respect. But

What If You and Your Adolescent Are Perpetually in Turbulent Waters?

Are you dealing with a son or daughter who is constantly irritable, negative, or disruptive? Do you spend most of your time simply trying to maintain some semblance of order? Are your requests or directives routinely met with passive indifference or outright rebellion? Do you feel a major sense of relief when you get away from your teenager for a while?

If so, some basic evaluation and course corrections are in order. Among other things, you may be dealing with one or all of the following:

- *A medical problem.* Many chronic conditions (for example, allergies, recurrent headaches, sinusitis, or anemia to name a few) can cause an adolescent to feel poorly enough to provoke ongoing irritability. Acute illnesses (such as the flu) or injuries (especially a blow to the head) can do likewise. In either case there are usually more specific symptoms or an event to suggest a medical problem. Nevertheless, a review of the situation by your teenager's physician can help determine whether a medical problem is responsible for your teen's behavior.
- *Medications and drugs.* Antihistamines or decongestant/antihistamine combinations may cause irritability, although usually the connection between the drug and the mood change is readily apparent. Drugs which themselves are intended to change behavior (for example, Ritalin or Dexedrine for attention deficit disorder) can sometimes backfire and worsen negative behavior. Illicit drugs and inhalant abuse now penetrate the school-age and adolescent population in many parts of the country, and their effect on behavior can be very significant. If you are concerned about a possible connection between your teenager's mood and medications or drugs—whether prescribed, over the counter, or bought on the street—a physician's evaluation is wise.
- *A neurochemical disturbance* such as attention deficit disorder.
- *A significant emotional disturbance.* Children and teenagers can suffer clinical depression, for example.
- *An innately strong-willed adolescent* who is going to challenge your leadership until the day he sets out on his own as a young adult.

even though you may risk a temporary decline in popularity, when it's time to take a stand, don't shirk your duty.

Consequences must occur consistently and in a timely manner. Not only should your adolescent know that you will back up your words with appropriate action every time, but she should also know that your response won't waver to any great degree. The same transgression shouldn't bring about a soft reminder one night and a harsh punishment the next. On-again, off-again discipline is confusing, and it generates both disobedience and

continued

- *A problem in consistent limit setting* during the first few years of life—perhaps brought on by parental turmoil, burnout, illness, or divorce—which now needs to be corrected.
- *Abuse*—by other teenagers or by an adult. Children and adolescents who have been abused emotionally, physically, or sexually will often demonstrate drastic changes in their behavior around other people, even those they love and trust. Withdrawal and ongoing hostility could be signs of a problem in this area.
- *Your own behavior as a parent.* Could your words, attitudes, or actions be contributing to your teenager's current behavior? Is your parenting style either excessively controlling or overly permissive? Are your responses to him unpredictable and disrespectful of his feelings? Is he getting enough of your time and attention, or could his negativity actually be a cry for more of it? A wise parent will periodically carry out prayerful self-examination, and a significant behavior problem in an adolescent is certainly an appropriate occasion for this task.

Your problem-solving approach will depend on your adolescent and the resources available to you. An evaluation by his or her physician would be a good start and, if appropriate, a referral for family counseling with someone who shares your values. Personal reflection and prayer, consultation with your pastor, and support in a group of parents with teenagers of similar ages would be wise as well. Repair work in relationships takes time, and you can expect this project to continue for a number of months.

Books that deal in more depth with problems of childhood and adolescent behavior include:

The New Dare to Discipline and *The Strong-Willed Child* by Dr. James Dobson (Wheaton, Ill.: Tyndale House Publishers, Inc., 1992 and 1985 respectively).

Making Children Mind Without Losing Yours by Dr. Kevin Leman (Old Tappan, New Jersey: Fleming H. Revell Company, 1984).

Parents' Guide to the Spiritual Mentoring of Teens. General Editors: Joe White and Jim Weidmann (Wheaton, Ill.: Tyndale House Publishers, Inc., 2001).

unhealthy fear. In a two-parent family, both parents should strive to dispense consequences in a similar manner. "Wait till your father gets home" is a phrase you should never have to use, because Mom and Dad should deliver the goods with equal conviction.

Most adolescents are experts at the game called "What happens if . . . ?" They have spent a lot of time observing cause and effect and can usually predict with some accuracy when (if not what) parental action is likely to occur. In many families, the odds depend upon which parent is playing the game, what else is going on, time of day, tone of voice, and numerous other factors. If a teenager hears a lot of talk about what he should or shouldn't do but little of it is backed up with action, he will probably pay little attention (unless he is extremely sensitive to tone of voice or verbal disapproval alone). The bottom line is that if and when your adolescent challenges your leadership (whether actively or passively), respond with action—calmly, respectfully, quickly, decisively, and consistently.

The consequence should be appropriate for the transgression. For discipline to be effective, an adolescent needs to know and understand what you want and, when appropriate, what will happen if he doesn't comply. Beware of issuing extravagant warnings that you are not likely to carry out. "If you don't stop arguing, we're going to cancel our trip to the lake!" is either an excessive or an idle threat, especially if the trip has been planned for months, with reservations and a deposit already mailed. After several grandiose warnings that never come true, your teenagers will catch on and not pay attention to you. But if you're truly willing to blow an entire vacation over an argument in the backseat, you need to reconsider whether your punishment really fits the crime. Like adults, adolescents care passionately about what is fair, and they become agitated when consequences seem to appear out of thin air. We have already noted the New Testament's warning that parents not exasperate their children. A steady stream of arbitrary or unjust punishments will not only exasperate them but reap a bitter harvest years later.

In many situations, **a verbal exhortation or reprimand** will suffice, especially when delivered in an even-handed tone. If you need to get your teenager's attention (for example, for a repeat offense), **withholding a privilege** is very often the most appropriate response. If she has ignored specific instructions about being home by a certain hour, for example, a week without phone or driving privileges can be a meaningful consequence.

Restitution is an important principle of discipline that can and should be used, especially with adolescents. If your teen makes a mess, he cleans it up. If he causes someone else's property to be damaged or destroyed, whether directly or through passive negligence, he participates in the repair and restoration. He may have to work to repay all or part of the costs involved.

Not all acts of restitution necessarily involve property. If your daughter lies to someone, for example, she should confess to that person. If she has broken a promise or failed to honor a commitment, she will need to apologize to the person(s) involved. These acts of humility are often far more difficult—but also more character building—than enduring any loss of privilege.

Allowing consequences to play out is a potentially powerful approach to discipline, especially during the preteen and early adolescent years. The basic principle is this: Look at mistakes as learning opportunities, and avoid rushing in to rescue your son or daughter from natural consequences (provided, of course, they are merely unpleasant and not potentially dangerous). For example:

- If he leaves his bicycle on the front lawn and someone steals it, don't replace it immediately. He'll be more careful with the next bicycle he owns.
- If she forgets to bring home the permission slip for the field trip, let her miss it. She won't forget the next time.
- If he damages or destroys one of his prized possessions through negligence or mistreatment, don't respond by buying him a new one. With a gentle reminder about taking better care of his possessions, let him mourn the loss and earn the money to replace it.
- If she dawdles every morning and then misses the school

bus or car pool, let her deal with the fallout from the unexcused absence.

Your motivation should not be anger or spite, and your tone should not be "I told you so," "Now you'll listen to me," or "That'll teach you!" If anything, this process should be painful for you; you should provide emotional support and comfort while you resist the urge to bail him out. Whatever you choose to teach during one of these episodes need not come with a flood of reprimands, because he has already felt the sting of wrongdoing.

Why should you and your adolescent endure these unpleasant experiences, especially when it is often within your capability to end them quickly and easily? Because what he learns from an uncomfortable episode now may save him from a disastrous or even lethal miscalculation later. A child or teenager who is allowed to become an expert on consequences will be more likely to think through the outcomes of his actions later on when the stakes are higher. Going without his lunch won't kill him, but getting involved with illegal drugs or premarital sex might. Furthermore, if he is repeatedly spared the consequences of his misbehavior throughout childhood and adolescence, he may never learn self-control or exercise good judgment as an adult.

Physical punishment is not an appropriate response to an adolescent's wrongdoing or a conflict. Slapping, punching, kicking, and beating are abusive, degrading, and illegal. Disciplinary spanking within very specific guidelines can be a useful tool in response to an episode of willful defiance by a toddler or preschooler.[2] It is inappropriate, however, for children older than ten years of age. (Indeed, it should be used very infrequently, if at all, after the age of five or six.)

A unified approach to discipline and conflict management, carried out regardless of who is responsible for an adolescent at any given time, should be a firm parental goal. An honest disagreement about principles and practices should not be discussed in front of children and adolescents. Under no circumstances (except an imminent threat to a teenager's life and health) should one parent openly contradict or overrule the instructions of the other. This is not only disrespectful, but it also undermines the other parent's authority. If necessary in the heat of the moment, parents should call a time-out and discuss their issues behind closed doors before taking further action. If mother and father are divorced, every effort should be made to maintain the same standards in each parent's household. Without such unity, teenagers will learn to play one parent or caregiver against the other ("Mom said no, so let's ask Dad").

Don't restrict teaching of values to times of confrontation. In many families, the only time moral principles are discussed is during corrective action resulting from an episode of wrongdoing. But this will tend to leave adolescents with a stunted or even repressive sense of values. Be on the lookout for "teachable moments," those conversations during which you can give your teenager a broader and deeper understanding of right and wrong.

When Mom and Dad Disagree:
Setting a Pattern for Good Communication

It is a sad fact that *few people have the opportunity to observe their parents resolve a conflict in a positive and mutually satisfying manner.* Instead, disagreements within a marriage all too often deteriorate into one of several unhealthy scenarios:

- *Suppression.* Fear of conflict causes husband or wife (or both) to allow issues to smolder and simmer—sometimes for years—into a stew of resentment. There may not be any fireworks in the home—but not much happiness either.
- *Repression.* One person dominates the other, winning every conflict through physical or verbal intimidation.
- *Guerrilla warfare.* Conflicts are manifested through quick jabs—indirect put-downs, subtle insults, sly sarcastic comments—that chip away at the other person without ever dealing with any issues directly.
- *Character assassination.* One person is subjected to name-calling, harsh remarks about appearance or intelligence, or ongoing scorn for his or her opinions or motives by the

other. Continuing direct assaults on an individual's identity and value create wounds that can take years to heal, and such behavior indicates that the relationship is in serious trouble.

- *Dredging up past grievances.* This tactic is manifested by counterproductive phrases such as "You *always* do this . . ." or "Here we go again . . ." or "This is just like that time when . . ." It is virtually impossible to settle today's issue when baggage from the past is continually dragged out of the closet.

- *All-out war.* Yelling, abusive language, shoving, and hitting are clear signs that the marriage is seriously damaged.

Children and adolescents who have repeatedly observed one or more of these destructive responses to conflict are likely to be ill equipped to manage disagreements that will inevitably arise in their own marriages. Unhealthy patterns may thus be perpetuated—either duplicating what was demonstrated by the older generation or perhaps moving toward opposite extremes. For example, someone who has lived through many intense and painful arguments may decide to ignore or sidestep issues to avoid the threat of an unpleasant altercation. But this course of inaction can allow anger and resentment to fester for years, leading ultimately to a sour—or dead—marriage.

If parents hope to demonstrate healthy conflict resolution for their children, they will need to practice—both before and after children are born. Some couples will have broached this subject during premarital counseling. Virtually every marriage could benefit from working on it in more formal settings—in small groups organized through churches (assuming they are properly led), in couples' communication classes, or in private counseling. While it is not possible to detail in this book all of the principles involved in settling disagreements in marriage, the following basic concepts can serve as a foundation for parents who desire to work on this important area.

Mutual respect is an absolute necessity. Without respect on both sides, any relationship will ultimately deteriorate or become destructive. With mutual respect, it is possible to have an intense disagreement with another person without causing damage to a relationship or those who are affected by it. Respect acknowledges the ultimate worth of the other person—as established by God and not by any other attributes or accomplishments—and affirms that worth in attitudes, words, and actions.

If parents do not respect one another or if respect flows only in one direction, attempts to resolve issues are likely to be unsuccessful or hurtful. This fundamental problem must be addressed—usually in a counseling setting—if a marriage is going to survive and thrive through the years of raising children and beyond.

When a disagreement arises, conversation should focus on the issue and not the person. If Mom feels she needs more help with the kids in the evening, it isn't productive to begin the discussion with the statement "You care more about that TV than your own children!" If Dad is getting worried about the family budget, he won't get very far by saying, "All you ever do is spend the money I work so hard to bring home!" Once the issue is defined (How do we care for the kids when we're both tired? or How can we keep better track of our finances?), the focus can shift toward generating and evaluating a potential solution.

When an issue needs to be discussed, pick an appropriate time and place. Not at the end of the day when energy is low and fuses may be short; not right before bed; not when anger is at a fever pitch; not when there isn't time to work through it; not when the TV is on, the phone is ringing, the kids are arguing, and the dog is barking. If it is clear that an issue needs to be addressed, it's quite all right for either person to call time and say, "This isn't a good time to discuss this" or "I don't feel like talking about it right now"—as long as a specific time is set to talk about it in the very near future. The best time to talk is when both parties are rested, focused, and attentive. It's helpful to work through an issue in a place that is relatively free of distractions and interruptions. This may be a particular room, somewhere out in the yard, or a place away from home. Many couples do their best negotiating at a coffee shop or on a long walk.

Pray together before discussing the issue. Laying the issue before God can help keep it in perspective and reinforce your common ground. Be careful not to use this prayer time unfairly to express your viewpoint or claim God's backing for your side of the conflict. Prayer should be an exercise in humility, not a power play.

Each person must be able to express his or her viewpoint fully, without interruption. A key element of respect is listening carefully to what the other person is saying, without thinking about one's own response. One technique that encourages attentive listening involves picking an object (such as a pen) and stipulating that whoever holds it is entitled to speak without any interruption. The other person cannot say a word until the pen is passed, and the pen will not be passed until the person receiving it can summarize what was just said to the speaker's satisfaction—without argument, rebuttal, or editorial comment. If the listener doesn't get it right, the pen doesn't pass. This approach may at first seem awkward and ritualistic, but it is surprisingly effective at improving listening skills.

Get in the habit of checking frequently to be sure that you understand what the other person is saying. "I hear you saying that . . ."

Avoid "You . . ." statements—especially those containing the words *always, never, should*, or *shouldn't*. Replace them with statements that express your own feelings. "You never spend any time at home anymore!" essentially demands a rebuttal ("That's not true!"). In contrast, "It seems as if the kids and I are spending more evenings by ourselves than ever before, and it makes me feel lonely" is a straightforward observation and an expression of a genuine feeling. Similarly, a statement such as "You shouldn't make commitments for both of us without talking to me first!" is likely to provoke a defensive response. The one way in which a "you" statement can legitimately enter a conversation is in this form: "When you say (or do) _____, I feel _____." (For example, "When you make commitments for both of us without talking to me first, I feel as if my opinion doesn't count.") This type of statement can help one person understand how specific words or actions are affecting the other person.

Avoid "Why . . . ?" questions—especially those (once again) containing the words *always* or *never*. "Why do you always leave the back door open?" can be answered in only one of two ways: defensively ("I don't either!") or sarcastically ("Because I'm an idiot!"). "Why . . . ?" questions immediately and automatically turn a discussion into a battle.

Avoid dragging events from the distant past into the current issue. "Here we go again. . . !" or "This is just what you did on our vacation in 1990, when you . . ." If current problems are indeed related to grievances from the past, then those specific concerns need to be discussed and resolved apart from any current problems.

Name-calling and other forms of insults are disrespectful and should be banned from all conversations within a family (or anywhere else). Verbal insults live in everyone's memory long after apologies have been made. One of the most powerful lessons your teenagers can learn from you is how to disagree or be angry with a person without labeling, name-calling, or insulting them in other ways. Remember that body language (sighing, rolling the eyes, etc.), gestures, and tone of voice can communicate disrespect as powerfully as the most explicit insult.

The discussion of an issue should eventually arrive at a point of exploring possible courses of action. "What can I do to help you not feel so tired at the end of the day?" or "How can we make Sunday morning less hectic?" It may help to list a number of possibilities and then talk through the pros and cons of each one.

Realize that on a number of issues you may have to "agree to disagree," and that in doing so, the other person's viewpoint is not to be subject to constant ridicule. This will mean compromising in some cases. There is usually, however, some solution that will allow for each person's needs to be met.

If your discussions of issues frequently deteriorate into shouting matches or glum stalemates, get some help. It takes courage and maturity to go to a counselor or to a mature couple whom you know to be experienced in conflict resolution, in order to determine what goes wrong when disagreements arise in your home. Constructive suggestions from an unbiased third party, if acted upon consistently, can drastically improve the quality and outcome of these conversations.

Should We Have Disagreements in Front of the Kids?

Parental modeling of respectful disagreements can be a powerful and useful life lesson for children and adolescents to observe, provided that a few cautions are kept in mind:

Consider your audience. The child(ren) should be old enough to comprehend what you are talking about and emotionally mature enough to grasp the concept that you can disagree with someone whom you deeply love and respect. Preschoolers and early-grade-school children can become terrified by the thought that Mom and Dad don't like each other and may misinterpret a spirited parental exchange as the unraveling of their world. They probably should rarely, if ever, witness a serious parental disagreement. Older children and adolescents, on the other hand, can benefit from seeing how two mature people can settle an issue in a positive way.

Play by the rules. If kids are going to watch or listen, you should be well versed in healthy conflict resolution, resolve to keep the tone of conversation respectful, and strive to come to a positive solution of your issue.

Consider demonstrating how you settled an issue. If you have had a particularly fruitful conversation about a problem, think about re-enacting it for your older children and adolescents to show how you dealt with it. You might even demonstrate some right and wrong ways to deal with an issue—especially if your kids are having some problems in this area themselves.

Beware of voicing a disagreement in front of a child or adolescent who is the subject of the disagreement. Parents should be united, even if they are not in total agreement, when dealing with basic issues—especially those relating to limits and discipline. A teenager must never get the idea that if Mom says no, he can go talk to Dad, or that one parent will veto the other's disciplinary measures. However, with some concerns that are not fundamentally important, an adolescent might benefit from hearing different viewpoints, as long as they are expressed appropriately. (For example, the pros and cons of going to a summer camp or joining an athletic team could be an excellent topic for discussion among teenager and parents, even if there is not total agreement about the best decision.)

Declare a cease-fire, if necessary. If your discussion is deteriorating into a shouting match and children of any age are within earshot, *call it off* until you can continue in private—after you have cooled down. It is devastating—and inappropriate—for children and adolescents to hear their parents yelling, insulting one another, or being physically aggressive. If your disagreement reaches this level, you should not only isolate it from them but seek counseling as soon as possible.

Divorce and Its Effect on Children and Adolescents

"What God has joined together, let no man put asunder."

In spite of this solemn admonition that concludes most wedding ceremonies, more than half of all marriages are eventually "put asunder" in the United States, which currently has the highest divorce rate in the industrialized world.[3]

Not too many decades ago, couples having significant marital conflict frequently saw children as a reason to stay together. Many would postpone divorce and strive to maintain the appearance of normalcy at home until their children were grown and gone. But in the wake of many cultural shifts of the '60s and '70s, children have come to be seen as beneficiaries of divorce and less often as an obstacle to it: "The children will be better off if we're not arguing/ we're not in a loveless marriage." In other words, "everyone will be better off if we go our separate ways." The advent of no-fault divorce laws, beginning in California in 1969 and spreading to forty-five states within five years and to all fifty states by 1985, was accompanied by a 34 percent increase in divorce rates between 1970 and 1990.[4]

The Pain Inflicted by Divorce

After more than two decades of widespread dissolution of marriages, research suggests that, in general, children of divorce are *not* as well off as those who grow up in intact families. According to the Family Research Council:

- Three out of four teen suicides are committed by adolescents from broken homes.
- Children of divorce are 70 percent more likely to have been expelled from school and are twice as likely to drop out of school, compared to their peers who are in intact families.
- Seven out of ten preteens and teenagers in long-term correctional facilities come from broken homes.

Judith Wallerstein, a therapist and former lecturer at the University of California, Berkeley, reported in *Second Chances: Men, Women, and Children a Decade after Divorce* that in a study of sixty families divorced between 1971 and 1981, ten years after the breakup of their parents the children felt "less protected, less cared for, less comforted" and still had "vivid, gut-wrenching memories of their parents' separation." A comprehensive analysis known as the California Children of Divorce Study found that more than a third of the children studied were dealing with moderate to severe depression five years after their parents' divorce. According to Wallerstein, almost all of the adolescent girls in the study "confronted issues of love, commitment, and marriage with anxiety, sometimes with very great concern about betrayal, abandonment, and not being loved."[5] Recent research also suggests that parental divorce may have long-term health consequences for children. A seventy-year longevity study reported in the *American Journal of Public Health* in 1995 indicated that individuals who were younger than twenty-one years of age when their parents divorced were more likely to have a shorter life span than those whose families remained intact.

Even when Mom and Dad's relationship has ongoing conflicts, from a child's perspective the breakup of the family is the end of life as she knows it. Depending upon the age and personality of the child, several immediate and long-term reactions are virtually inevitable, even when the divorce is amicable. These are likely to include fear, insecurity, sadness (in some cases overt depression), anger, and guilt. Younger children are particularly vulnerable to the idea that they were somehow at fault and that "Mommy and Daddy wouldn't have split up if I had been better." Older children and adolescents are often as angry as they are sad; in some cases they act out that anger, especially if the divorce is going to force them to move or cause some other significant change in their normal activities.

A more recent book by Judith Wallerstein, *The Unexpected Legacy of Divorce,* describes in vivid and poignant detail the powerful impact of their parents' divorce on adolescents and young adults as they struggle to establish and maintain stable relationships. According to Wallerstein, children of divorce experience not one, not two, but many more losses as their parents go in search of new lovers or partners. Each of these throws the child's life into turmoil and brings back painful reminders of the first loss.

Children observe their parents' courtships with a mixture of excitement and anxiety. For adolescents, the erotic stimulation of seeing their parents with changing partners can be difficult to contain. Several young teenage girls in the study began their own sexual activity when they observed a parent's involvement in a passionate affair.

Wallerstein followed 131 children of divorce for twenty-five years, and among them she observed significant damage to the "psychological scaffolding they need to construct a happy marriage"—often with disastrous results.

What prompts so many children of divorce to rush into a cohabitation or early marriage with as much forethought as buying a new pair of shoes? Answers lie in the ghosts that rise to haunt them as they enter young adulthood. They live in fear that they will repeat their parents' history, hardly daring to hope that they can do better. Dating and courtship raise their hopes of being loved sky-high—but also their fears of being hurt and rejected. This amalgam of fear and loneliness can lead to multiple affairs, hasty marriages, early divorce, and—if no take-home lessons are gleaned from it all—a second or third round of the same.[6]

Divorce has such serious consequences for all concerned, especially children and adolescents, that it should be considered an extreme measure. Sometimes there may be no alternative, such as in a marriage that has been severely damaged by repeated and unrepentant infidelity. A partner cannot be forced to stay in a marriage if he or she has decided to leave it—no matter how fervently the other partner desires to seek solutions and prevent divorce.

A commitment to avoid divorce at all cost does not mean that marital partners should drift silently through years of discontent without taking appropriate action when needed. In many ways a marriage is like a house—it needs a solid foundation, ongoing maintenance, intermittent repair, and perhaps major remodeling. Too many couples look at a marriage that needs a lot of repairs and conclude—often too quickly—that it can't be fixed, that they want to move out, or that they never wanted to live there in the first place. But when one or more children and teenagers have grown up in this family and see it as the center of their world, the process of leaving it is traumatic.

A detailed look at the process of marriage mending is beyond the scope of this book, but numerous resources—including books, seminars, support groups, and couples retreats—are available to help with this task. Most important, a couple whose marriage is in trouble should enlist the help of a counselor whom they trust and with whom they can work over a period of months or years if necessary. This process should also include a spiritual inventory. If both husband and wife have committed their lives to Christ, each should seek to submit to Him daily and consciously place the marriage under His authority. If one or both have not yet established a personal relationship with Christ, there can be no more crucial time to do so than during major marital reconstruction.

Additional accountability to a pastor, other couples (especially those who have built solid marriages over some years), or even mature relatives, assuming they are not contributing to the problem, may be necessary. In a society that seeks a quick fix for everything from cars to kids, making a commitment to an arduous process of restoring a marriage—especially when the possibility of a satisfying finished product seems hopelessly out of reach—may require both a leap of faith and a lot of small steps. But when we consider the damage that divorce inflicts upon children, this effort should become a couple's first priority. Ending the marriage should be considered only as the very last resort.

What If Divorce Is Already in Progress?

If a divorce is indeed going to take place, now is a crucial time for you to put your children's welfare ahead of your own emotions. *The divorce process itself can be brutal for both young children and adolescents if parents do not make very deliberate choices about their behavior—especially in regard to legal matters.* The following basic decisions can help keep the damage to a minimum.

Settle as many issues as you can outside the courtroom.
The adversarial nature of legal proceedings and the determination of attorneys to deliver the best outcome for their clients can bring out the worst in people, especially if there are many unresolved conflicts between the parents. One or both members of a divorcing couple may feel justified in attacking and blaming the other for what has happened or even taking revenge in a public courtroom for hurts that have been suffered. You owe it to your children to resolve as many issues as you can without turning the process into an endless nightmare of fights and name-calling, lawsuits and countersuits, and meetings with lawyers and judges.

Not only is this type of open warfare between Mom and Dad traumatic for their children and teenagers to watch, but it ultimately imposes a major financial burden on a family already beset with a great deal of stress. Do you really want to spend your children's future college funds on unnecessary and avoidable legal fees? No matter how much hurt a spouse may have inflicted, it is unwise to finance your retaliation with your children's (and your) future. When decisions have been reached by mutual agreement, expensive enforcement procedures are less likely to be needed later on.

A competent professional mediator or a divorce attorney who places a high priority on fairness and maintaining civility in family relationships may be able to help a couple come to an agreement without the pain and cost of a bruising legal battle. If a spouse is determined to "play dirty" in court, you will probably have no choice but to defend yourself—but don't assume that your only recourse is to "fight fire with fire." Your children will likely be burned in the process.

Do not ask your young children or teenagers to take sides.
When you feel you have been wronged by your estranged spouse, it is natural to want those closest to you to sympathize with your cause. But you must consider very carefully what is appropriate for your children or adolescents to hear about your difficulties with the other parent. Even if it is clear that you have not been treated respectfully or fairly, telling them all about your spouse's misdeeds may help you feel better for a while, but it could be devastating for them.

If you are going through a divorce, your children are already struggling with how to relate to both parents in a situation that feels very unnatural and threatening to them. It is inappropriate—and blatantly unfair—for them to be called upon to choose sides, to relay messages between warring parents, or to hear unpleasant details that are neither their responsibility nor under their control.

Children are born with the need and desire to love both parents. That need does not end during adolescence. It is not your prerogative to isolate them from their other parent's love, even when that person has hurt you. In some situations it will be necessary for children to have limited (or no) access to a parent whose lifestyle is unhealthy or dangerous. Even then, however, in many cases the children may be able to maintain a relationship within certain boundaries.

Do not allow your conflicts with a spouse to interfere
   with your responsibility for the children.
A skillful attorney might be able to win a settlement that is more favorable to one party than it is fair. But a loving parent may have

to consider relinquishing a few "points" in the divorce negotiations if doing so means that the children will receive better care and resources adequate to meet their needs.

A frightening number of otherwise reasonable adults become neglectful after a divorce settlement, and in doing so, act in a way that defies God's principles for caring for their families. If you owe child support, it is important—and right—to pay it when due. Furthermore, you need to make certain that your child's medical needs are properly met, even if doing so involves contributing more than is required of you. Your former spouse may be struggling to pay bills and provide a decent home for your children. That financial struggle usually intensifies as children enter and grow through their teenage years. Strive to be helpful and supportive in such a situation, rather than add to the problem.

Do not turn to your children or adolescents for emotional support. As vulnerable as you may feel while your marriage is ending, it is your responsibility to be the emotional anchor for your children— and not the other way around—whether they are young or on the verge of adulthood. While you can't avoid allowing them to see your sadness or even anger at times, you will need to make extra efforts to provide stability at a time when their world feels very unsafe. Providing stability will include repeated reassurances that the divorce is not their fault and ongoing confirmation that they are still loved by both parents.

Above all, it is not their job to take care of you or become your confidant, even if they appear to be adjusting well to the divorce. Because of their physical and intellectual capabilities, adolescents often fall into the role of "caretaker" for one or both divorced (or divorcing) parents. As a result, they may divert energy and attention away from working through their own issues. A teenager who is concerned about her parents' emotional stress, for example, may be reluctant to reveal difficulties she is having in school or the turbulence she is experiencing with her boyfriend. Make every effort to find the emotional support you need through relationships with other adults, so that you can in turn supply the emotional support that *they* need during these critical years.

What If Divorce Has Already Taken Place?

Even when a marriage has ended, it is critical to remember that parenting responsibilities have *not* ended. In the best situations, children of divorced parents should be able to continue a meaningful relationship with both mother and father through the teenage years, even if one has primary custody and the other's contact is more limited.

In reality, this does not always occur. One parent may abandon the other (and the children), move away, adopt a destructive lifestyle, or behave in an abusive manner. In such cases the other parent will need to carry on alone but supported by other adults who can help fill some of the gaps left by the parent who is gone. The following guidelines will help minimize the negative effects of divorce on your teen.

Maintain a civil and cooperative relationship
  with your former spouse.

Assuming that both parents remain involved with the children, every effort should be made to agree upon policies that affect them. Curfews, spending money, after-school jobs, trips, driving privileges, and disciplinary measures should be handled in a similar manner in both households. This can occur, of course, only if the parents cooperate. Unfortunately, it only takes one parent to create ongoing conflict by making new rules, abandoning the old ones, or disregarding the other parent's concerns or wishes. Parents may consider seeking the help of a counselor to help them arrive at appropriate mutual guidelines.

Help your child or adolescent work through her
  emotions about life after divorce.

Children and teenagers alike will need help processing the emotions that are an inevitable response to the divorce, as unpleasant as those feelings may be. Don't hesitate to connect your adolescent with an appropriate resource—a counselor, youth pastor, or a trusted relative—who can help her sort through her feelings.

Ongoing insecurity and sadness may cause a child or adolescent to become overly dependent on the parent who is providing the majority of the care. The parent might even reciprocate, allowing a son or daughter to assume the role of a confidant or surrogate spouse. As hard as it may be in the emotional storms that follow divorce, it is important for a parent to *remain* a parent—loving, affirming, compassionate, but also setting and maintaining appropriate limits for the child or teenager and boundaries for their relationship.

Keep discipline and order intact.
Children and adolescents need structure when life is stable and going well; in the wake of a parental breakup the security of loving boundaries is more important than ever. Parents are often tempted to "ease up" in the interest of relieving sadness or guilt. But abandoning your house rules and failing to take appropriate action when your teenager misbehaves will only compound the problem.

You may find it especially difficult to maintain discipline if the other parent becomes lax, because the children will be more than willing to point out the differences during a time of conflict ("Dad always lets us stay out later"). If at all possible, meet with your former spouse and attempt to establish consistent disciplinary policies. If the other person is in fact lackadaisical or inconsistent in this area, don't lower your own standards—but don't try to overcompensate by becoming more strict.

Take care of yourself.
Because of the significant physical and emotional consequences following divorce, men and women who have undergone this process should be mindful not only of their children's well-being but also of their own health. Basic self-care—a sensible diet, regular exercise, adequate sleep, and a balance of work and recreation—is a starting point. To this should be added the support of a network of friends, involvement in a church (if possible, one that has an active ministry for divorced individuals), and, above all, a day-by-day walk with God, who is the ultimate source of life and health.

What about Remarriage and Blended Families?

Forty percent of all marriages are actually remarriages for one or both parties, and approximately one in three Americans is a stepparent, stepchild, stepsibling, or in some way a member of a stepfamily. The formation of a new marital partnership in which children from one or both prior relationships come together under the same roof is no small undertaking. Idealized, "Brady Bunch" interactions are a sitcom fantasy, and in the worst situations conflicts between stepsiblings or between children and stepparents can undermine the remarriage or destroy it completely.

At the same time, there is the potential for building a new family that is loving and productive. This is possible with time, patience, and a lot of communication. Some principles to keep in mind include the following:

Remarriage should be preceded by effective counseling
  to prevent history from repeating itself.
Why did the previous marriage(s) fail? Was there anything that could or should have been done to prevent it? What understanding of God and moral values is each member bringing to this new partnership? What about goals, priorities, and expectations? What are the child-rearing styles of each parent? Does one tend to be more permissive or more authoritarian than the other? Will each person plan to discipline the other's children, and if so, how? All of these questions, and many more, need to be addressed in detail before wedding plans are made.

Beware of sexual involvement during this exploratory process. Not only can it cloud your judgment, but it will send older children—and especially your adolescents—a confusing mixed message ("Sex outside of marriage is okay for me but not for you") or a blatantly wrongheaded one ("Sex outside of marriage is okay for all of us"). Sexual entanglement outside of marriage is as bad an idea for adults as it is for adolescents.

The transition from acquaintance/friend to marriage partner
  and co-parent of someone else's children or teenagers cannot
  be made overnight.
Depending upon their ages and experiences, children may manifest intense—and at times contradictory—responses to the prospect of Mom or Dad (or both) getting involved with a new partner. The idea of having a "whole family" again can be appealing, especially if it seems to be making the child's own parent happy. But there will

also be anxiety or even agitation over a potential competitor for the parent's affection and attention. Becoming friendly with a new adult in the parent's life might bring up confusing feelings of divided allegiance—*if I like Mom's new boyfriend, does that mean that I'm not being loyal to Dad?* Children of divorce, both young and older, often maintain a fantasy that Mom and Dad will get together again, and remarriage to someone else will end that dream abruptly. Thus, another adult in the parent's life may be greeted by responses that are cool, if not hostile, from the children who are watching developments with great interest and concern.

The plot thickens when remarriage brings into focus the lines of authority. Should the new stepparent begin giving out orders or disciplining the partner's children? What happens when the child has a conflict with the stepparent and comes to the natural parent for support and comfort? All of these potential complications should be anticipated and talked over before a remarriage takes place. Even when this is done, the nuts and bolts of daily life will create new issues that must be worked through over many months.

At the outset, it is often best for each parent to handle disciplinary matters for his or her own children, while serving as backup and support for whatever the other parent decides to do. A stepparent's sudden application of a new set of rules can lead to serious conflict. Each parent can learn something from the other, and in doing so, strengthen his or her own child-rearing skills. A unified parental front in a blended family is every bit as important as in an intact family.

*When children from two different families are combined
through remarriage, be prepared for some turbulence.*
During the initial "getting to know you" process, sweetness and light may prevail. But some degree of conflict is inevitable. For example, a teenager who has to share his room with a new stepsibling may resent the sudden lack of privacy and will probably be very territorial about his possessions. Issues will arise over who uses the bathroom when, who picks up what, or who does which jobs around the home. Be sure that house rules, assignments of chores, administration of consequences, and granting of privileges are

carried out in ways that are scrupulously fair and open to respectful discussion. Children and adolescents alike become extremely indignant if they feel there is favoritism or injustice from either parent.

Be prepared to seek counseling when two families become one.
Given the number of potential conflicts within a blended family, you would be wise to see a counselor to expedite problem solving and troubleshooting. Depending on the damage incurred by the loss of the original family, whether through divorce or death, children and teenagers may need help adjusting to a new family. This should never be seen as strictly the child's or adolescent's problem but as an issue for the entire family. Family counseling can provide a safe forum in which every family member can share and be heard and, in turn, hear how the others feel.

You, as parents, will need outside support as well. A church family or local support group might provide this, but don't hesitate to see a counselor or pastor for more focused aid if you need it.

Reason to wait #1: STIs

Thirty years ago the typical high school health-education class discussed two sexually transmitted infections (STIs): syphilis and gonorrhea. They were described as potentially hazardous but nothing a little penicillin couldn't handle. But the sexual playground that opened during the late 1960s has resulted in an STI epidemic unprecedented in medical history, teeming with exotic, dangerous, and often incurable infections.

More than fifteen significant infections can be transmitted by exchange of body fluids or skin-to-skin contact during sexual activity. Some are fatal, a few are relatively harmless, and many have long-term physical and emotional consequences. A few can be successfully treated with antibiotics—but without creating any memory in the immune system. As a result, infections such as gonorrhea and chlamydia can be acquired over and over by the same individual. (For more information on this subject, see "STIs among Adolescents," beginning on page 182.)

Reason to wait #2: Sex is how babies get started

Each year 800,000 to 900,000 teenagers will become pregnant,[7] and of these one in three will end in abortion.[8] (Approximately 10 to 15 percent of teen pregnancies end in miscarriage.) The vast majority of the pregnancies are unplanned, and a sizable percentage begin even though a contraceptive is used. Three out of four teenage mothers are unmarried[9] (as opposed to 30 percent in 1970). Altogether, four out of every ten adolescent girls will become pregnant by the age of nineteen.

These statistics do not begin to communicate the profound effects of a pregnancy on a young woman's life. Whatever the circumstances of the sexual encounter that began it, a pregnancy cannot be ignored, and whatever is done about it will have a permanent impact on the young mother's life. Once she becomes pregnant, she will never be the same. Only two outcomes are possible: The baby will be born, or the baby will die before birth, whether through deliberate or spontaneous abortion (miscarriage).

Neither of these events is easy to deal with. There's no quick fix where human life is concerned, no way to "rewind the tape" and start over as though nothing happened.

If an unmarried teenager bears and brings up her child, her life (and probably the lives of other family members) will be affected for years to come. She must deal with the many challenges that all young mothers face, but nearly always with some additional difficulties. Her educational plans are likely to be postponed or significantly rearranged. Economic opportunities will probably be limited, and dependence upon welfare is common. (Seven out of ten adolescent mothers drop out of high school, and more than 80 percent of single mothers eighteen and younger eventually become dependent on welfare.[10]) Unless she has considerable help and support, a teenage mother will risk difficulties with parenting, difficulty in a future marriage relationship, and more unplanned pregnancies.

In some cases, one or both of the mother's parents choose to take on primary care of their grandchild. This situation can serve to forge new bonds in the extended family, allowing the baby to grow up loved and well cared for in his family of origin, while Mom manages part of his care and continues her schooling or vocation. But the added strain of such arrangements can take a significant toll on a family, and some families are simply too dysfunctional or lacking in material resources to provide adequate care for a new baby.

If a young mother gives up her child for adoption—an act of considerable courage—she will help bring about what is often a relatively positive combination of outcomes. Her baby will be reared by people who are usually better prepared to provide the time, attention, and resources. Then she can make a fresh start with her education and social life. But even this solution will not exempt her from pain. Her baby will never be forgotten, and a sense of loss, sometimes profound, will be felt for the rest of her life.

Women with unplanned pregnancies often feel a burning need to do something as quickly as possible. They may find the options of bringing up or giving up a baby highly uncomfortable, at least at first glance. For a teenager, a nine-month detour from normal activities may seem like an eternity. These and other factors (especially pressure from a boyfriend or parents) may lead to the wrong conclusion that abortion is the best alternative, one that offers a quick resolution, fewer personal complications, far less financial cost compared to having a baby, and usually confidentiality as well. (Many teenagers obtain abortions without parental involvement or consent.)

But abortion is not a completely risk-free procedure. Damage to the uterus that could jeopardize future pregnancies (or even require major surgical repair), infection, bleeding, future infertility, and even more serious events (including death) are possible complications. A number of research studies have raised concerns that having one or more abortions increases a woman's risk for breast cancer later in life. Furthermore, even if an abortion is carried out without any apparent hitch, a different type of pain may develop months or years later. Because they want so desperately for the crisis to go away, many women will undergo an abortion even though they are knowingly violating their own moral standards. Many come to realize later in life that a human being—a son or a daughter, not a shapeless wad of tissue—was destroyed through abortion. For these and other reasons, many women live with significant, long-term regrets after an abortion, especially if they have difficulty becoming pregnant later in life.

Reason to wait #3: The risk of infertility

An estimated 10 to 15 percent of couples (about 10 million people) have difficulty conceiving, and more than a million couples seek treatment for infertility each year in the United States. Statistics cannot begin to reflect the intense distress this problem creates in a couple's life. Dealing with infertility can be complicated, time-consuming, stressful, and expensive. Unfortunately, a significant number (but not all) of these infertility problems arise as a consequence of sexually transmitted infections and thus could have been avoided if both husband and wife had postponed sex until marriage.

Reason to wait #4: "Safe(r) sex" isn't

In spite of a relentless epidemic of sexually transmitted infections and unplanned pregnancies, far too few people are willing to accept the obvious: These problems and the heartaches accompanying them could be eliminated if adolescents (and single adults) would postpone sex, find and marry one partner, and remain mutually faithful for life. This idea is considered unrealistic by an influential cadre of individuals and institutions that, in response to the AIDS epidemic, began promulgating the notion of "safe sex." When it became clear that only mutually exclusive sex within marriage was truly safe, the concept was redubbed "safer sex."

Presentations that promote safer sex (including those geared to adolescents) usually advocate three precautions:

Myths of safer sex

Myth 1: *If I limit the number of partners with whom I have sex, I'll be safe.* It is true that having fewer partners means fewer chances for exposure to disease. But it only takes one contact to become pregnant or to be infected with a significant or lethal infection if that person has had other partners.

Myth 2: *If I know something about a potential partner's sexual history and I avoid having sex with someone who has had many partners, I'll be safe.* This sounds reasonable, but in fact taking a sexual history is tricky, even in a doctor's office. A prospective partner is often not willing to tell the truth if it means a pleasurable evening might be called off as a result. It is virtually impossible to discover the sexual history of the prospective partner's previous partners, or those partners' partners, and so on. *From an infectious-disease standpoint, one has sex not with just one person but with all of that individual's sexual contacts, and all of their contacts' contacts, and so on.* Furthermore, a significant number of people who are infected with STIs have no symptoms and do not know they are infected.

Myth 3: *If we use a condom every time, I'll be safe.* True, using a condom correctly (a multistep procedure) during each act of intercourse will reduce the risk of pregnancy and some STIs. But condoms are not a terribly effective form of birth control, with failure rates commonly estimated at 10 to 15 percent. This means that out of one hundred women who are sexually active, ten to fifteen will be pregnant within a year if condoms are the only form of contraception used. *Among adolescents, these failure rates are generally higher* for a variety of reasons. Not only are they more likely to forget or mismanage some of the fine points of proper condom use (including having one available in the first place) during the heat of the moment, but many teenagers, and older men as well, simply resist wearing them. Even if used correctly and consistently, condoms can break, leak, or fall off during intercourse.

These failure rates are even more alarming if one remembers that intercourse can lead to pregnancy only on a few days each month, while STIs can be transmitted *every day of every month*. Furthermore, infections such as syphilis, herpes, and human papilloma virus (HPV) are often spread through contact between skin surfaces that a condom cannot cover. (Condoms give almost no protection in preventing the transmission of HPV.)

Reason to wait #5: Devalued sex

Advocating that sex be kept within the boundaries of marriage is not based on notions that intercourse is "dirty" or "unholy" but on a true appreciation for sex as God's fine art. If the original Mona Lisa were entrusted to you for a month, you wouldn't leave it in your backyard, use it as a TV tray, or line a birdcage with it. Similarly, sex deserves more respect than our culture gives it.

- What truly devalues sex is the idea that intercourse is no more meaningful than a good meal or a drive in a fast car.
- What stifles sexual satisfaction is casual copulation with little or no emotional involvement.
- What people miss in nonmarital sex is the opportunity for enjoyment far greater than the immediate sensual experience.

While movies and television often portray casual sex as the epitome of sensual excitement, a healthy, long-term marital relationship is actually the best setting for satisfying sexual experiences. The security of commitment can free both husband and wife to relax rather than "perform," and their familiarity over a period of years allows them to please and excite one another with ever increasing expertise and finesse. In a growing and deepening marriage relationship, sexuality can encompass far more than the superficial, bumper-sticker mentality of merely "doing it." Sex becomes a comfort, a natural stimulant (or relaxant), a playground, a special means of communication, and a bridge that can connect individuals to one another after a difficult day or season. Short-term relationships provide few, if any, of these benefits, and those involved in casual sex cannot approach (or in some cases even comprehend) them.

Reason to wait #6: Distorted relationships

Adding sex to a nonmarital relationship, especially when adolescents are involved, is like throwing a one-thousand-pound weight into a rowboat. The center of gravity drastically shifts, forward motion becomes difficult, and the whole thing may eventually sink. Sex *never* enhances a teenage romance but almost always overwhelms and stifles it. Arguments, secrecy, stress, and guilt usually replace laughter, discovery, and meaningful conversation.

Indeed, sex has a way of wrecking good relationships and keeping bad ones going long after they should have ended. After a sexual relationship is broken off, there is likely to be a sense of loss (sometimes severe), regret, and awkwardness whenever the other person is encountered. Condoms can't prevent a broken heart, and antibiotics can't cure one.

When one or both partners have had prior sexual experience, what's to guarantee that tonight's coupling isn't just another notch on the belt? Trust has become so foreign to the sexual playground that the phrase "trust me" has become the caricature come-on, the phrase uttered by the predator who hopes the intended prey is too dumb to burst out laughing. Compare this with the experience of two people who have waited until marriage to initiate their sexual experience. For them the wedding night can be an ecstatic time of discovery and bonding, and whatever they might lack in technique can be learned pleasantly enough at their own pace. Additionally, prior sexual experiences create memories that may interfere with bonding and sexual intimacy in a future marital relationship.

Reason to wait #7: Damaged goods
An important warning for adolescent females: In the sexual revolution, women have been—and still are—the big losers:

- The woman virtually always pays a far bigger price than her partner when an unwanted pregnancy occurs.
- With the exception of syphilis and AIDS, sexually transmitted infections generally have more serious consequences in women.
- When women accept the "playboy" philosophy of "sex as recreation," they trade a number of sexual encounters for nothing. No ongoing relationship, no security, no commitments, no love, and—if they acquire a pelvic infection from a partner—possibly no children in the future.

Early sexual experiences never enhance self-esteem but usually leave a strong feeling of having been used, violated, and devalued. Instead of learning from experience and refusing to be burned again, the sexually experienced adolescent is likely to say, "What does it matter now? I might as well just go ahead the next time." Without specific counseling to counteract this damaged-goods mentality, resistance to continuing sexual activity may be seriously weakened—especially in adolescents who have had one or more pregnancies, whether ending in abortion or childbirth. This devaluation of both self and sexuality, while generally more common and profound in girls, certainly occurs in boys too.

Reason to wait #8: The moral high ground
Despite the rising tide of sexual anarchy in our society, a great many people still believe the words *right* and *wrong* apply to sexual behavior. Even someone with a casual exposure to traditional Judeo-Christian values should pick up an important message: The Designer of sex cares a lot about when it's done and with whom. Sex outside of marriage can be dangerous to one's physical, emotional, and spiritual health. Even for those who do not follow specific religious precepts, basic decency and concern for the well-being of others should curtail the vast majority of sexual adventures, which so often are loaded with selfish agendas.

Unfortunately, some adolescents who have had ongoing church experiences and explicit teaching about sexual morality may still become involved with premarital sex, which does nothing for spiritual growth. Intimacy with God on Sunday morning (or any other day) will be seriously impaired when there has been illicit physical intimacy.

What Can Parents Do to Reduce the Risk of Premarital Adolescent Sex?

Plenty. First, reread "Take on the tough topics: sex and substances" (pages 90-92). Then seriously consider the following measures (all of which are long-term projects):

Be aware of these specific risk factors for teen sex:
Alcohol and drug use. Aside from reflecting problem attitudes (rebellion, poor self-concept, invulnerability) that make sex more likely, intoxication also clouds judgment and weakens resistance to sexual overtures.

A steady boyfriend or girlfriend. Strong attachments and feelings of exclusivity invite nature to take its course, especially when physical expressions of affection begin early in the relationship. *This is a particular risk in a situation where the boy is more than two or three years older than the girl.* Ideally, a take-it-slow approach to relationships can be encouraged and set in motion through conversations both before and during the adolescent years. (This process is discussed at length later in this section.) If a teen romance appears to be getting hot and heavy and a lot of physical contact is already displayed, you will have a more delicate task. You will need to speak with both boy and girl diplomatically but candidly about the physical process they are setting in motion. If you're too easygoing about it, you will do little to discourage further progress down the road toward intimacy. On the other hand, if you come down too hard, you may drive the young lovers closer together, emotionally and physically. Forbidding further contact (which is much easier said than done) should be reserved for situations in which it is clear that the relationship is damaging, dangerous, or abusive.

Little parental monitoring. Adolescents aren't likely to remove clothing and get horizontal if parents are in the next room. Leaving them alone for hours at a time or not requiring accountability is a setup for sex.

A parental belief that adolescent sex is appropriate. If you think nonmarital sex is okay, your adolescent will too and will act on that belief.

A parental belief that adolescent sex is inevitable. Many parents who disapprove of teen sex have also concluded that it is as certain as death and taxes. Their approach to the subject will thus be double-edged: "Don't do it, but in case you do, use this condom." A few take their daughters to doctors or family-planning clinics to obtain birth control pills—*even if they have not become sexually active.* But in sexual matters, the venerable motto "Be prepared" communicates not merely precaution but expectation: "I know you're going to do it." Adolescents will get *that* message loud and clear and are likely to act accordingly.

Low grade point average/low attachment to school. While school performance is affected by a variety of factors, a basic desire to do well in school reflects (among other things) a more hopeful outlook on the future and a willingness to put off immediate gratification for long-term goals. Teen sex, on the contrary, is a here-and-now event, usually reflecting ignorance of or little regard for consequences. This doesn't mean, of course, that every scholar is a bulwark of morality or that all who are not academically oriented are destined to be promiscuous. What ultimately matters is a person's commitment to basic values such as responsibility, respect for self and others, and concern about the effect of today's decisions on the future.

A history of physical or sexual abuse. These acts against children and adolescents violate their bodies, minds, and hearts. Sexual abuse creates a grossly distorted view of sexual behavior, destroys boundaries, and drives a deep sense of worthlessness into the emotions. Whether the abuse occurred in the distant or recent past, adolescents with this history need ongoing support, counseling, and prayer to help them develop healthy attitudes about sex and about themselves.

Frequent family relocations. Moving generally stresses both parents and adolescents (especially if the kids resent the decision). This can erode parental authority and distract parents from involvement with their children. Bonds to social supports such as church groups that help prevent sexual activity are severed by multiple moves. Loneliness and loss of friendships may lead some teenagers to use sexual activity to gain social acceptance. These issues should be considered by parents who are thinking about a possible relocation.

Only one parent in the household. Parenting was meant to be a team effort, and some risks will naturally increase when one parent is left to do all the protecting and monitoring alone. Some studies do indicate that adolescents living with a single parent are more likely to become sexually active than those living with both parents. Work and household demands can prevent single parents from being as involved and attentive as they need and want to be. And the divorce and desertion that sometimes lead to a one-parent home can make teens uncertain about the value of marriage as the setting for sexual activity and about the role of sexuality in parental relationships.

This increased risk does not mean that adolescent sex is inevitable in single-parent families. But it does place an additional responsibility on single parents to send their teenagers clear and consistent messages about sexuality. And it is one more reason for single parents to enlist as much support as they can.

Understand these specific factors that lower the risk for teen sex.
- Religious commitment, which studies have shown consistently lowers the likelihood of adolescent sexual behavior.
- Educational accomplishment/commitment to school.
- Friends who have a similar commitment to abstinence.
- Presence of both parents in the home, especially the biological father. Positive involvement of a father with his teenage offspring has been shown to be an effective deterrent to early sexual activity.

- Parental and community values that support sexual abstinence until marriage and making them clearly known.
- A host of other interesting activities and passions. Adolescents who have other burning interests—such as earning academic honors; starting on a certain career path; traveling abroad; participating in ministry; or excelling in music, drama, sports, or other areas—will be less likely to allow premature sexual involvement to derail their plans and dreams. If they belong to a stimulating family that serves as a launching pad for fulfilling and fun activities, they will be less vulnerable to the boredom, purposelessness, and impaired self-concept that can sweep an adolescent toward unhealthy relationships.

Be a role model for the kinds of relationships you want your kids to develop with members of the opposite sex.
Parents should make every effort to keep their marriage intact and to nourish, enrich, and celebrate it, demonstrating respect and affection for each other on an ongoing basis. This gives adolescents a sense of security and a strong attachment to your values.

Fathers have a particularly important role to play. A boy who sees his father treat his mother with physical and verbal courtesies (which may range from fine points such as opening doors for her to broader strokes such as regularly seeking her opinions and advice and listening to and praising her) and is taught to do likewise will be more likely to carry this behavior and attitude into his own relationships with women. Girls who are consistently affirmed, cherished, and treated respectfully by their fathers aren't as likely to begin a desperate search for male affection that could lead to sexual involvement. Furthermore, they will expect appropriate behavior from the other men in their lives.

Single parents who are bringing up teenagers must repeatedly affirm them and create as stable a home life as possible. Values concerning nonmarital sex should be practiced as well as preached. A sexually active single parent or one who has a live-in partner is proclaiming in no uncertain terms that this activity is all right for teenagers as well.

Do your best to give your teen(s) a strong,
   positive sense of identity.

Teenagers who feel incomplete, inadequate, and unappreciated are more likely to seek comfort in a sexual relationship. But those with a life rich in relationships, family traditions, activities, interests, and—most of all—consistent love and affirmation are less likely to embark on a desperate search for fulfillment that could lead to unwise sexual decisions. Those who see their future as promising are more likely to protect themselves from physical or emotional damage arising from sexual activity. Those who have a healthy, productive faith in God are more likely to have deeply rooted reasons to respect and preserve the gift of sex and to respect rather than exploit others.

Create a special occasion to talk about abstaining
   from sex until marriage.

Early in your child's adolescence, plan a special evening (or a weekend away from home) during which the importance of preserving sex for marriage is the central focus. This time, shared by the teen and both parents, could culminate in the presentation of a special token—a necklace, ring, or key, for example—which symbolizes commitment to an abstinent lifestyle. It can be very meaningful if this item is carried or worn by your adolescent for years and then presented to his or her marriage partner on their wedding night.

If your adolescent has already had sexual experiences,
   make it clear that it is never too late to make a
   commitment to reserve sex for marriage.

This important concept is called "secondary virginity" and should be strongly encouraged among adolescents who have been sexually active. Some churches and parachurch organizations have formal programs organized specifically to promote the decision to remain sexually abstinent until marriage.

Continue sending healthy messages about sexuality throughout
   your son's or daughter's adolescent years.

The best time to build a solid foundation about sexuality is before puberty. But even if you've never discussed the subject directly, you still send all kinds of signals about your attitudes over the course of time.

- Your adolescent needs to know you are comfortable with the subject. If you seem embarrassed, flustered, ashamed, or unapproachable whenever the topic comes up, your teenager will look elsewhere for input.
- Don't hesitate to broach the subject yourself. Adolescents are reluctant to bring up sexual subjects with their parents, and your chances of having one or more conversations may be nil unless you take the initiative. Remember that the facts of sexuality are morally neutral. Anyone (even you) can teach them, but you have the opportunity to put the proper perspective on the subject.
- Be careful how you talk about someone else's sexual issues. News of a crisis pregnancy in another family can provide a powerful teachable moment, for good or ill. If you give a clear signal that the nonmarital sex was wrong but respond with compassion (and prayer) for the people involved, you make it clear that you can be approached if anyone at home has a problem. But if your response sounds something like "Don't you *ever* do something as stupid/shameful/evil as this," you could block potentially critical communication in the future. Crisis pregnancy centers routinely find that many of their most difficult clients are the daughters of good, moral, upright, churchgoing parents. "I can't tell Mom and Dad—it'll kill them (or they'll kill me)" is their common refrain as they head for the abortion clinic.

Talk about healthy and unhealthy relationships, and train your adolescent to avoid situations that increase the likelihood of a sexual incident.
Make them streetwise about the general course of relationships, dating, risky situations, and the ugly reality of date rape.

Encourage supervised, structured, nonpressuring group activities with the opposite sex as opposed to single dating situations, especially for adolescents in middle school and early high school. The object should be to learn how to talk and have fun without romantic expectations or sexual pressure. Group activities such as a church picnic or youth group outing are generally healthier than dances or other situations in which pairing up is necessary.

Talk to your adolescent about the qualities that ultimately matter in a relationship with a person of the opposite sex. Shared values (especially spiritual orientation), mutual respect, easy conversation, and enjoyment of everyday activities count far more heavily in the long run than good looks, money, popularity, or intense romantic attraction. Indeed, the best romances and marriages often come from relaxed friendships that progress gradually, with lots of conversations about everything under the sun. Accordingly, dating activities should be seen as experiences that are pleasant, enriching, and relaxing, not times of perpetual emotion.

Talk to your adolescent about unhealthy relationships, and have the courage to speak honestly if you see one developing:

- Relationships that ride a roller coaster of emotions—being madly in love one day, fighting like cats and dogs the next, crying and making up over and over—distract and drain a couple's time and energy and wear out everyone else for miles around. They also turn into difficult marriages.
- Relationships in which one person is intensely needy for the other, and thus clingy and smothering, are parasitic and draining. For example, a teenager who claims, "I'd kill myself if you ever left me" is putting unhealthy pressure on the other person.
- Relationships that have ongoing verbal disrespect in one or both directions are doomed.
- Relationships in which physical abuse occurs must be terminated immediately.

An important note: Unhealthy relationships carry a significant risk for sexual involvement.

Talk to your adolescent about physical demonstrations of affection. This is a natural desire when two people like each other, but how much (and how far) is okay? What about handling the desire—or some pressure—to push physical boundaries? You can lay down rules and regulations, but your adolescent needs a rationale for making good decisions without you. Here are some ideas that may help your teenager.

Set up your expectations and ground rules about dating
*   in advance—well before your teenager asks if he or she*
*   can go out with someone.*

Each family will have to set its own standards, but extremes are best avoided. Rigid parental control through high school and beyond (including selecting a limited number of "acceptable" candidates for courtship) stifles growth and independence and virtually guarantees rebellion. But a lax, anything-goes approach without parental guidelines is like handing the car keys to someone who has had no driver's training.

Think seriously about adopting a stepwise approach, especially for your adolescent's first socializing experiences with the opposite sex. Many parents have a policy that if someone wants to spend time with their son or daughter under age eighteen, the first step will be an evening at home with the family or joining in a family activity such as dinner and a movie or a ball game. This gives everyone a chance to get acquainted and broadcasts an important message: "The one you want to spend time with is deeply cherished by a family to whom you are accountable. We are happy to welcome you aboard, but nothing less than respectful and honorable behavior will do." Your expectation should be to make friends with the person, not to carry out a third-degree interrogation. In fact, you may develop a friendship that lasts long after your son or daughter has become interested in someone else. If anyone refuses or is extremely reluctant to spend time with the family in this way, however, consider it a red flag—and put further socializing with this person on hold.

If the first step goes well, group dating can be a good way to continue this process, assuming the other people involved are trustworthy. Many parents give the green light to single dating at age sixteen if there is ongoing evidence of maturity and responsibility and if the relationship appears basically healthy. Whenever this activity begins, you have the right and responsibility to know specifics every time about the intended companion(s), the activity and its location, who's providing transportation, etc. Have a clear agreement about the expected time to arrive home. Whatever time you set, talk about the importance of letting you know if they're going to be home later than planned. *Consistency and reliability about keeping you posted should be a bigger issue than abiding by an absolute time limit.*

While they may complain outwardly about some of these ground rules, most adolescents will feel more secure when you are appropriately involved in the socializing/dating process. This should extend beyond setting limits to offering some encouragement as well, such as quietly offering a little extra cash to help enhance a special occasion. Even more important is making it abundantly clear that your teenager can call you anytime, day or night, from anywhere, if any help is needed—including a ride home from a date that has gone sour.

How Much Touch Is Okay?: Guidelines for Teenagers on Dates and Other Occasions

Establish clear and unequivocal respect for your body, your life, and your future. Decide *before* the conversation, *before* the date, *before* the relationship gets more serious that physical intimacy is reserved for the wedding night.

Respecting yourself (and the person you're with) means setting your own limits for physical contact. Stick to them, and be ready to defend them if necessary. Sexual pressure can become a major problem if you are unclear about your boundaries, if you are afraid of rejection, or if you are worried about being called a prude because you won't go past a certain point.

Physical contact—even something as simple as holding hands—may be interpreted in ways you don't intend. What to you means "I like you" or "I think you're okay" might be received as "I'm madly in love with you" or "I want to go further." It's better to express how you feel in *words,* rather than through unclear and potentially powerful physical messages.

Remember that the events that lead to sex are progressive. Think of a car gaining momentum as it coasts down a steep hill. Once a given level of intimacy has been reached, it is very difficult to back up to a more conservative one. Also it is more difficult to defend a boundary in the heat of the moment.

Talk candidly to your daughter(s) about the unpleasant topic of date rape and how best to avoid it.

The odds are at least one in ten (some researchers say one in four) that a woman will be coerced into unwanted sex at some point in her life. In four out of five cases, the rapist is someone the woman knows—a fellow student, a business acquaintance, a neighbor, or (all too often) a date.

For your part, aside from issuing specific recommendations and warnings (see sidebar, pages 180-181), set some policies that will reduce the risk of a sexual catastrophe. First, veto any dating relationship between your adolescent daughter and someone who is more than two or three years older. The majority of teenage pregnancies involve relationships with men in their twenties or older. Object vigorously to her dating anyone who might have a position of authority or leverage over some part of her life, such as an employer, teacher, family friend, or business associate of yours. These situations are a setup for potential date rape.

continued

You are much better off setting very conservative limits for expressing affection (holding hands and perhaps a brief embrace or kiss) and progressing slowly, both emotionally and physically, in a relationship. This isn't old-fashioned but smart and realistic. More intense kissing, lying down together, touching personal areas, and increasing the amount of skin-to-skin contact sets off increasingly intense responses that are designed to lead to sexual intercourse—even when neither person intended this conclusion.

If you're not sure whether what you're doing physically is appropriate, ask yourself if you would be comfortable doing it in front of either set of parents or your pastor. Remember that the person you are with now will probably not be the person you will marry. Would you feel comfortable doing what you're doing in front of that person's future husband or wife?

If resisting physical intimacy is becoming more difficult, don't tempt fate. Stay away from situations where the two of you are alone together. Deliberately plan to be around other people or in places where nothing can happen. (It's difficult to have sex at a coffee shop.) Don't lie down on the sofa together to watch a video, and don't watch movies or videos with overt sexual content. Don't banter sexually provocative comments back and forth on the assumption that talk is safer than sex. Remember that your most important sexual organ is your mind, and where it goes your body will follow. (In some school sex-education programs, erotic conversations are actually recommended as an alternative to intercourse. Perhaps this idea works—on another planet.)

Here are some additional cautions to pass along:

Talk explicitly to your son(s) about respect for members of the opposite sex and about sexual responsibility.

Your mission is to embed some very important values deeply into his mind and heart, not only for the teen years but for the rest of his life:

- *Never become a sexual predator.* A male who specifically sets out to maneuver women into sexual encounters might be called a playboy, red-hot lover, or Don Juan, but he's basically a jerk. If and when you see this behavior depicted in a movie or TV program or displayed by someone you know, let your son know that this is no way to treat any woman.

- *Never push a woman's physical boundaries.* If she says no to anything, even holding hands, that statement is final and not to be questioned.

- *Respect a woman's body, integrity, and future, even if she is inviting intimacy.* Without question one of the most difficult challenges for a healthy teenage male is to hold his ground when a desirable female flashes a bright and explicit green light. *Talk through this situation, including what he might say and how to walk away from this situation immediately.* It is important that he not be flustered or embarrassed and that he be able to decline the invitation in a way that expresses a desire to protect each person's health and future.

- *Approach any activity or relationship with the opposite sex with the intention of enhancing the other person's life and not leaving a wake of regrets.* Thinking in terms of protecting the other person's long-term well-being rather than merely satisfying immediate needs or desires is a sign of maturity. Some thoughtful conversations between parents and sons can help establish these grown-up attitudes.

PART TWO: SEXUAL CRISIS SITUATIONS

What if—despite your best intentions, careful conversations, and earnest efforts—your adolescent slips, slides, plunges headlong, or is coerced into sexual experiences long before his or her wedding night? How will you respond?

As unpleasant as it might seem, it is important to think about the possibilities ahead of time. Parents would be wise to spend some time alone together (or single parents with a trusted and mature friend) talking through these difficult and emotional "What if . . . ?" questions.

What If You Discover Your Adolescent Is Sexually Active?

Many contemporary resources for parents of teenagers make the wrong assumption that premarital sex is inevitable and recommend that parents help their kids make "mature" sexual decisions—by which they mean wearing condoms and taking other contraceptive precautions. Some parents respond by bringing their teenage (or even preteen) daughters to a doctor or a family-planning clinic for various birth control measures and insisting that no one goes out for the evening without a supply of condoms.

These actions may seem responsible and open-minded to some parents, but giving tacit approval to teenage sex is foolhardy for many reasons: the risks of STIs, distorted relationships, damaged identities, and disrupted marital bonding later in life, not to mention the moral issues involved.

For a reality check, consider whether a responsible parent would carry out this sort of damage control in response to other risky adolescent behaviors:

- If your twelve-year-old starts smoking, would you teach him to buy low-nicotine brands?
- If your fourteen-year-old wants to move out of your home and get an apartment with a bunch of adolescent friends, would you pay the rent?
- If your sixteen-year-old begins downing six-packs every weekend, would you include a few intoxicated practice sessions as part of her driver's training?
- If your eighteen-year-old decides to try IV drugs, would you

supply sterile syringes and make sure he understands sterile injection techniques?

Each response would theoretically reduce risks but would also enable and promote misguided decisions.

If facilitating adolescent sex is a bad idea, so is ignoring it. Equally unproductive is blowing up, finger wagging, lecturing, or name-calling. This is a significant family problem deserving a loving and thoughtful response. The goal is to contain the damage and coach your adolescent toward more healthy and rational decisions. Therefore:

Think before you react. It is normal to feel upset and disappointed, and you will probably need a couple of days to settle down. Setting a time to talk about what has happened may be more appropriate than risking a more volatile, spur-of-the-moment confrontation. Ultimately, emotions should fuel appropriate action rather than ongoing angry outbursts.

Ask open-ended questions ("Can you tell me about your relationship with ____ ?") rather than judgmental ones ("How could you have done this?" or "What in the world were you thinking?"). *Listen* to the whole story (or as much as you are given) before offering your viewpoint. Eye rolling, crossed arms, finger drumming, and editorial comments will shut off communication in a hurry.

Put the emphasis on the big picture. You want your son or daughter to have a long life, good health, meaningful relationships, and freedom from unnecessary turmoil. Premarital sexual activity jeopardizes all of those goals. Be prepared to explain why. If you aren't convinced, review the reasons to postpone sexual involvement outlined earlier in this chapter. Based on your broader range of experience and knowledge, you must tackle one of the most important jobs of parenting—opening young eyes to life's many consequences.

Don't tear down the teenager's sense of worth with comments such as "I am so ashamed of you" or "How could you act like such a jerk/ tramp/lowlife?" This kind of rejection and judgment is what drives a lot of adolescents to sexual activity. A strong sense of identity and a conviction that one's future is worth protecting are deterrents to reckless or immoral behavior.

Stress the importance of new beginnings. Many teens who have been sexually active are willing to commit to secondary virginity, postponing any further sexual relationships until marriage. Actively encourage such a decision. Otherwise the feeling that "it doesn't matter anymore" may lead to more bad decisions.

Get medical input. A doctor's evaluation should be on the agenda to check for STIs (and for girls, to obtain a Pap test or perhaps a pregnancy test). *Choose your provider carefully.* It won't help your adolescent choose abstinence if he or she has a doctor who feels that teens can't control their sexual urges and who therefore emphasizes methods of contraception.

Strongly consider getting your son or daughter (and yourself) into counseling. A counselor whom you trust may be able to talk more candidly to your son or daughter about sexuality while promoting the decision to remain abstinent. Sexual activity may be a symptom of more basic problems that need ongoing work. Be prepared to put in time with the counselor yourself to deal with the causes and effects of this problem within your family.

Be prepared to take action appropriate for the situation and the age of your adolescent. Sexual activity in the elementary or middle-school grades deserves a highly concerted effort from parents, physicians, counselors, and others (a trusted youth-group leader at church, for example) to deal with the behavior and with underlying issues. A sexually active twelve- or thirteen-year-old has experienced a serious breach of physical and emotional boundaries, and considerable work will be needed to repair the damage.

You may need to have one or more candid conversations with your adolescent's partner(s) and, possibly, with the parents of the other individual(s) as well. More often than not, this will lead to one or more relationships being terminated and implementation of much tighter supervision and accountability. Parental schedules may need to be rearranged. If the situation involves an adult having sexual contact with a young adolescent, legal action may be necessary. (At the very least, the adult's sexual activity with a minor must be reported as required by law. Any indications of coercion and abuse must also be reported.)

Sexual activity in high school is no less significant, but the response (including medical and counseling input) should represent more of a parent-directed collaboration between the adolescent and the teachers, counselors, and physicians involved in his or her life. This does not mean abandoning efforts to curtail sexual contact but using strategies that stress a mature assessment of consequences. Dating and other socializing patterns that may have increased the chances for intimacy should be reassessed and restructured.

After the age of eighteen, you are essentially dealing with a young adult. This will necessarily modify your approach because your position of authority has changed somewhat, especially if your son or daughter is beyond adolescence. However, you can and should offer your input and concerns, and you have the right to stipulate what behavior is appropriate under your roof. If you are still paying the bills for an older adolescent/young adult, you have the right to decide whether such support will continue if it is helping to finance a lifestyle that runs counter to your basic values.

What If Your Adolescent Daughter Becomes Pregnant?

Before considering how you might respond to the news that your unmarried teenager is pregnant, take a brief tour of the emotions and thought processes that are likely to be swirling through her mind and heart.

Your daughter's experience

Fear is an overriding emotion in nearly every teen pregnancy. "I can't tell my parents. They'll kill me!" "How can I finish school when I'm pregnant?" "My boyfriend will take off if I don't have an abortion." The adolescent with a crisis pregnancy probably sees nothing but loss on the horizon—loss of love, time, education, and physical health. Fear of one or more of these losses propels most of her other responses.

Denial is common, especially during the early weeks of pregnancy when the only indication might be one or more missed periods, a little fatigue, possibly some nausea, or even a positive pregnancy test. The longing for things to be "the way they were" may delay acknowledging the problem and seeking appropriate help for weeks or even months.

Ambivalence about being pregnant may cause fluctuating emotions. One day the only solution may appear to be an abortion, while the next the prospect of a cuddly baby may seem appealing. Time spent with a friend's crying newborn may jolt the emotions in yet another direction. Indecision and apparent lack of direction in such an overwhelming situation are common.

Guilt. When a pregnancy results from the violation of moral values held since childhood, an adolescent will usually feel ashamed and worthless. Her growing abdomen becomes a constant reminder of her failure.

Pressure to have an abortion. This may come from several directions. A teenager may be weighing what appears to be a dismal future of hardship and remorse against a quick and relatively inexpensive procedure. "No one needs to know, and I can get on with my life." A boyfriend (who may be dealing with his own fear and guilt, along with concerns about future financial responsibilities) may exert considerable pressure to abort, even offering to pay the bill. He may also threaten to bail out of the relationship if the pregnancy continues. Some parents, worried about their daughter's future or perhaps their own reputation in the community (or even the prospect of being responsible for the actual child rearing), may also find abortion attractive.

The "cuddly doll" mentality. Some unmarried teenage girls see their pregnancy unrealistically as an escape from a difficult and unpleasant home situation. They may envision a baby as a snuggly companion who will require roughly the same amount of care as a new puppy, not realizing the amount of energy a newborn will take without giving much in return (especially during the first few weeks). Teens with this mind-set need to adjust their expectations of child rearing—not to drive them to abort but to help them make more appropriate plans. If adoption is not chosen as a solution, some careful groundwork should be laid to prevent serious disappointment and even the mother's abuse of the baby.

Your experience as parent(s)

If a pregnancy is an upheaval for a teenager, it is also no picnic for her parents. Discovering that your adolescent daughter is pregnant is a trial like few others, and reactions—fear for her future, denial, guilt—may parallel hers with equal intensity. Parents are likely to feel anger in a number of directions—anger toward their daughter for being careless, not taking their advice, not using good judgment, and disobeying both them and God. They may be angry with the boy (or man) involved, who has violated their trust and their daughter's well-being. They may be angry with themselves for a number of reasons: They were too narrow or too permissive, too busy or too tired to tune into their daughter's world for the past several months—and now look what has happened.

Anger is such a classic parental response that the daughter may try to keep her pregnancy a secret. In fact, many states allow minors to obtain abortions without parental consent or knowledge, based on the presumption that the mother and/or father will be so disruptive and unreasonable that the teenage daughter can better deal with her pregnancy without them.

Your most difficult (and character-building) task is to show how much you really love your daughter, even though you don't approve of what she has done. The classical Chinese symbol for the word *crisis* has special meaning in this situation. It consists of two symbols: one representing *danger,* the other, *opportunity.* The danger is that your response to the pregnancy may open wounds in your family that will take years to heal, if they ever do. Your opportunity is rising to the occasion in such a way as to earn your daughter's lifelong respect and gratitude.

Your mission is to remain calm when panic is in the air and to be more concerned about her embarrassment than your own, which may be enormous. It is to be comforting when you feel like saying, "I told you so!" It is to help organize everyone's conflicting impulses into a thoughtful plan in which the family can work as a team. It is to guide the baby's father into responsible participation if he is willing, when you would just as soon enlist him in the Marines. Most of all, it is to channel your intense feelings into productive outlets—through planning, prayer, vigorous exercise, and blowing off steam to a tolerant friend rather than at your child.

Your daughter will need help, and lots of it, but not a total rescue. She must make a fast transition to adulthood, a state about which you know a great deal more than she does. You must resist the temptation to throw her out or keep her stuck in childish irresponsibility by making all of her decisions. She needs to face all the tough decisions and demands of pregnancy but with you at her side as a confident ally.

You may have one very critical decision of your own to make. What role do you intend to take in the child's upbringing? If the mother-to-be is very young, you may see another parenting job on the horizon and perhaps resent the idea. Or you may be excited about having the nest occupied for several more years. Your feelings on this issue need to be sorted out, and your course of action planned accordingly.

In the midst of your family's deliberations, be sure ample consideration is given to adoption. A pregnant teenager may be torn by the thought that "if I had the baby, I couldn't handle giving her away." But adoption can provide a livable solution for all parties involved. The baby is raised by a couple who intensely desire to be parents, and the birth mother can pick up and move on to complete her education and career goals, postponing her own parenting until she is ready.

You will also need to address the question of abortion. Many voices will be calling your daughter to the abortion clinic, claiming this simple procedure will bring the crisis to a swift and straightforward resolution. Some parents may be tempted to give this option serious consideration for similar reasons. But before lending encouragement to ending the pregnancy this way, remember that abortion is not a procedure like an appendectomy that eradicates a piece of diseased tissue. It ends a human life that is designed to develop in a continuous process from conception through birth and beyond. Because this life is unseen for now, its identity and significance may pale in comparison to the problems and concerns of the moment. That developing person, whose life is in the hands of her mother and those influencing her, cannot speak for herself. Like it or not, even under the most trying circumstances, that new person is not better off dead.

Your daughter should consider making an appointment with a local crisis pregnancy center (CPC) in order to sort through the issues, gather information, and consider her options in a compassionate setting. Even if she has strong opinions about what her course of action should be, a CPC can be an extremely valuable resource. Services available at most CPCs include a realistic assessment of the long-range impact of each option, ongoing counseling support, assistance with medical and other referrals, and maternity clothes and baby supplies. Many CPCs also provide some on-site medical services such as prenatal screening exams. All of these services are normally provided at no charge. (In recent years a number of CPCs have adopted names such as "Women's Resource Center" or "Pregnancy Help Center." For the name and location of a CPC in your area, check the yellow pages under "Abortion Alternatives," or contact 1-800-A FAMILY.)

It is important that capable and compassionate medical care be maintained throughout the pregnancy. Many pregnant teens delay or avoid seeking appropriate care for a variety of reasons. *But adolescents have higher rates of complications related to pregnancy and childbirth compared with older women.* Most of these problems can be significantly reduced (or at least anticipated) with consistent prenatal visits and appropriate medical follow-up.

What If Your Adolescent Son Is Involved in a Pregnancy?

If your son has had a sexual relationship from which a pregnancy has resulted, remember that he will probably be experiencing many of the same emotions as his girlfriend, including fear, guilt, and ambivalence. In addition, he will feel considerable conflict and confusion over the role he should play.

Usually the relationship with the mother-to-be has not, until this point, involved any long-range plans. Now he must make a decision about the level of commitment he intends to assume, and the issues are significant. What does he owe this young woman? Can he walk away from this situation? Should he make a lifelong commitment to her because of this unplanned pregnancy?

He does not bear the biological consequences, of course, and the mother of the baby has the legal right to have an abortion or carry the pregnancy to term with or without his input. This may leave him with the impression that he has no control over the un-planned pregnancy and therefore no responsibility for it. As his parents, you are one step further removed from the situation and may have similar questions about the role you should play.

Above all, your son will need encouragement and guidance to assume the appropriate level of responsibility for his role in the pregnancy. He should not be allowed to abandon his girlfriend with a cavalier, hit-and-run attitude. "It's her problem now" or "She should have protected herself" or even "She should just get an abortion" are shallow and disrespectful responses to a serious situation. Pushing for a quick marriage may seem honorable but is probably unwise. Teenage matrimony carries with it very short odds of long-term success, and the combination of immatu-rity, lack of resources, and the intense demands of a newborn baby will usually strain an adolescent relationship to the breaking point.

In a best-case scenario, the families of both participants will co-operate to find a productive balance among several tasks: facing the consequences of the sexual relationship, accountability of ado-lescents to the adults in both families, short- and long-term plan-ning, and mature decision making.

Your son will need encouragement to acknowledge his responsi-bility to the girl's family and to accept with humility their response, whether it is measured or angry. All of you may have to face the pos-sibility that the other family will choose to deal with the pregnancy on their own, even if you are willing to participate in the process. And if that decision includes forbidding your son to have further contact with someone about whom he cares very deeply, he will have to find the strength to abide by the other family's wishes. If he is allowed to continue their relationship and support her when the going gets tough, clear ground rules (including abstaining from sexual contact) will need to be established and respected.

Having a pregnant girlfriend is tough and painful. But it also can be an opportunity for your son to mature, to find out what he is made of. In the long run, the pregnant adolescent girl isn't the only one who has to make important choices.

What If Your Adolescent Isn't Sure of His or Her Sexual Orientation?

Few parenting concerns during adolescence generate as much emotional turbulence as the possibility that one's child might have a homosexual orientation. For many parents, especially those deeply committed to traditional values, the thought of a child becoming involved in homosexual relationships raises unsettling moral questions. For some, reactions to homosexuality extend into the darker emotions of hatred and loathing.

In contrast, many influential voices in media, government, and health care state that sexual orientation is inborn and unchangeable; however, that has never been proven. In their view, if your child is destined to be attracted to members of the same sex, nothing can or should be done about it other than to accept it. Gay and lesbian activists proclaim that adolescents who feel same-sex inclinations should explore, embrace, and celebrate their homosexual identity and that their parents should celebrate it along with them.

The vast majority of parents, while neither hating homosexual individuals nor applauding homosexuality, deeply desire to see their adolescents eventually bear and rear children. They anticipate the joys of watching the next generation's courtships, marriages, and family life. Therefore, contemplating a child's involvement in homosexual acts and in unconventional relationships for decades into the future is enough to provoke considerable concern, if not ongoing insomnia.

What should you do if your adolescent's sexual orientation is uncertain or if he or she has had one or more homosexual experiences?

Don't assume that characteristics that fall outside your gender expectations indicate homosexual tendencies. A boy who has a slight build and prefers painting over pitching or fabrics over football may disappoint a father who envisioned bringing up a burly, athletic hero. A daughter who isn't shapely or petite and who excels at basketball rather than ballet may not fulfill a mother's expectations of magazine-cover femininity. But both need unconditional affirmation of their worth from parents who accept and encourage their particular strengths as appropriate.

What may drive a teenager toward same-gender sexuality is *ongoing rejection* from parents or peers. Cutting remarks about a child's or teenager's size, shape, or other attributes merely reinforce the idea that "I'm different from everyone else." If genuine acceptance is eventually offered by someone with a homosexual orientation, the teenager may conclude that "I'm different, so that must mean I'm gay—and furthermore, I've always been this way."

Remember that adolescents may feel transient confusion about sexual identity, especially if they have had a sexual experience with someone of the same gender. Whether as a phase of rebellion and experimentation or as the result of sexual abuse in childhood, your child may have one or more same-sex encounters, which may raise questions in an adolescent about his or her ultimate sexual destination. It is therefore important for children and teens who have had such experiences to receive appropriate counseling that (among other things) will clarify the fact that these events have not destined them to a lifelong homosexual orientation.

If you discover that your child has had one or more homosexual encounters, whether coerced or voluntary, you need to remain his strongest ally. A child or young adolescent who has suffered sexual abuse needs to know that what happened was not his fault and that you are not in any way ashamed of him. He will need comfort, reassurance that his physical boundaries are now secure, and time to sort out his experiences, both with you (which will be very uncomfortable) and with a professional counselor. It is crucial that the damage done by the abuser to a child's sexual identity and sense of self-worth be contained.

If the activities involved one or more peers and were not the result of coercion, your response should parallel what was outlined in connection with premarital heterosexual activity. You will need to make a particular effort to maintain a balance between taking a clear stand for moral principles and demonstrating that you and your adolescent are still on the same team. Harsh expressions of revulsion and condemnation are counterproductive, will probably confirm an adolescent's feelings of alienation, and may very well provoke more of the same behavior. At the same time, a resigned and passive nonresponse ("Nothing can be done about this, so I might as well get used to it") squanders an opportunity to bring about change. As with other early and midadolescent sexual activity, conversation and counseling with someone who shares your values is in order.

If your late adolescent moves into adulthood and becomes overtly involved in a homosexual lifestyle, your balancing act will become even more delicate—but no different from the approach you must take to any other of your grown child's choices that you find ill advised or contrary to your values. It is possible and necessary—but at times also very difficult—to express love and acceptance without condoning the behavior. You have the right and responsibility to insist that sexual activity be off-limits under your roof. But decisions about a number of other situations will be tough. For example, should your adult offspring's homosexual lover be included at the family Thanksgiving dinner?

You must commit to patience, prayer, and perseverance. You may shed rivers of tears, but you must not allow animosity or bitterness to take root in your emotions. Most of all, you will need generous amounts of wisdom, because you may be the only voice expressing love while encouraging your child to begin the difficult process of disengaging from ongoing homosexual behavior.

What If Your Daughter Is the Victim of a Sexual Assault?

In the sidebar on pages 180-181, several recommendations are made that could reduce an adolescent's risk of date rape. But even when appropriate precautions have been taken, it is possible that your daughter will be the victim of a sexual assault. The odds are at least one in ten (some researchers say one in four) that she will be coerced into unwanted sex at some point in her life. As unpleasant as it may be to discuss this topic, she should know what (and what not) to do if this occurs, whether the attacker is an acquaintance or a stranger.

First, she should get to a safe place as quickly as possible and then contact a family member and the police *immediately*. In the emotional aftermath of an assault, the urge to deny what has happened may cause a victim to wait days or weeks to report it. But doing so reduces her credibility and makes prosecution of the attacker more difficult. Reporting the assault right away can help her regain a sense of control, obtain proper medical care, and guarantee personal safety. Furthermore, it is important that all physical evidence of the attack be preserved. She should not shower, bathe, douche, or even change clothes, even though it is normal to feel an overwhelming urge to rid herself of every trace of the attack.

Because of embarrassment, fear of reprisal, or apprehension over dealing with police, doctors, and attorneys, only 5 to 10 percent of rapes are reported. The attacker has assumed that he could have his way without any consequences, and he must not be allowed that unjust satisfaction. He has committed a serious crime and deserves punishment for it. Furthermore, most rapists are repeat offenders, and taking action may help prevent someone else from being assaulted.

The officers who take the report will need to ask about specific details of the rape that may be painful to answer but are necessary for proper documentation of the crime. It is important that your daughter be completely honest and candid about what happened, even if she feels that she made a mistake or even violated her own moral standards prior to the rape. If her story changes later on, the case against the attacker will be weakened.

The police will advise that a medical evaluation be carried out, even if your daughter does not believe she was injured. A thorough examination is necessary to assess her physical condition, to collect important evidence, and to provide counseling regarding the possibility of pregnancy or sexually transmitted infection. This should be done in a hospital emergency room where the physicians and staff are equipped to deal with rape victims or in a rape treatment center (assuming that its services include appropriate medical evaluations).

As with the police report, parts of this examination will be difficult and uncomfortable, especially if she has not had a pelvic exam before. But cooperation with the physician and nurses is important, and the temporary discomfort will be worth the long-term benefits of proper medical care.

Protecting Yourself from Date Rape

- You are much better off dating someone you know fairly well rather than someone who is a casual or chance acquaintance.
- In general, multicouple or group activities are less risky (and more fun) than single dates.
- Single dates—especially the first time with someone—should take place in public places. An invitation to a play or a sporting event is far preferable to "Come to my place to watch a video." Be especially leery of the suggestion that it would be nice "to go someplace private to talk." Enjoyable and meaningful conversation can happen anyplace where two people can hear each other's voices.
- Consider accepting a blind date only if the person carries a strong endorsement from someone you trust. Even then, this should not be a single date.
- Bring your own money. Paying your own way in the early stages of a relationship can help establish your independence. Even if your date picks up the tab, you might need cash for transportation home if things get out of hand.
- Stay sober. Alcohol and drugs cloud judgment and put you off guard and off balance.
- Pay attention to your beverage. A sexual predator may attempt to spike a woman's drink—even a glass of ice water—with a drug (such as Rohypnol) which can temporarily incapacitate her, facilitating a sexual assault and preventing her from remembering the experience. You are safest with a beverage from a can or bottle that you yourself open and dispense.
- Never leave a restaurant, party, or other get-together with someone you just met.
- Trust your instincts. If you don't feel right about the way the date is progressing, bail out. A little awkwardness is far better than a sexual assault. Call home at any time, and a parent will come get you, no questions asked.

Finally, your daughter should receive counseling from an individual who is qualified to deal with the impact of the rape experience on her life. This event cannot be ignored and will not be forgotten. She will need both time and support to recover from the physical, emotional, and spiritual aftereffects of a sexual assault. Many powerful emotions must be sorted out, including guilt or mistaken feelings of blame.

It is important that your own anger and frustration not boil over and cause more damage. This is not the time for comments such as "I told you so" or "How could you have let this happen?" Even if your daughter used extremely poor judgment or flatly disobeyed your explicit instructions, she in no way "asked for" or deserved a sexual assault. She will need your help to rebuild her sense of dignity

continued

- Avoid situations in which you do not feel on equal footing with your companion. If you feel unequal, intimidated, awestruck, or indebted to your date in some way, your willingness to assert yourself may be weakened or delayed. Unhealthy situations include relationships with men more than two or three years older than you, an employer, a teacher, or someone to whom you or your family owes a debt.
- Beware of expensive gifts and lavish dates. Too many guys still carry the Neanderthal notion that picking up the tab for a nice evening entitles them to a sexual thank-you. If your date presents that message, don't hesitate to straighten him out. Declining a present that appears to have strings attached is a healthy way to set boundaries.
- Look out for the control freak, someone who insists on his way and ignores your likes and dislikes. If he shows contempt for your tastes in restaurants, movies, and music, he may also have little regard for your physical boundaries.
- Beware of the person who tries to isolate you from your other friends and your family or who constantly bad-mouths them. If he is extremely possessive and wants you all to himself, chances are he will eventually want all of you sexually as well.
- Steer clear of guys who tell raunchy jokes, listen to sexually explicit music, enjoy pornography, or make degrading comments about women. These men have an attitude disease about women and sexuality, and they don't belong in your life.
- Don't waste your time with anyone who won't accept your limits; who begs, pleads, and haggles for physical contact; or who trots out worn and pathetic lines such as "If you loved me, you'd do it" or "Trust me." Anyone who pressures you for sexual favors is a loser and an abuser and most certainly doesn't love you.

and worth. Without this important repair work, she will be vulnerable to sexual pressure and abuse in the future.

What If Your Son Is the Victim of a Sexual Assault?

The vast majority of information and advisories regarding rape are directed toward women, who are most commonly—but not always—the victims of sexual assault. In a less frequent (but no less serious) situation, an adolescent or young adult male may be the sexual target of one or more other men. Should this happen to your son, you will need to muster all the same strength and support you would offer a daughter who had been attacked.

In particular, it is critical that appropriate medical assessment, evidence collection, preventive measures for sexually transmitted infections, and counseling be provided in a timely fashion, just as in the case of a female victim. If possible, the perpetrator(s) should be identified, arrested, and prosecuted. Even if a parent learns about an assault months or years after it took place, medical care and counseling should be provided. It is particularly important that such an event not be allowed to confuse an adolescent's sense of sexual identity or integrity.

PART THREE: STIs AMONG ADOLESCENTS

In the United States, over 15 million people are newly infected with STIs each year, and more than two-thirds of these are younger than age twenty-five.[11] Although teens comprise less than 10 percent of the total population, one in four STIs occur among them—approximately three million cases per year.[12]

In 1997, the Centers for Disease Control (CDC) reported that five of the ten most common reportable infectious diseases in the United States were STIs: chlamydia, gonorrhea, AIDS, syphilis and hepatitis B. These five accounted for 87 percent of *all* reportable infections.[13] One in five Americans between fifteen and fifty-five is infected with one or more sexually transmitted viruses.[14] Many of these people are unable to rid themselves of the virus(es) they have acquired, and some are plagued with recurrent, prolonged, or even lethal manifestations of their infection.

Pelvic inflammatory disease (PID), in which one or more sexually transmitted organisms invade the uterus, fallopian tubes, ovaries, pelvis, or all of these, is experienced by more than one million women in the United States each year. More than 75 percent of the infections occur in women younger than twenty-five, and at least one in five cases involves an adolescent—and the rate at which teenagers are affected continues to rise. More than one hundred thousand women require hospitalization for PID each year in the U.S. at an estimated cost of $7 billion.

At least 12 to 14 percent of women become infertile after an episode of PID, usually because of scarring of the fallopian tubes. Repeated infections increase this risk dramatically.

Adolescent girls are particularly susceptible to STIs. *A fifteen-year-old is ten times more likely to develop PID than a twenty-four-year-old involved in the same type of sexual behavior.*[15] This vulnerability is the result of two physiologic realities. First, the cervix (opening of the uterus) in a teenager is covered by a lining of cells called **ectropion** that is more fragile, produces more mucus, and is more easily invaded by organisms that cause STIs than is the lining in an older woman. After a woman has had a baby or reaches her twenties, the ectropion is replaced by a tougher lining that is more resistant to infection. Second, during the first several months after the onset of menses, many menstrual cycles occur without ovulation. This causes the mucus in the cervix to be thinner and thus a friendlier environment for STI organisms.

When STIs are discussed in health-education classes and public-service messages geared to teenagers, the emphasis is on preventing the transmission of HIV/AIDS. As serious as this epidemic is, a number of other significant predators should not be ignored.

Syphilis is caused by a spiral-shaped organism known as a spirochete. It is usually curable with penicillin, but resistant strains are now emerging. The initial sign of infection is a single painless ulcer, or **chancre,** which appears in the genital area (or wherever the initial point of contact was made). The chancre heals in two to six weeks without treatment and may even go unnoticed by the infected individual. A secondary phase occurs in six weeks to six months, producing a mild (and nonspecific) rash or more serious changes in various parts of the body. If untreated, a third stage may develop years later, with life-threatening heart disease and central nervous system disturbances, even insanity. Syphilis can be detected by a blood test. If the initial screen is positive, additional tests will be necessary to confirm the diagnosis and determine the proper course of treatment.

Gonorrhea is a bacterial infection that affects approximately 650,000 Americans each year. Symptoms in males tend to be dramatic: a thick discharge from the penis accompanied by significant pain during the passage of urine. Many infected women have no symptoms, while others experience problems ranging in severity from mild vaginal discharge to abscesses in the pelvis requiring surgical treatment. In some cases extensive scarring of a woman's tubes may occur. Depending upon the extent of damage, infertility may result.

Once uniformly responsive to penicillin, gonorrhea strains resistant to penicillin are now present in all fifty states.

Chlamydia infection has risen from obscurity in the 1970s to become the most common bacterial STI in the United States. Estimates of infection rates range from 20 to 40 percent of sexually active singles, with the highest rates among teenagers. In some studies, more than 30 percent of sexually active females were found to be infected with this organism.[16] Assuming it is detected (which may not always occur because symptoms may be subtle or nonexistent), a chlamydia infection normally responds to antibiotics.

In men chlamydia often causes a discharge from the penis that tends to be more watery and less profuse than with gonorrhea. Pain with the passage of urine is also less severe. In women 85 percent of those with chlamydia show no symptoms. Those with symptoms may experience vague pelvic discomfort or pain with urination. Whether or not symptoms are present, chlamydia can infect and damage a woman's reproductive organs and create a significant risk of infertility later in life. A single teenage sexual encounter that transmits chlamydia may cause untold emotional pain and major medical bills years later for infertility treatments.

Herpes simplex virus (HSV) is notorious for a property it shares with a number of other viral organisms: Once it enters a person's body, it has the capacity for reoccurrence, although the manifestations of this prolonged infection may vary considerably from person to person. HSV type 1 typically causes cold sores or fever blisters around the mouth or nose, although it can also cause genital infections through oral-genital contact. HSV type 2 is most commonly spread by genital sexual contact.

The first outbreak of genital herpes is usually the worst, with an irritating, sometimes painful, cluster of blisters that gradually crust and fade over ten to fourteen days. Men usually see an eruption on the penis, although they may not realize its significance because it resolves without treatment. Women are frequently unaware of the infection, but some suffer extreme discomfort in the genital area. The virus is sometimes transmitted through the skin or mucous membranes *even when no blisters are present.* This undoubtedly contributes to its high prevalence. In the United States, one in five individuals over the age of twelve is infected.

At least 90 percent of those infected will have recurrent outbreaks for months or years. Stress, intercourse, or other local irritation of the genital area (even from tight clothing) may trigger an outbreak, although these normally are not as severe as the first episode. Recurrences may occur several years after the initial contact, often causing concern and consternation in a subsequent relationship. For many the primary discomfort from a herpes infection is psychological, arising from the knowledge that this virus can never be eradicated and that any future sexual partner will probably become infected as well.

Antiviral medications such as **acyclovir** (Zovirax), **valcyclovir** (Valtrex), and **famcyclovir** (Famvir) can limit the severity of the first or subsequent herpes outbreaks, assuming that they are started at the outset of the eruption. When taken on a daily basis, they can reduce the frequency of recurrences, although this treatment can become expensive on a long-term basis.

Herpes outbreaks are rarely life threatening for adults. Unfortunately the same cannot be said for newborns. A baby born vaginally to a mother with HSV may be infected during delivery if there is a herpes outbreak on the mother's genital area, especially if it's her first HSV infection. If the newborn is infected with HSV, the results can be disastrous. About 20 percent of infected infants will have surface (skin and mucous membrane) involvement only. In the other 80 percent, the virus spreads throughout the body and central nervous system, with a strong likelihood of major consequences including blindness, mental retardation, and death.

Genital warts are caused by the **human papilloma virus (HPV).** This is one of the most common sexually transmitted diseases in the United States. Infection with human papilloma virus (HPV) is now considered to be more common than herpes. (One study of sexually active college females showed that roughly 60 percent were infected with HPV at least once during a three-year period.) Like herpes and many other STIs, HPV can be transmitted by an individual who has no visible signs of disease. *Condoms offer little, if any, protection against HPV, a fact that has not been widely publicized.*

Most who are infected with HPV never have any problem with it. However, the virus frequently causes soft, wartlike growths in the genital area. Small growths, which are usually the most common, respond to topical chemical treatment, but they can become quite large in size, requiring laser or other methods to remove them.

Of greater concern is that HPV has been clearly demonstrated to be the underlying cause of most cervical cancer and is implicated in cancers of the vulva, vagina, and penis. While the male cancer is rare, cancer of the cervix causes almost five thousand deaths each year. This cancer risk is specifically increased by early onset of sexual activity and contact with multiple partners. The cancer is also more aggressive among teenagers than in older adults; a disturbing recent trend has been an increasing number of precancerous abnormalities of the cervix among adolescent women. The aggressiveness of HPV appears to be enhanced by nicotine—yet one more reason to avoid smoking. Any woman who has had genital warts (or for that matter, any woman who has been or is sexually active) should have regular Pap smears to detect early changes in the cervix, which can be treated before they develop into a cancerous growth.

Acquired immune deficiency syndrome (AIDS) is caused by the **human immunodeficiency virus (HIV).** The virus is transmitted through semen, vaginal secretions, blood, and breast milk. Most HIV infections are transmitted during sexual contact (in all forms—heterosexual or homosexual, vaginal, oral, or anal), through accidental injection of infected blood, by contaminated needles, or by transfer from infected mother to baby during pregnancy. A small number of cases in infants have been attributed to nursing from an infected mother. Some early cases of IIIV resulted from transfusions of blood from infected donors. Revised blood-bank procedures and scrupulous screening of donors have reduced the likelihood of this happening to less than one in one hundred thousand.

At highest risk for this disease are people who have many sexual partners (especially male homosexuals) and/or who are intravenous drug users. But HIV infections are not limited to those with high-risk lifestyles. *The virus can be transmitted during a single sexual encounter,* even to someone having sex for the first time. For a variety of reasons, the rate of new HIV infections has been steadily rising among heterosexuals, especially adolescents. Twenty-five percent of all newly reported HIV infections occur in people younger than twenty-two, and 50 percent occur in those under twenty-five.[17]

After causing an initial flulike illness, HIV multiplies quietly within the immune system for years. The infected individual may feel perfectly well during this period but will be capable of transmitting the disease to others. Eventually the virus destroys the competence of the immune system, resulting in full-blown AIDS. Without adequate defenses, the body becomes vulnerable to a variety of devastating infections and some forms of cancer.

Screening tests for HIV detect a person's antibody response to the virus, not the virus itself. Once HIV enters the body, it will take a minimum of three weeks, and in some cases several months, to generate a detectable antibody response. An infected individual whose blood tests remain negative for HIV can still transmit the virus to others.

Hepatitis B is a viral infection of the liver transmitted through the same mechanisms as HIV. The majority of cases resolve completely following a flulike illness with fever, nausea, and jaundice (a yellow discoloration of skin caused by a buildup of a compound called bilirubin, which an inflamed liver does not process normally). However, about 1 to 5 percent develop a chronic infection that can lead to cirrhosis (scarring) or even cancer of the liver. Chronic carriers—there are about one million in the United States—can transmit the virus to sexual partners or from mother to baby during pregnancy or delivery. Most babies infected at birth become chronic carriers as well and risk developing long-term complications if not treated.

Hepatitis B is the only STI for which a reliable vaccine has been developed. Because efforts to vaccinate those at highest risk did not substantially reduce the number of new cases and because many cases of hepatitis B occur in people who do not have a history of risky behavior, current recommendations call for immunizing all infants, children, and adolescents against this virus.

In the midst of an enchanted evening at a secluded rendezvous, with romance in the air and hormones in high gear, it's easy to forget (or ignore) the unpleasant facts about STIs—including how prevalent they are. In most instances, an infected sexual partner will show absolutely no evidence of any illness. He or she may be a wonderful, intelligent person—dressed for success, impeccably groomed, attractive, and well mannered—but still capable of transmitting an organism that can impair health or threaten life itself. In other words, there is no way to look at a potential partner and determine if sex with that person might be safe or not. Furthermore, as was discussed in the section entitled "Safe(r) sex isn't" (pages 151-153), the protection offered by condoms is far from foolproof. When dealing with these diseases, the only sex that is safe takes place within a mutually exclusive relationship with an uninfected life partner.

Tobacco, Alcohol, and Drug Abuse—Resisting the Epidemic

Not too many generations ago, our ancestors regularly watched in horror as bubonic plague, diphtheria, smallpox, and other lethal epidemics swept through their towns and families, taking rich and poor alike to the grave. Today, the consumption of alcohol, tobacco, and a host of addicting drugs has become a modern-day plague ravaging many of our youngest citizens.

Like the scourges of old, the drug epidemic spreads without regard to economic, racial, geographic, educational, religious, or family boundaries. More recently, it has become particularly aggressive among preteen children, dipping freely into the primary grades for new consumers. While all of us should work and pray toward ending this blight in our nation and our communities, we must ultimately be concerned about preventing it from moving across our own doorsteps.

No child whom you bring into the world will be automatically immune from the drug epidemic. Therefore you must work diligently over the years to "drugproof" your child(ren). This project involves various tasks that cannot be tackled haphazardly. First, you must understand what draws kids toward drugs. You also need basic information about the substances that are currently prowling your neighborhood. You should become familiar with the signs that a drug problem might be developing in your home. Finally, and most important, you must be prepared to take long-term preventive measures and to respond appropriately if one or more of the toxins should breach your family's defenses.

Why Do Kids Start (and Continue) Using Drugs?

Four factors set the stage for adolescent drug use:

- *Attitudes of parents* toward tobacco, alcohol, and other substances. Children learn what they live. Smoking, drinking, and other drug-related behaviors among parents will usually be duplicated in their children.
- *Attractiveness of drugs.* Smoking and drinking are widely promoted as habits enjoyed by sophisticated, fun-loving, attractive, and sexy people—what most adolescents long to become. Illegal drugs are "advertised" by those using them in an adolescent's peer group.
- *The high induced by drugs.* If drug use wasn't pleasurable, it would be relatively easy to keep kids and harmful substances separated. But the reality is that many kids enjoy the way they feel on drugs—at least for a while.
- *Availability of drugs.* Finding drugs is not difficult for children and adolescents in most communities, but tougher local standards can help keep drugs out of less-determined hands.

Once the stage is set, the following factors exert a more direct influence on who will and who won't try drugs. The consequences of early experiences (whether pleasant or disagreeable), the drug used, and one's genetic predisposition will determine whether a problem is nipped in the bud or blossoms into addiction.

Peer pressure. Peers play a huge role at each stage of a child's or adolescent's drug experience—whether resisting them, experimenting, becoming a user, or confronting withdrawal and recovery. The need for peer acceptance is especially strong during the early adolescent years and can override (or at least seriously challenge) the most earnest commitments. "Just say no" may not mean a whole lot when smoking, drinking, or taking drugs determines who is included in highly esteemed ranks of the inner circle.

There are three obvious implications:

- *It is important that kids find their niche in the right peer group(s),* among friends who are not only committed to positive values (including drug-free lifestyles) but also involved in worthwhile and enjoyable pursuits.
- *You may have to intervene if your adolescent (especially in the early teen years) is hanging out with the wrong crowd.*
- *Children and adolescents with a healthy, stable identity and an appropriate sense of independence will be more resistant to peer pressure.* This will be discussed later.

Curiosity. Unless your family lives in total isolation, your child will be aware of smoking, alcohol, and drug use well before adolescence from discussions at school, watching TV and movies, or direct observation. Some curiosity is inevitable: *What do these things feel like?* Whether this leads to sampling and whether an experiment progresses to addiction will depend on the individual's mind-set and physical response.

Thrill seeking. This desire for excitement is in all of us to some degree and propels us toward all kinds of activities: skydiving, roller coasters, movies (where sights and sounds are "bigger than life"), fireworks displays, sporting events, and so on. Some of these are more risky than others, but none require chemical alteration of the senses to be satisfying. Unfortunately, many children and adolescents seek drug experiences to produce thrills that normal consciousness can't duplicate.

Rebellion. Wayward children may engage in smoking, alcohol, and drug use as a show of "independence" from family norms and values.

Escape from life/relief from pain. This is often the driving force in drug use. If everyday life seems boring, meaningless, oppressive, or painful (physically and/or emotionally), alcohol and drugs may appear to offer a powerful time-out. The strongest resistance to drug abuse therefore arises from an ongoing sense of joy and contentment that transcends circumstances. These attitudes are usually acquired, not inborn. Early positive experiences in the family and an active, wide-awake relationship with God play the most important roles in molding such attitudes.

The "Gateway" Drugs: Tobacco, Alcohol, Marijuana, and Inhalants

Few children and adolescents start a career of drug use by snorting cocaine or injecting heroin. The path usually begins with products from the corner store—tobacco, alcohol, or household products that are inhaled—or with marijuana, which some mistakenly consider safe.

Tobacco—the smoking gun

No drug habit has a greater negative impact on our national health than tobacco, which is implicated in more than four hundred thousand deaths in the United States each year. The list of disorders caused or aggravated by tobacco is staggering. Among these diseases are cancers of the lungs, mouth, vocal cords, and other organs; chronic lung disease; asthma; ulcers; clogging of the vessels that supply blood to the heart and other organs, causing heart attacks, strokes, amputations, and premature deaths. Babies and children who breathe smokers' exhaust at home are at risk for respiratory infections, asthma, and sudden infant death syndrome (SIDS).

The vast majority of diseases related to tobacco take their toll later in life after subjects have had years of exposure. So why is adolescent tobacco use such a major concern?

Nicotine is extremely addictive. Nicotine's hook is set quickly and, once in place, is extremely difficult to remove. A few hits of nicotine produce a unique combination of relaxation and alertness, and withdrawal produces unpleasant physical and psychological symptoms. As a result, fewer than 10 percent of smokers can limit their habit to five cigarettes or fewer per day.

Almost every long-term smoker first lights up during adolescence. Nearly 30 percent of any high school graduation class are regular smokers, as are more than 70 percent of their peers who dropped out of school. Over the past two decades, the average age at which tobacco use begins has dropped from sixteen to twelve. The younger one becomes nicotine dependent, the more cigarettes will be smoked as an adult.

A huge amount of money is spent every year to make smoking appear glamorous and exciting. The tobacco industry's annual multi-billion-dollar advertising budget is supposedly intended to encourage adults to switch brands, but the cartoon characters, sexy young couples, macho men, and liberated women in cigarette ads have clearly been shown to influence children and adolescents. Heavy visibility of these ads at sporting and cultural events also sends definite signals that tobacco is hot stuff. Warnings issued in health-education class pale in comparison. In one survey of high school smokers, more than 95 percent were aware of health risks, but 70 percent claimed they were not concerned enough to stop.

Cigarettes keep very bad company. Smoking is associated with significantly poorer school performance and a higher likelihood of sexual activity. Because the use of alcohol and marijuana is significantly greater among adolescent smokers, tobacco is identified as a "gateway" drug—one that increases the odds of using even more dangerous substances. It is the last of these points that should sound the alarm for parents of adolescent smokers. If your teenager is smoking cigarettes, he is seven times more likely to be using illicit drugs[18] and eleven times more likely to be drinking heavily than his nonsmoking counterparts.[19]

Smokeless (chewing and snuffing) tobacco, which has been made highly visible (and glamorized to some degree) by users who are - professional athletes, is not a safe alternative to cigarettes. Surveys show that about 12 percent of male high school students currently use smokeless tobacco. Usage rates are even higher in many Native American populations. Chewing tobacco is clearly associated with damage to the gingiva (the soft tissues surrounding the teeth) and with aggressive cancers of the mouth. Furthermore, both chewing and snuffing deliver powerful jolts of nicotine. A 1993 report from the National Institutes of Health indicates that a typical dose of snuff contains twice the amount of nicotine in a cigarette, while a wad of chewing tobacco contains *fifteen times that amount.* Needless to say, addiction to these substances is very common, as are withdrawal symptoms when use is stopped.

Alcohol—the most dangerous gateway drug

In all fifty states, it is illegal to sell alcoholic beverages to anyone under age twenty-one. This is no accident, because for teenagers alcohol is a gateway to a lot more than other drugs.

Alcohol causes more deaths among adolescents than any other substance. Alcohol is involved in one third of all traffic deaths for young people aged fifteen through nineteen.[20] Overall, driving under the influence is the leading cause of death for people between the ages of fifteen and twenty-four. Alcohol also frequently plays a role in adolescent deaths from other causes: homicides, suicides, drownings, and motorcycle and bicycle accidents.

In addition, alcohol plays an important role in adolescent crime, sexual promiscuity, and date rape. According to research compiled by Mothers Against Drunk Driving (MADD), 95 percent of violent crime on college campuses is alcohol related, and 90 percent of reported campus rapes involve alcohol use by the assailant, the victim, or both. In one study cited by MADD, 60 percent of college women diagnosed with a sexually transmitted infection were drunk when they became infected.

Another sobering reality about drinking is the early age at which it frequently begins.

- According to the American Academy of Pediatrics, about one in five fifth-graders has already experienced alcohol intoxication. Four out of ten sixth-graders say they feel pressure from other students to drink.[21] More than 50 percent of eighth-graders and eight out of ten twelfth-graders have tried alcohol at least once. One in four eighth-graders and half of all twelfth-graders have used alcohol within a given month.[22]
- More alcoholic products that specifically appeal to kids are hitting the marketplace. Wine coolers are increasingly popular with younger drinkers, as are a new wave of alcoholic

concoctions billed as "thirst quenchers," often containing lemon or other fruit flavors.

A significant number of drinkers (about 20 percent) develop full-blown alcohol addiction and struggle with it for years. Ironically, the person who prides himself on the ability to "hold his liquor" is at the greatest risk for alcoholism. If large quantities of alcohol must be consumed to produce intoxication, he is demonstrating a *tolerance* for alcohol—something all alcoholics have in common—and addiction is likely to develop. Tolerance of alcohol and the risk of addiction are thought to be genetically predisposed and usually run in families. *Adolescents with family members who have had alcohol-abuse problems must be warned that they are at higher risk for becoming addicted to alcohol if they ever start drinking.*

Marijuana—inhaled intellectual impairment
Parents who experimented with marijuana during the 1960s may not be terribly concerned about this drug. But what kids are smoking today bears little resemblance to what flower children were inhaling three decades ago. The average batch of marijuana in the 1960s contained 0.2 percent delta-9-tetrahydrocannabinol (or THC for short), its main mood-altering chemical. Today's vintage contains at least 5 percent THC, or twenty-five times the old concentration, which—along with four hundred other assorted chemicals—adversely affects the brain, lungs, heart, gonads (ovaries or testes), and immune system. In preteens and young adolescents, heavy use of marijuana can also impair growth and development.

Most kids who use marijuana or take THC capsules experience a sense of euphoria, relaxation, and calm. Some feel it enhances perception. The reality is that it impairs intellectual function, specifically concentration, memory, judgment, and motor skills. Short-term fallout can include injuries and death from motor-vehicle accidents or other trauma as well as sexual misadventures resulting from loss of inhibition and rational thinking.

Long-term users are known for an "amotivational" syndrome in which goals and self-discipline and the activities that require them (especially school performance) literally go up in smoke. During the teen years a child should be learning how to think and act more maturely, but frequent marijuana use can halt that process. Worse, it introduces kids to the harrowing world of illegal drugs and the criminals who produce and distribute them.

Inhalants—cheap (and dangerous) thrills
This form of substance abuse is particularly hazardous because:

- The materials involved are inexpensive and readily available in any garage or hardware store. Model glue, contact cement, gasoline, lacquers, paints, toiletries, cosmetics, and dozens of other aerosol and volatile products can have mind-altering effects if inhaled deeply.
- Substance inhalers are generally very young. The age of peak use is typically twelve to fourteen, with first experiences as early as six to eight years of age. Most adolescents who have experimented with inhalants do so before their second year of high school,[23] and nearly twenty percent of eighth graders have tried some form of inhalant.[24]
- The potential effects are disastrous. The most serious by-product of chronic use is permanent damage to the brain and nervous system, causing loss of intellectual function and coordination. In addition, a variety of products can be lethal during or after inhalant use. One study of inhalant deaths revealed that over 20 percent occurred among first-time users. One consequence known as **sudden sniffing death syndrome** can occur when a user is surprised or suddenly frightened during the act of inhaling. Many inhalants temporarily increase the sensitivity of the heart muscle, and an abrupt adrenaline surge in response to being startled can provoke a lethal irregular heart rhythm.

Depending upon the substance used, several deep inspirations bring on a sense of euphoria—frequently with hallucinations—as well as stimulation and loss of inhibition (which may lead to other dangerous behavior). Drowsiness and sleep may follow.

Like other drug users, inhalant abusers may display erratic behavior, poor self-care, and declining school performance. Parents may notice specific clues such as the aroma of the inhalant (which can persist in the breath for several hours), stains and odors in clothes, and an unusual stash of products (such as gasoline or aerosol cans) in a child's room. An adult who discovers children or adolescents in the act of inhaling should avoid surprise tactics or a sudden confrontation that might cause a startle reflex, since this could precipitate a sudden lethal heart-rhythm disturbance.

Beyond the Gateway—Dead-End Drugs

Beyond these gateway substances lies a dark world of more powerful drugs that assault bodies and minds more quickly and savagely. These may be grouped into four categories: **stimulants, sedatives/ hypnotics, narcotics,** and **hallucinogens.**

Stimulants—the fast track downhill

Cocaine is one of the most addictive drugs on the street and in many ways the most dangerous. It directly stimulates pleasure centers in the brain, creating an overwhelming desire for the same experience again and again. Its powerful jolt to the central nervous system also triggers a rapid heart rate, constricted blood vessels, and elevated blood pressure. Even in young, well-conditioned bodies, these events can cause stroke, seizures, or cardiac arrest.

When the drug wears off, cocaine users become anxious, irritable, depressed, and desperate for the next dose. Bigger and more frequent doses are needed to produce the same effect, and progression from first use to desperate addiction can be rapid.

All of cocaine's routes of entry into the body pose unique hazards. Snorting cocaine up the nose can lead to destruction of the septum (the structure separating the two nasal passages) and eventual collapse of the bridge of the nose. Injecting cocaine into the veins can transmit dangerous microorganisms, including the viruses that cause hepatitis and AIDS, when needles or syringes are shared with other users. The cheapest form of cocaine, at five to fifteen dollars per dose, is **crack,** which produces a response so sudden and powerful that addiction frequently begins with the first dose. Crack is a form of freebase cocaine, a purified version of the drug that can only be smoked. (When heated, it produces a crackling sound; hence its name.)

Amphetamines ("speed") and their derivatives, whether swallowed, smoked, or injected, rev up the central nervous system and produce a sense of energy, excitement, and invincibility. But with this come a number of serious risks and consequences. Excitement may deteriorate into excitability, irritability, paranoia, delusions, and even violent behavior. When these drugs wear off, profound fatigue and depression are left in their wake. Tolerance results in a need for higher doses, and so addiction is not unusual. Chronic use leads to physical deterioration caused by malnutrition (from decreased interest in food) and loss of sleep. Heavy use can result in permanent brain damage, stroke, or heart attack.

The potential for abuse of these drugs has recently increased for two reasons. First, the widespread use of Dexedrine and Ritalin in treating attention deficit/hyperactivity disorder (ADHD) has placed more of these stimulants in circulation, thus increasing the likelihood of potential misuse through sharing with or selling to others. (Those with ADHD who receive proper doses of these drugs appear to have little risk of addiction to them.)

Second, and more important, the abuse of a form of amphetamine known as **methamphetamine** (also called "ice," "crank," "crystal meth," and "poor-man's coke," among other names) has reached epidemic levels. Methamphetamine is relatively cheap to manufacture in home laboratories, and an inexpensive dose gives users a more sustained high than cocaine. Teenagers and young adults use this drug to boost mood and self-confidence, suppress appetite to lose weight, and enhance sexual experiences. But ongoing use commonly leads to insomnia, agitation, psychosis, and violent behavior. Methamphetamine-induced emergency-room visits, crimes, and deaths have increased dramatically, and some experts fear use of this drug will become a plague dwarfing the cocaine epidemic that began in the 1980s.

Sedatives and hypnotics—escapes to the land of nod
These agents in small doses produce a pleasant sense of relaxation and sleepiness. In some cases they may be misused to offset the sleepless excitation from stimulants taken earlier in the day. Prolonged use usually leads to psychological and physical dependence.

High doses of these medications, particularly when combined with other drugs (especially alcohol), can produce stuporous intoxication, depression of the drive to breathe, coma, and death. Withdrawal can be hazardous, with symptoms including anxiety, tremors, panic, and seizures.

A few decades ago, **barbiturates** were commonly prescribed by physicians as sedatives and sleeping pills. Because of problems with overdoses, abuse, and withdrawal, few doctors recommend them, so they are more widely marketed on the street than in pharmacies. Two exceptions are **phenobarbital,** used to treat seizure disorders, and **butalbital,** which is combined with caffeine and aspirin in headache remedies such as Fiorinal and Esgic. Despite their relative safety, both of these forms are still potentially habit-forming. **Benzodiazepines** (Valium, Librium, Xanax, Tranxene, Klonopin, and others) are widely prescribed to treat anxiety disorders. More sedating forms (Dalmane, Restoril, and Halcion) are often used to induce sleep. These drugs are not commonly sold on the street, but legitimate prescriptions can be misused or overused and lead to dependence.

An extremely potent, fast-acting benzodiazepine called **Rohypnol** produces significant short-term memory loss. This drug, which is sold legally in Europe, has been implicated in numerous date rapes in the United States. Sexual predators slip Rohypnol tablets (called "roofies") into an unsuspecting victim's drink; this leads to rapid onset of deep sleep and amnesia for whatever happens during the next few hours. Rohypnol has become the rapist's best friend—obliterating the victim's ability to resist or remember who did what.

A newer drug of abuse, **gamma-hydroxybutyrate or GHB,** is unrelated to traditional prescription sedatives. Identified with a colorful variety of street names ("blue nitro," "cherry fx bombs," "nature's Quaalude," and many others), this compound has been advertised in body-building magazines, health food stores, and on the Internet as a muscle builder, weight loss aid, aphrodisiac, and mood elevator. It has also been popular among those who frequent nightclubs and all-night "rave" parties. Unfortunately, GHB is highly dangerous. Variablility in the product manufactured by homegrown labs, a wide range of individual sensitivity, and a narrow margin for error in dosing can lead to disastrous consequences. The drug can rapidly bring on a severely altered mental state and seizurelike activity, progressing to coma or even death in some cases. Because of its powerful sedative effects, it has been used by some sexual predators as a "date-rape drug." Needless to say, manufacture and sale of GHB is now illegal in the United States.

Narcotics—painkillers with a hook

Derivatives of opium, known as **opiates,** such as **codeine, hydrocodone** (Vicodin, Lortab, and others), **oxycodone** (Percodan, Percocet, and others), and morphine are used widely in medicine to relieve pain. But they can also create a general sense of well-being and relief from psychological pain, leading to long-term use and dependence. Adults are more likely than teenagers to have problems with narcotic prescriptions for chronic problems such as headache or back pain.

Adolescents involved in high-risk drug behavior may be drawn into the snare of **heroin,** a derivative of morphine that is injected into the vein to produce an intense euphoria. Repeated use always leads to addiction, as well as to the perpetual risk for accidental overdose and transmission of hepatitis and AIDS viruses from contaminated needles and syringes.

Narcotic addicts deprived of their drug experience a host of unpleasant symptoms they will desperately seek to avoid. These include sweats, cramps, vomiting, and diarrhea. As miserable as narcotic withdrawal may feel, it is far less dangerous than abruptly stopping a long-term barbiturate or benzodiazepine habit, which can lead to convulsions.

Hallucinogenic drugs—checking out of reality

LSD (lysergic acid diethylamide), which seemed to be a faded relic of the psychedelic sixties, has made a disturbing comeback. Tiny amounts swallowed or licked off paper can produce intense hallucinations, which may be exhilarating or terrifying. The worst of the "bad trips" can bring on profound anxiety, confusion, panic, or self-destructive behavior, such as jumping off a building or stepping in front of oncoming traffic. **Mescaline, peyote,** and other hallucinogens have similar effects and risks. Long-term use can damage the brain, resulting in defects in memory and abstract thinking.

Phencyclidine (PCP, "angel dust"), originally formulated as an animal tranquilizer, is an extraordinarily dangerous hallucinogen. It can induce profound alterations of all sensory perceptions (sight, sound, touch, smell, and taste), essentially jerking its users far from normal consciousness. But this dissociation from reality can also provoke marked anxiety, depression, paranoia, and acts of horrific violence against oneself or others. An agitated PCP user may demonstrate incredible strength and no apparent sensation of pain, making him extremely dangerous to those who might try to restrain him.

Physical consequences of large doses of PCP can be severe—heart failure, seizures, coma, and lethal strokes. Users also risk direct brain damage, leading to alterations of speech, loss of memory and intellectual function, and in some cases, psychosis. PCP can be swallowed or smoked (if sprayed onto tobacco or marijuana). It can also be injected, at times with tragic results.

Designer drugs—the worst of all worlds
The incredibly misguided creativity of those who seek new and different drug experiences has led to the synthesis of a variety of powerful, addictive, and extremely hazardous substances. Most of these are spin-offs of other drugs such as PCP, amphetamines, or meperidine (Demerol, a potent painkiller). Those who experiment with **ecstasy** (the most well-known designer drug) and the other designer drugs literally play Russian roulette with their brains every time they swallow, snort, or inject. These drugs come aboard with the dangerous baggage of their parent compounds and then add unpredictable side effects. Irreversible brain damage, with long-term disabilities such as tremors, paralysis, and speech disturbances can be the pathetic legacy of a season of thrill seeking with designer drugs.

What Are the Stages of Involvement in Substance Abuse?

Experts in adolescent substance problems have identified a common progression of alcohol- and drug-related behaviors that moves from bad to worse. While it is not a foregone conclusion that everyone who experiments with drugs will progress to the worst stages of involvement, a child can already have incurred a lot of damage before parents or others notice that something is wrong. Secretive adolescent behavior and skillful lying, combined with parental denial ("No one in *our* family could have a drug problem!"), may delay identification of the problem. While paranoia and daily inquisitions around the breakfast table are counterproductive, wise parents will keep their eyes and ears open and promptly take action if they see any signs that a problem may be developing.

Stage one: experimentation—entering the drug gateway
Characteristics:
- Use is occasional, sporadic, often unplanned—weekends, summer nights, someone's unsupervised party.
- Use is precipitated by peer pressure, curiosity, thrill seeking, desire to look and feel grown-up.
- Gateway drugs are usually used—cigarettes, alcohol, marijuana, possibly inhalant abuse.
- A drug high is easier to experience because tolerance has not been developed.

Parents may notice:
- Tobacco or alcohol on the breath or intoxicated behavior.
- Little change in normal behavior between episodes of drug use.

Stage two: more regular drug use—leaving the land of the living
Characteristics:
- Alcohol and other drugs are used not only on weekends but also on weekdays, not only with friends but when alone.
- Quantities of alcohol and drugs increase as tolerance develops; hangovers become more common.
- Blackouts may occur—periods of time in which drugs or alcohol prevent normal memories from forming; "What happened last night?" becomes a frequent question.
- More time and attention are focused on when the next drug experience will occur.
- Fellow drinkers/drug users become preferred companions.

Parents may notice:

- Son or daughter will be out of the house later at night, overnight, or all weekend.
- School performance worsens—unexplained school absences.
- Outside activities such as sports are dropped.
- Decreased contact with friends who don't use drugs.
- Disappearance of money or other valuables.
- Child withdraws from the family, is increasingly sullen and hostile.
- User is caught in one or many lies.

Stage three: waist deep in the mire of addiction—and sinking
Characteristics:

- Alcohol and drugs become primary focus of attention.
- Becoming high is a daily event.
- There is a use of harder, more dangerous drugs.
- More money is spent each week on drugs; theft or dealing may become part of drug-seeking behavior.
- Adolescent displays increasing social isolation; no contact with nondrug using friends; more drug use in isolation rather than socially.

Parents may notice the behaviors listed above, plus:

- Escalation of conflicts at home.
- Loss of nearly all control of the adolescent.
- Possible discovery of a stash of drugs at home.
- Arrest(s) for possession of and/or dealing drugs or for driving while intoxicated.

Stage four: drowning in addiction
Characteristics:

- Constant state of intoxication; being high is routine, even at school or job (if there is any attendance at all).
- Blackouts increase in frequency.
- Physical appearance deteriorates—weight loss, infections, poor self-care.
- Injectable drugs are possibly used.
- Involvement in casual sexual relationships (at times in exchange for drugs).

- User will likely be involved with theft, dealing, and other criminal activity.
- Guilt, self-hatred, and thoughts of suicide increase.

Parents are likely to be dealing with:
- Complete loss of control of adolescent's behavior; escalation of conflict, possibly to the point of violence.
- Ongoing denial by user that drugs are a problem.
- Increasing problems with the law and time spent with police, attorneys, hearings, court officials, etc.
- Other siblings negatively affected because the family is pre-occupied or overwhelmed by consequences of drug user's behavior.

This descent into drug hell is a nightmare that no parent envisions while rocking a newborn baby or escorting an eager five-year-old to kindergarten. But it can happen in any neighborhood, any church, any family, even when parents have provided a stable and loving home environment. In fact, it is often in such homes that a drug problem goes undetected until it's reached an advanced and dangerous stage. "This can't be happening, not in my house!" But if it does, parental guilt, anger, and depression can undermine the responses necessary to restore order.

What Can Parents Do to Reduce Their Child's Risk of Developing a Substance Problem?

Drug abuse is so widespread in our culture that you cannot expect to isolate your child from exposure to it. However, as with diseases caused by bacteria and viruses, you can institute infection-control measures. Specifically, take steps to reduce the likelihood of contact with drugs, and build your child's immunity to using them. These measures should be ongoing, deliberate, and proactive.

Model behavior you want your children to follow.
When it comes to drugs, two adages are worth noting: "Children learn what they live" and "What parents allow in moderation their children will do in excess." While not absolute truths, these maxims reflect the reality that kids are looking to their parents for cues

as to what is acceptable behavior, while at the same time developing the discernment required to understand what moderation is all about.

If you smoke, your offspring will probably do likewise. But it's never too late to quit, and your decision to give up cigarettes will make an important statement to all the members of your family—especially if you are willing to hold yourself accountable to them.

If you consume alcohol at home, what role does it play in your life? Does it flow freely on a daily basis? Do you need a drink to unwind at the end of the day? Is it a necessary ingredient at every party or family get-together? If so, your children will get the picture that alcohol is a painkiller, tension reliever, and the life of the party, and they will likely use it in a similar fashion. For their sake (and yours), take whatever steps are necessary to live without alcohol.

If you drink modestly—an occasional glass of wine with dinner, a beer every other week, a few sips of champagne at a wedding—think carefully about alcohol's role in your family. Many parents decide to abstain while rearing their children in order to send an unambiguous message to steer clear of it. Others feel that modeling modest, nonintoxicated use of alcohol (while speaking clearly against underage drinking, drunkenness, driving under the influence, and other irresponsible behaviors) equips children and teenagers to make sensible decisions later in life.

Each family must weigh the options carefully and set its own standards. But if you or any blood relatives have a history of alcohol addiction (or any problem caused by drinking), make your home an alcohol-free zone and warn your adolescent that he or she may have a genetic predisposition toward alcoholism.

Also think about the impact of your family's habits on visitors or guests, including your teenager's friends. What might be perfectly harmless for you could prompt someone who has a potential for alcohol addiction to make a bad decision. All things considered, nothing is lost and much can be gained by abstaining.

What about the medicine cabinet? If you are stressed, upset, or uncomfortable, are d-r-u-g-s the way you spell r-e-l-i-e-f? Have you accumulated prescription narcotics and tranquilizers that you utilize freely when the going gets tough? Kids aren't blind. If they see the adults around them frequently taking "legitimate" drugs to dull their pain, why can't they use their own drugs of choice to do the same?

Even if you feel you have a legitimate need for painkillers (recurrent headaches, chronic back pain), you can become addicted to prescription drugs. Finding other ways to cope and working diligently to minimize the use of drugs for *symptom* relief should be priorities. Note: The appropriate use of antidepressants to treat the biochemistry of mood disorders does *not* represent a potential abuse situation. These medications are not addicting or habit-forming and are not sold on the street to create an artificial drug high.

Finally, if you use marijuana and other street drugs, whether for recreational purposes or because of an addiction problem, you are putting the parental stamp of approval not only on the drugs but also on breaking the law. For your own and your family's sake, seek help immediately and bring this dangerous behavior to an end.

Build identity and attitudes that are resistant to drug use.
This is an ongoing project, beginning during the first years of your child's life. Specifically:

- Create an environment that consistently balances love and limits. Children and teenagers who know they are loved unconditionally are less likely to seek "pain relief" through drugs, and those who have learned to live within appropriate boundaries will have better impulse control and self-discipline.
- Instill respect and awe for the God-given gift of a body and mind—even one that isn't perfect.
- Help children and adolescents become students of consequences—not only in connection with drugs but with other behaviors as well. Talk about good and bad choices and the logic behind them. "Just say no" is an appropriate motto for kids to learn, but understanding *why* it is wrong to use harmful substances will build more solid resistance.
- Build a positive sense of identity with your family. This means not only openly affirming and appreciating each

member but putting forth the time and effort for shared experiences that are meaningful and fun. A strong feeling of belonging to a loving family builds accountability ("Our family doesn't use drugs") and helps prevent loneliness, which can be a setup for a drug experience.

- Encourage church-related activities (including family devotions) that build a meaningful, personal faith. *Reliance on God is the cornerstone of many drug treatment programs, and it makes no sense to leave the spiritual dimension out of the prevention process.* A vibrant faith reinforces the concept that the future is worth protecting, stabilizes the emotions during turbulent years, and provides a healthy response to the aches and pains of life. In addition, an awareness of God's presence and a desire not to dishonor Him can be strong deterrents to destructive behavior.

Begin talking early about smoking, alcohol, and drugs.
Because experimentation with drugs and alcohol commonly begins during the grade-school years, start appropriate countermeasures in very young children. A five-year-old may not be ready for a lecture about the physiology of cocaine addiction, but you should be ready to offer commentary when you and your child see someone smoking or drinking, whether in real life or in a movie or TV program. If intoxication is portrayed as humorous (as in the pink-elephant sequence in the movie *Dumbo,* for example), don't be shy about setting the record straight.

Keep talking about smoking, alcohol, and drugs
as opportunities arise.
Make an effort to stay one step ahead of your child's or adolescent's knowledge of the drug scene. If you hear about an athlete, rock star, or celebrity who uses drugs, be certain that everyone in the family understands that no amount of fame or fortune excuses this behavior. If a famous person is dealing with the consequences of drug use (such as being dropped from a team or suffering medical or legal consequences), make sure your kids hear the cautionary tale.

Be aware of current trends in your community and look for local meetings or lectures where abuse problems are being discussed.

Find out what's going on—not only from the experts but from your kids and their friends. If you hear that someone is smoking, drinking, inhaling, or injecting drugs, talk about it. What are they using? What consequences are likely? Why is it wrong? What help do they need?

All this assumes that you are available to have these conversations. Be careful, because the time when you may be the busiest with career or other responsibilities may also be the time one or more adolescents at home most need your input. If you're too overworked, overcommitted, and overtired to keep tabs on the home front, you may wake up one day to find a major drug problem on your doorstep.

Don't allow your child or adolescent to go to a party, sleepover,
  or other activity that isn't supervised by someone you trust.
Don't blindly assume that the presence of a grown-up guarantees a safe environment. Get to know your kids' friends' parents, not just your kids' friends. Make certain your child knows you will pick him up anytime, anywhere—no questions asked—if he finds himself in a situation where alcohol or drugs are being used. And be sure to praise him for a wise and mature decision if he does so.

Have the courage to curtail your child's or adolescent's
  contact with drug users.
The epidemic of drug abuse spreads person to person. Whether a recent acquaintance or a long-term bosom buddy, if one (or more) of your teenager's friends is known to be actively using alcohol and/or drugs, you must impose restrictions on the relationship. You might, for example, stipulate that your adolescent can spend time with that person only in your home—without any closed doors and when you are around.

However, even with these limits in place, you will need to keep track of who is influencing whom. If your family is reaching out to a troubled adolescent and helping to move him toward healthier decisions, keep up the good work. But if there is any sign that the drug-using friend is pulling your teenager toward his lifestyle, declare a quarantine immediately. By all means, if your teenager feels called to help a friend climb out of a drug quagmire, don't let him try it alone. Work as a team to direct that person toward a recovery program.

Create significant consequences to discourage
  alcohol and drug use.

Teenagers may not be scared off by facts, figures, and gory details. Even the most ominous warnings may not override an adolescent's belief in her own immortality, especially when other compelling emotions such as the need for peer acceptance are operating at full throttle.

You may improve the odds by making it clear that you consider the use of cigarettes, alcohol, or illegal drugs a very serious matter. Judgment regarding punishments fitting crimes will be necessary, of course. If your adolescent confesses that he tried a cigarette or a beer at a party and expresses an appropriate resolve to avoid a repeat performance, heart-to-heart conversation and encouragement would be far more appropriate than summarily grounding him for six months.

But if your warnings repeatedly go unheeded, you will need to establish and enforce some meaningful consequences. Loss of driving, dating, or even phone privileges for an extended period of time may be in order. You can make the bitter pill less threatening by pointing out the following:

- He can easily avoid the penalty by staying clear of drugs and the people who use them.
- Consistent responsible behavior leads to more privileges and independence. Irresponsible behavior leads to decreased independence and more parental control.
- The drastic consequence can be used as a reason to get away from a bad situation. If a friend starts to exert pressure to smoke, drink, or use drugs, he can say, "Sorry, but I don't want to be stuck without transportation for the next six months."

What If a Problem Has Already Developed?

Even in families that are closely knit, hold strong values, and practice ongoing drugproofing, there are no guarantees that substance abuse won't affect one or more of your children. The problems may range from a brief encounter with cigarettes to an episode of intoxication (perhaps with legal consequences) or even involve addiction. As you begin to cope with the chemical intruder(s) in your home, keep the following principles in mind:

Don't deny or ignore the problem.
If you do, it is likely to continue to worsen until your family life is turned inside out. Take the bull by the horns—but be sure to find out exactly how big and ugly the bull is. The marijuana cigarette you discovered may be a onetime experiment—or the tip of an iceberg. Talk to your child or adolescent about it—but also talk to siblings, friends, and anyone else who knows what he's up to. You may not like what you hear, but better to get the hard truth now than a ghastly surprise later.

Don't wallow in false guilt.
Most parents assume a great deal of self-blame when a drug problem erupts in their home. If you do carry some responsibility for what has happened (whether you know about it immediately or find out later on), face up to it, confess it to God and your family, and then get on with the task of helping your child. But remember that your child or adolescent must deal with his or her own responsibility as well.

Seek help from people experienced with treating drug problems.
Talk to your physician and pastor. They should be part of your team, even if in a supporting role. It is likely that you will receive a referral to a professional who is experienced in organizing a family intervention. This may include educational sessions, individual and family counseling, medical treatment, and long-term follow-up. When the user's behavior is out of control and he is unwilling to acknowledge the problem, a carefully planned confrontation by family members and others affected may need to be carried out under the supervision of an experienced counselor. The goal is to convince the drug user in a firm but loving way of the need for change—*now.* The confrontation should include specific alternatives for the type of treatment he will undergo and a clear-cut "or else . . ." if he is not willing to cooperate.

Be prepared to make difficult, "tough love" decisions.
If you have a drug-dependent adolescent who will not submit to treatment and insists on continuing the drug use and other destructive actions, you will need to take a stomach-churning step of informing him that he cannot continue to live in your home while carrying on this behavior. This will be necessary not only to motivate him to change but to prevent his drug-induced turbulence from destroying the rest of your family.

If you must take this drastic step, it would be helpful to present him with one or more options. These might include entering an inpatient drug-treatment center, halfway house, boot-camp program, or youth home, or staying with a relative or another family who is willing to accept him for a defined period of time. More ominous possibilities may need to be discussed as well, such as making him a ward of the court or even turning him over to the police if he has been involved in criminal activity. If you continue to shield him from the consequences of his behavior or bail him out when his drugs get him into trouble, he will not change, and you will be left with deep-seated anger and frustration.

Don't look for or expect quick-fix solutions.
It is normal to wish for a single intervention that will make a drug problem go away. But one conversation, counseling session, prayer time, or trip to the doctor won't be enough. Think in terms of a comprehensive response encompassing specific treatment and counseling and the gamut of your child's life—home, school, friends, and church.

Remember the father of the Prodigal Son.
"Tough love" means allowing the consequences of bad decisions to be fully experienced by one who is making them. It also means that he knows your love for him is so deep and secure that it will never die. Never give up hope, never stop praying, and never slam the door on reconciliation and restoration when he comes to his senses.

Recognizing Depression and Preventing Suicide in Adolescents

DEPRESSION—AS COMMON AS THE COMMON COLD

Depression is by far the most common and important emotional health problem in America. In terms of its frequency among the population, depression could be compared to the common cold. But the similarity ends there.

- The sneezing and hacking of a cold is readily apparent to the person who has it, as well as to everyone around him. But depression can be manifested in a bewildering array of symptoms, many of them physical, and these may not be recognized by the individual himself or by those closest to him.

- Cold viruses are usually vanquished by the immune system within a week, while untreated depression can continue for months or even years.

- Cold remedies are simple to use and readily obtained at the nearest supermarket. But appropriate treatment of depression is a prolonged process that nearly always involves one or more professionals and sometimes carefully chosen medication.

- A person with a cold isn't considered defective or weak-willed or in need of "getting his act together." But depression is a diagnosis no one wants to acknowledge or accept because of the stigma associated with having a mental disorder.

- While colds never have a fatal outcome except in the most physically frail individuals, depression can lead to the sudden and tragic ending of a life that would most likely have continued for many more years.

All of the difficulties and heartaches arising from depression apply not only to adults but also to children and adolescents, often with greater intensity. At any given time, nearly 2 percent of prepubertal children and 5 percent of teenagers are estimated to have a major depressive problem—not a brief case of "the blues" or a temporary mood swing—and that number may be conservative. What is more disturbing is that depression kills the young more frequently than it does adults. Suicide is the sixth leading cause of death in children between the ages of five and fourteen and the third leading cause of death among those between the ages of fifteen and twenty-four, claiming the lives of at least five thousand teenagers every year in the United States. The number may actually be higher, because many accidents (such as drug overdoses, drownings, or fatal automobile crashes involving a lone teenage driver) may in fact be suicides. The suicide rate among the young has risen dramatically since the late 1960s; among fifteen- to nineteen-year-olds it has doubled, while among ten- to fourteen-year-olds it has tripled.[25]

A 1991 study by the Centers for Disease Control and Prevention found that 27 percent of the high school students surveyed had considered suicide, 16 percent had made a specific suicide plan, 8 percent had made a suicide attempt, and 2 percent had inflicted enough damage during a suicide attempt to require medical attention. Females attempt suicide four times more frequently than males. However, because young males are more likely to utilize violent methods (such as leaping from an overpass or using a gun), their suicide attempts are four times more likely to be fatal than those of females.

What Is Depression?

In our culture the term *depression* is applied to a broad spectrum of situations in which a person feels unhappy. Here, however, we are dealing specifically with **clinical depression**—not a temporary emotional slump, such as after watching a sad movie or receiving a traffic ticket or even after a day in which one thing after another goes sour. Clinical depression involves a *persistent* and usually *disruptive* disturbance of mood and often affects other bodily functions as well. As we list the common characteristics of depression, it is important to note that these may manifest themselves quite differently in children and adolescents from how they appear in adults. In fact, because the behaviors provoked by depression are frequently confused with the normal emotional and physical upheavals of growing up, at one time it was erroneously assumed that this condition occurred rarely, if at all, before adulthood. In each symptom category we will mention some of the unique variations seen in young people who are depressed.

A persistent sad or negative mood

Most parents may at some point, if not frequently, complain that their teenager has a "lousy attitude." As described in chapters one and two, it isn't at all unusual for adolescents to experience emotions and mood swings that seem out of proportion to the circumstances. But the depressed teenager seems to be in a perpetual slump.

Unfortunately, you won't hear a young person say, "In case you haven't noticed, I've been depressed for the past several weeks." Instead, you may see any of a number of the following signals that would appear disconnected:

- Continued overt sadness or moping, which may be accompanied by frequent episodes of crying.
- A loss of enthusiasm or interest in things that were once favorite activities.
- Increasing withdrawal and isolation from family and friends.
- Poor school performance: plummeting grades, loss of interest in schoolwork, and frequent absences.
- Outbursts of anger, arguing, disrespectful comments, or blatant hostility toward everyone at home.
- Repeated complaints about being bored or tired.
- Overt acting out: drug or alcohol use, running away, sexual activity, fighting, vandalism, or other antisocial activity.

This does not mean, of course, that all negative attitudes and actions are manifestations of depression. But a component of appropriate parental corrective action should be a willingness to entertain this possibility when an adolescent displays an unexpected and persistent disturbance in behavior.

Painful thoughts

If we compare depression to a very long, sad song, the mood disturbance just described is the mournful or agitated music. But accompanying the unhappy melody are painful lyrics—words that express, over and over again, a view of life that is anything but upbeat.

People who have experienced both depression and bodily injuries (for example, a major fracture) usually will confirm that physical pain is easier to manage than emotional pain. Usually one can expect physical pain to resolve or at least become tolerable. But no such hopeful expectation accompanies painful thoughts, which can roll into the mind like waves from an ocean that extends to a limitless, bleak horizon.

Painful thoughts, like a disturbed mood, can have several manifestations:

- *Relentless introspection.* Adolescents tend to be highly self-conscious during the normal (and necessary) process of establishing their identity during their transition into adulthood. But depression magnifies and warps this natural introspection into a mental inquisition. The inward gaze not only becomes a relentless stare, but it focuses exclusively on shortcomings. It can also move into some dangerous territory: "Wouldn't I and everyone else be better off if I weren't here? Why does it matter at this point whether I live or die?"
- *Negative self-concept.* Physical appearance, intelligence, competence, acceptance, and general worth are all subject to relentless and exaggerated criticism. This is not a healthy examination of areas that need improvement, nor repentance for wrongdoing that might lead to improvements in attitude and behavior. Instead, unrealistic self-reproach for whatever isn't going well in life—or, at the opposite extreme,

spreading blame to everyone else—is likely to dominate a depressed adolescent's thoughts and interfere with positive changes.

A depressed teenager slumps into a lunchroom chair and moans, "I'm fat. I'm never gonna get a date. I'm stupid. I'll never pass algebra. I feel miserable. I'm never going to feel good again." Her friends, if they bother to hang around and listen to this litany of woe, may argue with her. "You're not stupid. Stop talking that way." If she persists in her lament, they may become fed up and agree with her, if only to end her complaints: "Okay, so you're fat and stupid. C'mon, we're gonna be late for class." Her parents might unwittingly make a similar mistake in trying to bolster her spirits: "What are you talking about? You look fine to us, and you're smart. That's enough of this negative talk!" Such responses only build feelings of rejection and a conviction that "no one understands me."

This state of affairs will be drastically worsened for those who have been subjected to emotional, physical, or sexual abuse during childhood or adolescence. Whether these assaults attack the heart ("You're so stupid!" "Why can't you be like _____ ?") or the body, they create a sense of worthlessness that supplies powerful fuel for an ongoing depression.

- *Anxiety.* Persistent worry, whether focused on a specific issue or a free-floating apprehension that encompasses most daily activities, frequently accompanies depression. While a modest level of concern is not only normal but in fact necessary to motivate appropriate precautions for everyday activities, the anxiety associated with depression is disabling and actually interferes with effective responses to life's challenges.

- *Hopelessness.* This is particularly troublesome for adolescents, not only because they may feel emotions so strongly, but also because they haven't lived long enough to understand the ebb and flow of life's problems and pleasures. Most adults facing a crisis will think back to the last twenty-seven crises they have already lived through and will have gained enough perspective to know that this current trial will probably pass as well. But when young people collide with a crisis (or at least what appears to be one from their perspective), they usually have far fewer experiences with which to compare it and a limited fund of responses. If they can't see a satisfactory route past the current problem, it is no wonder they might begin to think that their "life is over" or "not worth living." This dark view of life isn't helped by some powerful voices in adolescent popular culture (especially in music) that focus on rage, alienation, despair, and death.

Physical symptoms

No emotional event occurs without the body participating, and it should come as little surprise that physical symptoms accompany depression. Common problems include:

- *Insomnia and other sleep disturbances.* Difficulty falling asleep at night, awakening too early in the morning, and fitful sleep in between are very common in depressed individuals. This may be accompanied by a desire to sleep during the day. Some have **hypersomnia** (sleeping for excessively long periods of time), in which sleep seems to serve as an escape from the misery of waking hours. An important sign that depression is improving is the normalization of sleeping patterns.
- *Appetite changes.* Loss of appetite and weight or nonstop hunger and weight gain are not uncommon during depression. Such changes can complicate an adolescent's normal concerns about appearance.
- *Physiological problems.* Depressed individuals often have a variety of physical complaints. Fatigue is almost universally present. Headaches, dizziness, nausea, abdominal cramps, episodes of shortness of breath, and heart palpitations are not at all unusual. Sometimes poor concentration, unusual pain patterns, or altered sensations in various parts of the body will raise concerns about a serious medical disorder. Very often an evaluation for an assortment of symptoms will uncover no evidence of an underlying disease but will lead an attentive physician to suspect depression. The absence

of a serious diagnosis may bring a sigh of relief to a young patient (and most certainly to his parents) but can also cause dismay. "Are you saying all of this is in my (my kid's) head?" is a typical response. In fact, the symptoms are very real and a predictable component of depression. When depression improves with treatment, so do the physical symptoms.

Delusional thinking

Very rarely, a severe case of depression will also involve delusional thinking, in which the individual's beliefs and sensory experiences do not match with reality. He may hear voices or have hallucinations. He might believe that others are trying to harm him or entertain grandiose ideas about his identity or purpose in life. This is not merely a depression but a **psychosis,** a serious disorder of neurochemical function in the brain that must be treated with appropriate medication. (Hospitalization is often required at the outset.) Many psychotic individuals require lifelong medication to prevent a relapse.

Why Do Adolescents Become Depressed?

A complex blend of genetic, biochemical, personal, family, and spiritual factors can interact to cause depression. These include:

- *Genetics and biochemistry.* For a great many individuals, depression is primarily the result of a malfunction of **neurotransmitters,** compounds (such as serotonin) that participate in the electrochemical communication between nerve cells in the brain. Very often the vulnerability to a neurotransmitter disturbance appears to have a genetic origin, such that a number of members of the same family may be affected. This vulnerability, among other things, accounts for an individual becoming depressed for no apparent reason or struggling with depression throughout life.
- *Personal and family events.* A person who is brought up in an atmosphere of love, stability, encouragement, and consistent boundaries will usually see his world differently and interact with it more successfully than one who has lived with abuse, indifference, or chaos. For many individuals depression is

deeply rooted in early childhood experiences that taught them that the world is a dangerous place where no one can be trusted.

- *Recent stresses and reversals.* One or more major losses or traumatic events can set off a depressive episode (often referred to as a **reactive depression**) that is more prolonged and profound than the normal grieving process. Examples of such stressful events are a severe illness or death of a parent or other loved one (or even a pet); parental separation, divorce, or remarriage; a move from a familiar home; one or more episodes of physical or sexual abuse; a natural disaster; war or violence in the community; difficulty or failure in school or an athletic pursuit; the breakup of a close friendship or romantic relationship; a severe or chronic illness.
- *Personal and family faith.* A meaningful relationship with God and a sense of His love and involvement in an individual's life can have a significant stabilizing effect on mood and behavior. An ongoing personal commitment to God and positive connections with others who are caring and like-minded in faith serve to build a teenager's emotional world on a firm foundation, such that it will not crumble when the inevitable strains and storms of life arrive. Unfortunately, some religious situations involving intense legalism or an atmosphere of continuing condemnation can contribute to anxiety and depression.

What Can Be Done about Depression?

A parent's role in dealing with depression can be broken down into three key tasks:

Be alert for signs of depression.

These have already been listed, but it bears emphasizing that *parents are often caught off guard by their adolescent's depression.* This disorder can occur even in the most stable home where teenagers have been reared by devoted parents who provide consistent love and limits. Remember that for many individuals depression is caused primarily by a biochemical imbalance in the brain and not by bad parenting or a personal crisis. Don't assume that "it can't happen in our home" because in doing so, you might ignore or write off as a "bad attitude" significant changes in mood or behavior that desperately need your attention.

If you suspect that your adolescent might be depressed or suicidal, seek appropriate help immediately.

Depression is not a character weakness or a sign of parental failure. It is as important and *treatable* a problem as diabetes or asthma, and like those conditions, it can lead to serious consequences—including death—if it is ignored. The approaches to this problem include:

First and foremost, listen carefully to your teenager, and take his feelings and problems seriously. One study of suicidal adolescents indicated that 90 percent felt that they were not understood by their families. Expressions of worry or a sad mood should never be met with indifference or (worse) a shallow rebuff ("You'll get over it" or "Snap out of it!"). Sit down, shut off the TV, look your son or daughter in the eye, and hear what he or she has to say—without judging, rebuking, or trivializing it. It might help enormously if you can say honestly that you (or others you know and respect) have struggled with some of the same feelings.

Get a physician's evaluation. Usually a number of physical symptoms such as fatigue or headaches will need to be assessed, and rarely a specific disorder (for example, thyroid abnormalities) will be responsible for the entire gamut of emotional and physical complaints.

Get counseling with a qualified individual about the issues of life, including past problems, family interactions, stressful situations, and other concerns. This should be carried out with someone who is trained to do this type of work with young people and who also shares your basic values. Do not assume that a depression can be "straightened out" in one or two counseling sessions. Normally several weeks (sometimes months) of work will be necessary. Be prepared to become involved yourself at some point in the process. No depression occurs in a vacuum, and family dynamics very often are part of both the problem and the solution.

Be willing to consider medication. This can play a very important role in the treatment of depression. **Antidepressants** can normalize disturbances in neurotransmitter function and are neither addictive nor an "escape from reality." On the contrary, more often than not they allow the individual to tackle life issues much more effectively, and they greatly accelerate the recovery process. The decision to use medication and the choice of a particular agent will involve careful discussion with a primary-care physician or psychiatrist who can prescribe it and monitor its effects. Assuming that positive results are obtained, it is common to continue medication on a maintenance basis for a number of months. (The neurochemistry of depression is not like a streptococcal throat infection that can be resolved with ten days of treatment.)

Be willing to consider hospitalization. In severe cases, where the emotions have been extremely unstable or there has been suicidal behavior, hospitalization will usually be recommended in order to initiate treatment and ensure safety. The type of program utilized will vary considerably, depending on community resources, health insurance benefits, and the needs of the depressed individual.

Continue to support and pray for your depressed teenager. He needs to know that you are there for him and that you do not think of him as "crazy" or a colossal failure for having this problem. Prayer serves as an acknowledgment by parent and child that God alone has a complete understanding of this complex situation. Counseling and medication may serve as useful tools, but they are best used under His guidance.

Be on the lookout for risks of suicide and signs of suicidal behavior. Many of the unique features of depression among young people also increase their risk of suicide. In particular, the intensity of their emotions and a shortage of life experiences that might allow them to imagine a hopeful future beyond an immediate crisis may give rise to self-destructive behavior, especially on an impulsive basis. In order to reduce the chance of a tragic loss of life, be aware of not only the signs of depression, which have already been listed, but also of the following risks and warning signs:

- *A previous suicide attempt.* This is considered the most significant predictor of a future suicide; more than 40 percent of adolescents who commit suicide have attempted it at least once in the past.
- *A family history of suicide.* Compared to their nonsuicidal peers, teenagers who kill themselves are five times more likely to have a history of a family member who has committed suicide.
- *Expressions of intense guilt or hopelessness.*
- *Threatening, talking, or joking about suicide.* It is important to have a heart-to-heart conversation with any adolescent who makes comments such as "I would be better off dead" or "Nothing matters anymore." Find out what is going on in his life and how he is feeling, and make it clear that you are committed to obtaining whatever help he might need to work through his problems. Broaching the subject of suicide does *not* encourage it, but rather increases the likelihood that a successful intervention can be started.
- *"Cleaning house."* You should be very concerned and should investigate immediately if a teenager—whether your own or a member of someone else's family—begins to give away favorite possessions, clothing, entire CD or tape collections, etc. This is a common behavior among young people who are planning suicide.
- *A gun in the home.* Among young people, more suicides are carried out using firearms than by any other method. If anyone in your family—especially a teenager—is having a problem with depression, remove all guns from the home and keep them out.
- *Alcohol or drug abuse.* One frightening aspect of substance abuse is that it can trigger erratic, self-destructive behavior for which little or no warning was given. A mild depression can suddenly plummet to suicidal intensity with the help of drugs or alcohol. Because of the unpredictable actions of chemicals on the system, a number of deaths occur among youngsters who did not intend to hurt themselves.

- *Suicide among other adolescents in your community.* Occasionally one or more suicides in a community or school will precipitate a disastrous "cluster" of self-destructive behavior among local teens.
- *A sudden, major loss or humiliation.* All of the stressful life events that were listed earlier in this section—death of a loved one, parental separation, failing an important test, etc.—not only can provoke a depressive episode but can also precipitate an unexpected suicide attempt.

If you feel that there is any possibility of a self-destructive act by your teenager, it is important that you not only express your concern but also *seek help immediately.* You may want to contact your adolescent's physician for advice or referral. If anyone in your family has dealt with a counselor, this individual may be the appropriate initial contact. Many communities have a mental-health center that offers on-the-spot assessment of an individual's suicide risk or even an assessment team that will come to your home. *Stay with your adolescent* (or make certain that he or she remains in the company of a responsible adult) until you have reasonable assurance from a qualified individual and a clear commitment from your son or daughter that suicide is not going to be attempted. In situations where assurance cannot be obtained, the suicidal individual may need to be hospitalized for safety, further assessment, and the initiation of treatment. You will also need to take appropriate safety precautions, including removing any guns from the home and controlling access to medications.

What If a Teenager Attempts Suicide?

Fortunately, the vast majority of suicide attempts by adolescents are unsuccessful. Some of these result in significant medical problems, while many are considered gestures or cries for help. *Any deliberate self-destructive act, whether planned or impulsive, should be taken very seriously, regardless of the severity of the outcome.* An evaluation at an emergency department should be carried out; subsequent hospitalization for medical treatment or observation is not uncommon.

After any medical problems have been resolved, a formal assessment by a qualified professional is mandatory. The course of action to be taken will depend upon a number of factors and may range from ongoing counseling while the adolescent remains at home to a formal treatment program in a psychiatric hospital setting. The latter approach is usually chosen both to ensure safety and to begin intensive treatment. While the details of treatment that might be used in such settings are beyond the scope of this book, it is important for parents to understand and approve of the approaches that will be used and to play an active role in their adolescent's recovery process. As upset or guilty as you might feel under such circumstances, this is the time to draw close to your teenager who is in such pain and not to communicate shock and dismay ("How could you do such a thing?"). Above all, he will need loving and optimistic people on his team, and it will help immensely if his parents are at the top of the roster.

CHAPTER 10

Nutritional Issues in Preteens and Adolescents

In a world of hectic schedules that tend to replace home cooking with entrées from the freezer or meals from the nearest fast-food franchise, it can be challenging for teens to obtain the proper nourishment for their bodies on a day-to-day basis. Poor eating choices combined with physical inactivity can also lead to excessive weight. Additionally, poor nutrition can result in slowed growth, loss of appetite, decreased energy and endurance, and increased susceptibility to colds and other types of infection.

To help individuals make healthy food choices, the U.S. Department of Agriculture, in conjunction with the U.S. Department of Health and Human Services, has developed the **Food Guide Pyramid** (see following page). This diagram illustrates the various components of a healthy diet, based on five broad categories of foods. Food groups are arranged so that those from which more servings should be eaten daily are at the bottom. At the base of the pyramid, corresponding to a proper foundation for a healthy diet, are grain foods, including breads, rice, pasta, and cereals. Next come the fruit and vegetable groups. Higher up the pyramid is the dairy group, which includes milk, yogurt, and cheese. Also at this level is the meat, poultry, and fish group (which also includes beans, eggs, and nuts, other good sources of protein). At the top of the pyramid are fats, oils, and sweets, which should be consumed sparingly.

Proper energy consumption (intake of calories) is essential for adolescent growth and development. About 2,800 calories per day is appropriate for most teenage boys; 2,200 calories per day will be sufficient for most teen girls. These amounts may need to increase if your teen is more active or athletic. There is a great temptation among weight-conscious young people to avoid calories as much as possible. While weight control depends upon keeping caloric intake equal to energy expenditure (or less than expenditure for weight loss), a drastic reduction in calories—even when weight loss is needed—can be harmful at this time of life.

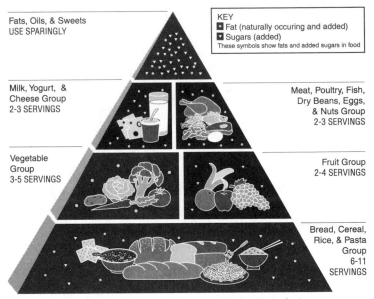

SOURCE: U.S. Department of Agriculture/U.S. Department of Health and Human Services

Below are the daily numbers of servings recommended by the USDA for the given caloric requirements.

	Daily Intake 2,2000 Calories	Daily Intake 2,800 Calories
Grain Group Servings	9	11
Vegetable Group Servings	4	5
Fruit Group Servings	3	4
Dairy Group Servings	2-3	2-3
Meat Group Servings (ounces)	6	7
Total Fat (grams)	73	93

Food labels indicate how much of a given food makes up a single serving.

While the Food Guide Pyramid provides broad guidelines, each adolescent's nutritional needs are ultimately determined by growth and developmental stage, as well as height, weight, gender, and level of physical activity. Your teenager's physician or a registered dietician can provide more specific information about your teen's nutritional needs and the foods which will best meet them. In addition, a number of Web sites provide useful and straightforward information about nutrition for all age groups. These include the American Dietetic Association's Web site (www.eatright.org) and the USDA's dietary guidelines at www.usda.gov/cnpp/DietGd.pdf. To review **the recommended daily allowance (RDA)** for a number of nutrients (including vitamins and minerals) check the American Society for Nutritional Sciences' Web site at www.nutrition.org/nutinfo.

A few nutritional requirements are worthy of special note:

- *Protein.* The body breaks down dietary proteins into their component building blocks called amino acids, which are then converted into new proteins used for building and maintaining a variety of structures, including muscle. If your child is growing, athletic, or extremely active, he may need more protein than usual. Meat, poultry, fish, nuts, milk products, and eggs are good protein sources. Legumes and beans are among the best vegetable sources of protein. However, vegetable proteins generally do not supply essential amino acids (amino acids that the body cannot produce and must obtain from the diet) in the optimal ratios. Therefore those who follow a vegetarian diet must consume vegetable sources of protein in greater quantity and variety to make up for any potential deficit.

- *Iron.* This mineral is vital to the production of red blood cells. Young people, especially girls who are menstruating, may become anemic—that is, suffer from a deficiency of red blood cells—if they fail to obtain sufficient iron from their food. Dietary sources of iron include meat, poultry, fish, grain products, leafy green vegetables, legumes, and soy. Although most iron obtained from vegetable sources is not easily absorbed, Vitamin C can enhance its uptake.

- *Calcium.* This mineral is required for healthy teeth and bones. Calcium can be obtained from a variety of sources, including skim milk, fortified soy milk, fortified orange juice, cottage cheese, yogurt, and dark leafy vegetables.
- *Fats.* While everyone needs some amount of fat in their diet, most Americans eat far too much. Overconsumption of fats is linked with obesity, heart disease, and increased risk for certain types of cancer. Adopting an informed view of dietary fats at an early age may yield dividends for your teen for decades to come.

Nutrition experts suggest that adults and older teens keep their dietary calories from fat at 30 percent or less of their total caloric intake. Many teens and adults consume a lot more than that—indeed, avoiding a surplus of dietary fat in our culture requires some degree of effort, despite the fact that supermarket shelves seem to abound with low-fat products. A typical fast-food meal—a favorite choice among teens because of convenience and/or hectic schedules—can easily contain more than one thousand calories, of which about half are derived from fat. The problem is intensified by the fact that most Americans, teenagers included, simply like the taste of fats. In addition, compared ounce-per-ounce to carbohydrates, fats contain more than twice as many calories. In other words, a relatively small amount of fat contains a lot of calories—a problem when fat calories should represent a minority of calories in the diet.

Helping your teen avoid fat might seem daunting, but it can be simpler than you think. When buying groceries, be careful in your selection of foods and read the labels on the packaging. Substitute fish and chicken for red meat when possible, and when choosing meats, buy only lean cuts. Use low-fat or skim milk instead of whole milk. Likewise, encourage teens to be discriminating when dining out.

While the majority of the world's children suffer from a chronic lack of adequate food to sustain normal growth and development, the most common nutritional disorder among children and adolescents in developed countries is an excess of body fat. In some ways, this is not surprising. When food is abundant, it is not unusual to eat more than is really needed to relieve hunger. Furthermore, eating will occur for a host of reasons that have little to do with appetite, such as providing emotional pleasure and comfort. Eating is also a common response to excitement, boredom, anger, depression, or simply an accompaniment to virtually any form of relaxation or social gathering.

Our bodies are designed primarily for surviving the ebb and flow of an unstable food supply. When more food arrives than is immediately needed, intricate biochemical processes see to it that the leftovers are stored as fat for use during the next famine. If a famine never arrives, the excess fat becomes a permanent resident and continues to accumulate.

Modern technology has provided a multitude of labor-saving devices and beguiling passive entertainments, all of which promote much more sitting and watching than active muscle motion. A great many grade-school children, adolescents, and adults have thus moved from the perpetual motion of their toddler years to a sedentary lifestyle that does not maintain even a basic level of exercise. As a result, excessive body fat is a continuing physical and emotional problem for millions of children and adolescents.

At the same time, powerful cultural forces provoke behaviors that pose even more serious threats to the young. We are saturated night and day with powerful images of beautiful, shapely, impossibly sleek women or buff, tight-muscled masculinity. This leads many, especially prepubertal and adolescent girls, into dangerous thinking: *If only I could look like* that, *my problems would be over.* Often this fantasy fuels a deeply felt desire for physical perfection that collides rudely with the imperfect appearance of a very real body seen in the mirror. The conflict can lead not only to erratic eating habits and dieting, which are not without some risks, but also to the more severely disordered eating patterns known as bulimia and anorexia nervosa, which can rob an adolescent of health or life itself.

What If Your Teenager Becomes a Vegetarian?

In recent years, vegetarianism has become a more popular trend among American teens. A 1995 Roper poll commissioned by the Vegetarian Resource Group found that 11 percent of girls aged thirteen to seventeen years old do not eat red meat, while the number of boys in that age-group abstaining from meat is 5 percent. The percentage of teens abstaining completely from meat, poultry, and seafood is lower—1.4 percent.[6] To some, adolescent vegetarianism represents an encouraging trend toward health consciousness among young people. Others are concerned about eating disorders or, at the very least, inadequate nutrition.

Why do some adolescents choose vegetarianism? Surveys have determined a number of reasons:

- Vegetarianism appears to be a healthier choice.
- Controlling weight seems easier on a meat-free diet.
- Dislike for the taste of meat.
- Ethical aversion to the killing of animals.
- Influence from vegetarian friends.

Additionally, some religions emphasize the merits of vegetarianism. These include Seventh-day Adventists as well as Eastern religions such as Buddhism and certain forms of Hinduism.

Not all vegetarians follow the same dietary pattern, and several options of vegetarianism are available. Individuals who abstain from all forms of animal flesh (meat, poultry, and seafood) and other animal products (dairy and eggs) are known as *vegans*. Some extreme vegans even refuse to eat honey or foods prepared with yeast. Other forms of vegetarianism are less strict. *Ovolactovegetarians*, for example, avoid animal flesh but will consume eggs and dairy products. *Ovovegetarians* and *lactovegetarians* will eat, along with plant foods, eggs or dairy products, respectively. *Pescetarians* include fish in their diet.

The benefits of a vegetarian diet

Professional groups such as the American Dietetic Association affirm the healthful benefits of *appropriately planned* meat-excluding diets. Vegetarian nutritional regimes are generally low in saturated fats and cholesterol, and high in fiber. Additionally, vegetarian teens are more likely than their nonvegetarian counterparts to eat more fruits and vegetables and eat fewer foods that are high in salt, fats, and sugar.

Research indicates that vegetarian diets offer protection against coronary artery disease and tend to lower serum cholesterol and triglyceride levels. Vegetarians enjoy lower rates of hypertension, type II diabetes, and gallstones; risks for lung cancer and colorectal cancer are substantially reduced as well. Vegetarians also have a lower incidence of obesity and constipation.

So what's to worry about?

Given the potential benefits of a well-balanced vegetarian diet, why are many parents concerned about their teens' avoidance of meat? One reason is that many teens who adopt vegetarianism do so to cut calories from their diet. While this may be an accept-

continued

able option in certain circumstances, reports suggest that some teens use vegetarianism as a façade to hide anorexic eating behaviors. By going vegetarian, teens with eating disorders legitimize their behaviors by increasing the number of foods to be excluded from their diet. One study showed that although vegetarian teens ate more fruits and vegetables than their nonvegetarian peers, vegetarians were twice as likely to diet frequently, four times as likely to diet intensively, and eight times as likely to abuse laxatives—all behaviors associated with eating disorders.

Even if a teen is not disposed toward an eating disorder, parents may rightly be concerned about whether their child would get proper nutrition from a vegetarian diet. Adolescence is a time of rapid growth and change, and nutritional needs are high. Indeed, most American kids are getting less than optimal nutrition, whether or not they eat meat. One study showed that only 1 percent of children aged two through nineteen ate enough from the five food groups, and 16 percent met none of the USDA's nutritional guidelines.[7] When animal foods, and possibly eggs and milk products as well, are removed from the diet, there may be reasonable concern that a teen's nutritional needs will not be satisfied.

Adolescent development requires adequate amounts of various nutrients as well as a caloric intake that might not be obtained from a poorly planned vegetarian pattern of eating. Vegan diets, for example, generally have a lower total protein content than omnivorous diets, and unless proper steps are taken to ensure the inclusion of the right foods in their diet, teens might lack the protein their changing bodies need. The need for protein is even greater if an adolescent is athletic. Fortunately, protein and essential amino acid requirements can be met with a proper assortment and intake of plant foods. In the same way, nutritional deficiencies of iron, calcium, zinc, and Vitamins D and B-12—valuable nutrients that might not be adequately obtained with a haphazard vegan diet—can be avoided when a proper balance of foods is eaten regularly. The key to healthy vegetarianism is, as with any diet, variety and careful planning.

What should you do if your child wants to adopt a vegetarian diet?

First, it's important to learn why she wants to pursue vegetarianism. Most vegetarians choose this lifestyle because of personal tastes, health reasons, or because of ethical concerns over the treatment of animals—not because they have an eating disorder. To gain a better understanding of her perspective, sit down with her and talk about it. If she launches into a discourse about the immorality of eating animal flesh, you might not share her viewpoint but at least her response is less likely to suggest an eating disorder than if she goes on at length about the number of calories and grams of fat in a slab of beef. Likewise, observe your teen's eating habits, before and after the exclusion of meat. If you notice any behaviors or trends that raise concerns (see pages 238-241), contact your teen's physician for help.

If your teen is serious about exploring vegetarianism in a healthy fashion, talk with her about her nutritional needs. Allow her as much freedom as possible in drawing up plans to meet her body's requirements. As you do so, bear in mind the following dietary necessities.

continued

- *Calories.* Many people think of calories as an attendant evil of food that serves only to widen hips. In fact, calories represent energy, which is especially needed in young men and women. Calories are necessary for growth in all teens, and active or athletic teens need even more calories. The USDA recommends that most teen girls need to consume about 2,200 calories each day; most teen boys require around 2,800 calories.

  Vegetarian diets tend to be lower in calories than omnivorous diets, and high-fiber fruits and vegetables may fill the stomach without providing necessary calories. Avocados, nuts, seeds, dried fruits, and soy products are all concentrated sources of calories.

- *Protein.* Protein is necessary for building and maintaining muscle. When protein intake is neglected, muscle mass may decrease relative to body fat. Good sources of protein include peanut butter, nuts, legumes, grains, and soy products. Dairy products and eggs are also excellent sources of protein.

- *Vitamin D.* This vitamin, normally produced in the body in response to exposure to sunlight, is necessary for building strong bones and teeth. Most teens who are regularly exposed to sunlight have adequate amounts of Vitamin D. Darker-skinned adolescents and those who spend less time in the sun may need supplemental Vitamin D. Sources include fortified cow's milk and certain brands of soy milk, as well as some cereals.

- *Vitamin B-12.* While animal foods are often rich in this vitamin, there are no good vegetable sources. Vegans are at high risk for Vitamin B-12 deficit, and even ovolactovegetarians may not get as much as they need. Fortified soy milk, breakfast cereals, and nutritional yeast can provide necessary amounts of this nutrient.

- *Calcium.* Required for healthy teeth and bones, calcium can be obtained from a variety of sources, including cow's milk, fortified soy milk, fortified orange juice, and dark leafy vegetables.

- *Iron.* Anemia is a common problem among individuals deficient in this mineral. Iron is available from many plant sources, including fortified grain products, legumes, and green leafy vegetables. Although iron contained in plant foods is not as readily available to the body as that found in meat, eating foods rich in Vitamin C can help improve the body's absorption of iron from vegetable sources.

- *Zinc.* Deficiencies of this trace mineral, found primarily in animal foods, may be linked to poor appetite and slowed growth. Good vegetarian sources of zinc include tofu, nuts, whole grains, wheat germ, and legumes.

Note that the vitamins and minerals listed above can also be obtained from most multivitamin supplements.

Keeping a food diary is an excellent way to track dietary patterns and can help your teen make sure she's getting enough of what she needs. For more information about healthy vegetarian options and foods, consult the American Dietary Association (www.eatright.org). Consulting with your teen's doctor or a registered dietitian may also be very helpful.   *by David Davis*

While the issues relating to excessive weight and eating disorders cannot all be covered in depth in this book, this section will review key concepts that can help adolescents—and their parents—begin moving in the right direction if one of these problems is already present.

Dealing with Excessive Weight

Twenty to 30 percent of American children and adolescents are estimated to be **overweight**, which is traditionally defined as 10 to 20 percent over "ideal" (a better term would be "appropriate") weight[26] for age and height or **obese** (more than 20 percent over appropriate weight). It is important to understand that the significance of a given weight depends not only upon age and height but also on general build and percentage of body fat. For example, a muscular, well-conditioned athlete may technically weigh more than the ideal amount for his height, but his percentage of body fat may be normal or even low. For this reason, another indicator of weight is often used which compensates somewhat for variations in build. Body Mass Index, or BMI, is the ratio of a person's weight to the square of her height ($\frac{wt.}{ht^2}$).

Normally height and weight are entered on a growth chart as part of routine physical examinations, and very often a look at the pattern of these measurements over a period of time can clarify concerns about an adolescent's weight. If your teenager is more than 20 percent overweight, or in the 95th percentile or higher for BMI, a medical evaluation is appropriate, whether as part of a regular checkup or during a special visit. While it is unlikely that the doctor will find a treatable disease that is responsible for the weight problem, it is most important to seek help and begin to work with the teen on this problem for the following reasons:

- Eating and weight patterns established in childhood and adolescence tend to persist into adulthood. The longer the problem continues, the more the odds against reaching a normal adult weight worsen. One in four obese children entering adolescence will eventually reach a normal weight, but only one in twenty-eight who are obese at the end of adolescence will accomplish this goal.[27]

- Long-standing obesity is associated with a host of health problems later in life, including elevated blood pressure, stroke, diabetes, gall bladder disease, and painful destructive changes in joints.
- Even more significant for adolescents is the cruel and relentless psychological (and at times even physical) abuse that they nearly always receive from peers. Name calling, isolation, and other forms of social brutality are the order of the day for the overweight adolescent, leaving emotional wounds that could take years to heal—if they ever do.

Once medical causes and/or effects of obesity have been assessed, specific nutritional guidelines should be obtained from a qualified professional. If at all possible, this input should be provided by a registered dietitian who works with young people, since weight management for adolescents who are still growing is not a simple matter of "just eat less" or "just go on a diet." *Indeed, food restrictions that leave a preteen or teenager constantly hungry are potentially harmful, both physically and emotionally.* Even if you or some other member of the family has benefited from a specific eating plan or weight-loss program, do not impose that program on your adolescent. Her physiology and situation are unique, and any program she undertakes should be under the guidance of a physician and/or nutrition counselor. The amounts and types of foods must be adequate to meet her ongoing needs for growth and development, while at the same time allowing either for gradual loss of weight, holding it level, or slowing its rate of increase. Mapping out the appropriate changes requires some expertise.

A dietitian might ask you and your teenager to keep a detailed food diary for two or three weeks before attempting any dietary modifications. This can provide insight into the relationship between eating patterns and the current weight. Often the overweight adolescent is not consuming more calories than her lean counterpart, and this observation will need to be considered in the course of nutritional planning. The diary may also reveal specific food choices that are contributing to the weight problem.

How parents can help their overweight teenager

Once reasonable goals have been set and a basic course mapped out, there are a number of contributions parents can make to help their teen achieve a proper weight:

Be supportive and matter-of-fact about what needs to be done. *The last thing an overweight adolescent needs is another critic.* Whatever insults he hasn't heard from an insensitive cohort at school he has probably said to himself. Harping on the weight problem not only adds to the shame, guilt, and self-loathing, but it may even push him toward more extreme and destructive eating behaviors.

Instill the concept of making wise food choices for life rather than just "going on a diet." A diet has a lot in common with a jail sentence— a time of deprivation resulting from a crime (eating too much). When the sentence is served, very often it's back to business as usual. Furthermore, after the body has been deprived through a diet, it may become even more efficient at storing fat. As a result, the dieter can actually gain back more weight than she lost.

Give your teenager as much responsibility as possible in his food choices, appropriate with his age. You can only push the right food choices for so long. Eventually he will need to make the process his own and enforce his own decisions. The sooner this happens, the better.

Model healthy eating habits. Leading by example is much more effective than giving a lot of directions. Because of genetics, lifestyle, or both, it is not unusual for more than one family member to be struggling with extra pounds. The choices that benefit the overweight adolescent will most likely be helpful for everyone else around the table.

Help your teenager avoid temptation. It's easier to make healthy food choices when healthy foods are the only kinds available. If the shelves at home are stocked with calorie-dense, high-fat snacks and sweets, don't expect any great progress. Are there family habits or traditions, such as eating continuously while watching TV or playing a video game, that are contributing to the problem?

Encourage and model physical activity. Many overweight adolescents are also very inactive. The goal should be to find an activity such as walking, cycling, jogging, swimming, or basketball that increases oxygen consumption continuously for fifteen to thirty minutes most days of the week. If this means converting some time spent in front of TV and video games into exercise, all the better for both body and mind. Needless to say, all of your encouragement to "go outside and get some exercise" will be much more meaningful if you are doing likewise.

Eating Disorders

While eating and body image are sources of concern or exasperation for millions of people, for some they become the focus of extreme and potentially dangerous behavior. According to the American Psychiatric Association, at any given time roughly a half million people in the United States are affected with an eating disorder. Of these, 95 percent are young women between the ages of twelve and twenty-five, most from middle- or upper-income families. (These conditions are rarely seen in developing countries.) Athletes, models, dancers, and others in the entertainment industry are at particular risk, usually because of intense concern over maintaining a particular, often unrealistic, appearance or level of performance.

The two most common eating disorders, other than obesity, are **anorexia nervosa** and **bulimia nervosa.**

Anorexia nervosa

Anorexia nervosa is a condition of self-imposed starvation that eventually leads to a body weight at least 15 percent below the expected level for an individual's age and height. It is characterized by an extreme fear of gaining weight and a striking disturbance of body image; the anorexic who appears grossly emaciated will look in the mirror and see herself as overweight. This distorted perception typically is stubbornly resistant to feedback from families, friends, and health professionals, even in the face of serious physical and medical consequences.

As more weight is lost, the fear of gaining weight intensifies rather than diminishes, leading to nonstop preoccupation with eating and weight. Behaviors that are called **obsessive-compulsive** often attend this disorder. What little food is eaten will usually be derived only from "safe" low-calorie sources, often measured out in precise quantities and then consumed in an exacting, almost ritualistic manner. Food might be cut into tiny pieces and then arranged and rearranged on the plate to give the impression that some of it has been eaten. Anorexics may obsess over the number of calories they consume from medication or even from licking a postage stamp. Often they carefully monitor body measurements such as upper arm circumference. The fervor with which calories are restricted is frequently applied to burning them as well, and an anorexic individual might exercise vigorously for hours every day. Other efforts to rid the body of calories may include "purging" behaviors, such as self-induced vomiting, which are seen more commonly in bulimia nervosa (see below).

It should come as no surprise that medical consequences, most arising from the body's attempt to conserve energy, become more serious as starvation and weight loss continue. With loss of fat and circulating estrogen, the intricate hormonal interplay of a woman's monthly cycle shuts down. (The absence of three consecutive menstrual periods is one of the diagnostic criteria for anorexia nervosa.) This, combined with an ongoing inadequate intake of nutrients and calcium, leads to loss of bone density, which can cause stress fractures, especially in the presence of intense exercise.

Starvation leads to reduced capacity of the stomach, delays in its emptying of food, and constipation, all of which may be falsely interpreted by the anorexic as gaining weight. Dry skin, thinning of the scalp hair, and development of a fine hair growth on the body called **lanugo** typically occur. Loss of fat stores and metabolic energy conservation lead to a lower body temperature, often causing the anorexic individual to wear more layers of clothing to keep warm. More serious complications arise from the heart, which typically slows its contraction rate and decreases in size in response to efforts to conserve energy. Heart rhythm might become irregular, sometimes to a degree that is life-threatening, especially in the presence of purging behavior, which depletes the body of potassium.

For all these reasons, anorexia nervosa should be considered a very serious condition with lethal risks. Between 5 and 20 percent of anorexics die from starvation, cardiac arrest, or suicide. (The higher death rates are observed among those with a long duration of anorexia, more severe weight loss, poor family support, and multiple relapses despite treatment.)

Bulimia nervosa

Bulimia nervosa is characterized by behavior known as **binging** and **purging,** which may continue for decades. During a binge, an individual quickly consumes an enormous amount of food containing many thousands of calories, often without even chewing or tasting it. The resulting physical and emotional discomfort will then provoke a purge, usually involving self-induced vomiting. Bulimics often use laxatives and diuretics (so-called water pills, medications that increase urine output)—sometimes in dangerous quantities—in a misguided belief that the medications will somehow help rid the body of the food that isn't lost through vomiting. The binging and purging cycles may occur a few times a week or, in severe cases, several times daily.

Bulimia is much more common than anorexia, but it frequently goes undetected because most episodes take place in secret and typically do not lead to significant weight loss. (However, some individuals with anorexia may engage in binge-and-purge behaviors.) Nevertheless, bulimia can have many serious medical consequences. The repeated exposure of teeth to stomach acid (during vomiting) can erode enamel, cause a yellowish discoloration, and lead to decay. The throat and esophagus might become chronically inflamed, and the salivary glands—especially the parotid glands that lie directly in front of the ears—can become enlarged in response to continuing episodes of vomiting. Repeated use of laxatives can lead to severe constipation, while heavy diuretic use may have an adverse effect on kidney function.

Potentially dangerous disturbances in heart rhythm can arise from the repeated loss of potassium from vomiting, as well as from excessive ingestion of diuretics and laxatives. Other equally serious (but fortunately uncommon) events include bleeding and even rupture of the esophagus or stomach from frequent vomiting. Food aspirated into the airway during vomiting can cause choking or pneumonia.

What Causes Eating Disorders?

What influences cause such seemingly unrewarding and even dangerous behaviors? While each case is unique, potential contributing factors include the following:

- *Cultural factors.* In developed countries, advertisements, films, videos, and TV programs continually display images of bodily perfection, especially for females. Those who are shapely, sleek, and most of all *thin* are seen as successful, sophisticated, desirable, and apparently free of emotional or personal pain. A vulnerable individual who desperately desires these attributes but cannot attain them through normal means may buy into this and thereby set in motion unhealthy and extreme behaviors.
- *Personality and psychological factors.* A typical profile of an anorexia patient is a perfectionistic, high-achieving, adolescent female. She may be seen as a compliant, "good" girl by her parents (one or both of whom might be perfectionistic also), and she usually does not rebel or even have much of a social or dating life. While excelling in many areas, she may berate herself over any performance that falls short of perfection. Some researchers theorize that refusing to eat may serve as a form of rebellion or that it may represent one area of her life over which she can exercise total control. Bulimics, on the other hand, are less predictable in personality and attributes, although alcohol or drug abuse may be a concurrent issue. In nearly all individuals with either type of eating disorder, anxiety and depression play a significant role.
- *Biochemical factors.* Chemical messengers in the brain called neurotransmitters are known to be associated with mood, emotional stability, appetite, and sleep. Many people are genetically vulnerable to changes in neurotransmitter levels,

which can lead to overt depression and anxiety disorders, as well as a condition called **obsessive-compulsive disorder (OCD)**—performing certain repetitive acts or ritualistic behaviors to relieve anxiety. Neurotransmitter imbalances appear to play a role in the origin of eating disorders, and many features of anorexia bear a striking resemblance to those of OCD.

Because eating disorders can put health and even life in serious jeopardy, they should be taken very seriously. Initiating treatment can be difficult for the bulimic, because so much of her disordered behavior goes on in secret, and for the anorexic, who may stubbornly deny that she needs help or may undermine therapeutic efforts.

In order to be effective, treatment must address a variety of issues and will often require a team approach. A thorough medical evaluation is extremely important and will sometimes reveal a variety of problems that need attention. Counseling will be needed on a long-term basis and should involve the entire family. Antidepressant medication that normalizes neurotransmitter levels can help stabilize mood, relieve depression, and reduce the obsessive component of anorexia. A dietitian should be involved to provide nutritional input and accountability. Pastoral counseling should be sought in an effort to work through issues of guilt and shame, as well as to provide a reorientation to life from God's perspective. In severe cases of anorexia, hospitalization and medically supervised refeeding may be necessary to prevent a fatal outcome.

How parents can help

It is impossible to predict who might develop an eating disorder, but it is possible for parents to reduce an adolescent's risk in the following ways:

Beware of perfectionism, especially in regard to weight or physical appearance. Your adolescent must understand that her worth and your acceptance of her are not based on physical beauty or perfect performance; your love and acceptance are, in fact, unconditional. If you have difficulty expressing this idea to your teenager, you might need to address this issue in counseling on your own.

Beware of demands on an adolescent to "make weight" for an athletic team, slim down for a cheerleading or dance team, or in some other way subject the body to stringent dietary restrictions.

Help your child understand that body shape and build have a strong genetic basis and that few are capable of attaining cover-girl status, even with intense effort.

Eliminate from your own and your family's conversations jokes or other demeaning comments about the appearance of others.

Point out to your children how advertising and other media put forth images of beauty and body image that are out of reach for nearly everyone.

Be a good role model in your own eating and exercise habits, and be careful about openly criticizing your own body appearance.

Focus on relationships and building emotional intimacy in your family, rather than on food-related issues. Be aware of the purposes beyond relieving hunger that food might be serving in your home. Is it used for comfort or reward? Is it used to relieve boredom? Be careful not to use food as a substitute for hugs and saying, "I love you."

CHAPTER 11

Preparing for Independence

If you think of parenting in the simplest of terms, it is in essence a twenty-year process of nurturing and guiding a precious human being from the utter helplessness of infancy to the independence and maturity of adulthood. Over time, it is easy to become buried in everyday concerns and lose sight of this sweeping perspective. This is unfortunate, because seeing the big picture often inspires mothers and fathers to commit themselves wholeheartedly to their parenting assignment as they grasp its profound significance and relative brevity. Two important components of this perspective are worth noting here as we begin to discuss the process of releasing your adolescent from the nest.

Parenting is a process of working yourself out of a job.
While you will probably always *feel* like a parent, your role of guidance and authority has a very definite time limit and must eventually end. You should experience a major payoff when this occurs; instead of having a dependent child for the rest of your life, you will have an adult friend whose company and conversation you will savor and who can help *you* grow as an individual. One of the most important tasks of parenting will be working with your adolescent, step by step, through this gradual release. Each teenager's pathway toward independence and each parent's willingness to grant it will be unique, and the process will not always be smooth. Judging your

adolescent's readiness for new freedoms and responsibilities is one of parenting's fine arts and should be shaped by awareness of his or her strengths and weaknesses, collaboration with your spouse (or a trusted adult if you are a single parent), soul-searching, and prayer.

Passing the baton: What will your teenagers carry
with them into adulthood?

In one very significant respect, parenting is like a relay race: One generation completes a very long lap and then passes a crucial baton to the runners in the next generation. In an Olympic relay, the gold medal usually hinges on the skill with which the baton is passed between the runners. If the baton is fumbled, the runner will still arrive at the finish line but probably with some disappointment over the final result.

Parents, grandparents, and others who are responsible for rearing the citizens of the next generation must repeatedly ask themselves some critical questions: Will this adolescent carry with him into adulthood the values that are truly important? Will these values play a significant role in his life, his career, and his own family? Will they be passed on to his own children?

Jesus asked a question which has given pause to men and women for twenty centuries: "What good will it be for a man if he gains the whole world, yet forfeits his soul?" (Matthew 16:26). A similar

What If Your Grown Child Doesn't Leave the Nest?

For all their chomping at the bit, when the moment of truth arrives, many adolescents aren't so eager or willing to leave Mom and Dad. If a grown child remains at home after the age of twenty-one or so, two important principles should be observed.

First, the arrangement must be mutually agreeable. It's one thing to let the kids know the porch light will always be on, but they also need to know that having a key to the door is a privilege, not an eternal right.

Second, and more important, the relationship between parent and adult child must be redefined. This means that you will need to insist subtly (and sometimes not so subtly) that she function as an adult. She must treat you and your property with respect, assume responsibility for her own expenses and perhaps some household expenses, do her own laundry, and clean up her messes. In other words, she must live in your house more or less with the status of an adult boarder. Treating her as though she were still in junior high school will stifle her emotional maturity and ultimately frustrate everyone under your roof.

question should be pondered regularly by parents: "What good is it if I achieve all my aspirations but my children reject the values I care about?" (For more information about raising your teens to become spiritually strong men and women, see the *Focus on the Family Parents' Guide to the Spiritual Mentoring of Teens.*)

The Basic Goals

As a parent you have been entrusted by God to help mold your adolescent's character, values, and spirituality, while preparing her for such practical matters as choosing a career, handling finances, and finding a husband or wife. This is a tall order, and we sometimes lose sight of these bigger issues while dealing with the daily details. But the important assignment of preparing her for the future can be accomplished—one small step at a time.

The first step is to define what your specific goals should be. This chapter is intended to help with that process by serving as a basic road map, one that can be reviewed every year to gauge whether your race is still on course and your baton ready to be passed. You may find the length and breadth of this endeavor daunting. *How can I instill all of my values and virtues in my teenagers? I'm still trying to develop them in my own life!* If you realize that you can't accomplish all of these goals perfectly and that you can't be an

---

continued

But requiring that she take on adult responsibilities at home also means you can no longer be in charge of her decisions. You can't set curfews, tell her what to wear, or pass judgment on her friend(s). You do have the right, however, to ask—not insist—that she keep you posted on her whereabouts as a matter of common courtesy.

You also have the right—and responsibility—to set and enforce codes of conduct under your roof. If your postadolescent offspring is making bad decisions about smoking, drinking, sex, or disorderly conduct, you can insist she do it elsewhere. You are under no obligation to facilitate self-destructive or antisocial behavior.

If house rules are respected and there is a deliberate shift from a parenting to a "benevolent landlady" mode, the situation can be both pleasant and mutually beneficial. You might even develop a nice, grown-up friendship with your child—something that usually requires not only time but a little physical distance between you.

infallible guide to life for your adolescent (because you're still figuring out a few things yourself), congratulations! Acknowledging this fact is the beginning of parental wisdom. You can be certain that God knew your shortcomings before entrusting you with a child, and you would be wise to seek His counsel on a regular basis.

As you think about these concepts, you may experience misgivings or even remorse. You probably haven't cherished every moment with your teenager (few parents do), and you may have felt burdened with—or even resentful of—the demands of parenting. Perhaps your children are already in the midst of stormy adolescence or are grown and gone, and you are painfully aware that you have not exactly been the world's best cheerleader, teacher, or coach. But it is never too late to make course corrections—and amends—as a parent. Even if your children are already grown and living as independent adults, what you have learned (sometimes the hard way) can still benefit *their* children. What ultimately matters is that you ask for forgiveness where it is needed and then move forward, providing input and support that is appropriate for their current stage of life.

Chapter 5 ("Encouraging Spiritual Growth and Building Character") presented a number of specific goals to pursue in encouraging spiritual maturity and character development in an adolescent. The following pages will focus on four other key areas of your child's life: driving, handling finances, choosing a vocation, and preparing for marriage.

The Teenage Driver

Driving is one of the most momentous steps that a teenager takes toward personal independence. Being able to drive provides mobility, the gratification of not having to rely on parents or friends for a ride, and a definite sense of prestige (even if the vehicle involved is the family "fixer-upper"). Like every increase in freedom, however, driving is fraught with risk. Because of the safety issues involved with driving, new drivers and their parents should prepare for this next phase of life with the utmost diligence.

Parental apprehension about teen driving is not unfounded. (The fact that automobile insurance rates are greatly increased for adolescent drivers—especially for males—is also no accident, so to speak.) Motor-vehicle accidents are the leading cause of death in young people ages fifteen through twenty, killing more than five thousand youths in America each year.[28] Even though this age group comprises less than 7 percent of the driving population, it accounts for 14 percent of vehicle-related fatalities.[29] Over the past decade, over sixty-eight thousand teens have died in car crashes.[30]

Inexperience is a major risk factor for teens involved in accidents. Driving is, after all, an amazingly complex task. New drivers must learn to control their vehicle and its speed, while at the same time detecting and responding to hazardous driving conditions and emergency situations. Teens are learning to operate a large and dangerous piece of equipment at a time when their judgment and decision-making ability may not yet be fully developed.

Another factor contributing to teen accidents is a tendency to engage in risky behaviors. Each year, speeding—a major temptation for the teenage driver—is a factor in about 30 percent of all traffic fatalities.[31] Alcohol is involved in one third of all traffic deaths for young people aged fifteen through nineteen.[32] One survey found that at least 13 percent of high school students reported driving after drinking alcohol, and more than 33 percent of teens had ridden with a driver who had been drinking.[33] Having a passenger in the car increases a sixteen-year-old driver's chance of being killed by 39 percent; the likelihood of a fatal accident is 86 percent greater if there are two passengers in the car and 282 percent higher if three or more passengers are in the vehicle.[34] Sixteen percent of high school students report that they never or hardly ever use a safety belt when riding in a car driven by someone else.[35] All of these behaviors increase the odds of a teenager being involved—and injured or killed—in an automobile accident.

After reading such information some parents may vow not to let their children sit behind the wheel of a car until they are in their twenties and living on their own. Aside from being unrealistic, such a mind-set is counterproductive and insulting to teens who really want to learn to drive safely. A more constructive outlook views the adolescent years as a time when adults can teach safe driving habits and influence a young driver's behaviors for life, imparting skills and knowledge that will perhaps save lives many years in the future. Becoming an expert driver requires years of experience, and being able to oversee the first few years of that experience is a wonderful, though at times ulcer-generating, privilege.

As a parent you can pass on a wealth of driving wisdom in many ways. First, be patient with your teen. His learning to drive may be nerve-racking for you, but it's much more so for him! Give all instructions calmly and clearly. Second, as with other practices that they want children to adopt, moms and dads must model safe driving habits. For better or worse, teenagers will imitate their parents. Also, parents should not only learn the traffic laws for their state but also be prepared to enforce additional limits and expectations based on their adolescent's attitude and skill.

Realizing that driver's education courses by themselves are not a complete preparation for novice motorists, a number of states have instituted graduated driver licensing for teens. Such a system is designed to phase teens into full driving privileges by allowing them to mature and develop their driving skills in steps. Each state's system is different, but the typical graduated licensing model involves three stages. Beginners must remain in the first two stages for a minimum amount of time, demonstrating a mastery of basic skills under less challenging driving conditions. (For example, the stage-one teenage driver might not be allowed to drive after dark, while in stage two he might drive at night, but only with adult supervision.) Even if your state has not yet enacted graduated licensing, you may wish to grant your teen's driving privileges in a stepwise manner that allows him to acquire the experience he needs while reducing some of the risks. For example, you might require your teen driver to be accompanied by a parent or other responsible licensed adult driver at all times for a set period of time. You may also wish to set specific rules to reduce his chances of being involved in an accident, such as limiting the number of passengers he may have in the car or restricting driving to daylight hours.

Always require your teen to buckle up before the engine is started, whether driving or riding. (This is an area where your example speaks louder than your words.) Your adolescent should never drive if he is drowsy. Additionally, while there are many good reasons for him to abstain from alcohol and drugs, don't fail to drive home the message that drinking kills thousands of people every year—many of them teens. Not only should your teenager never drink and drive, but he also should never get into a car if the driver has been drinking. And no matter how strongly you might feel about the use of alcohol, let your adolescent know that he can *always* call you for a ride in order to avoid being in a car with an intoxicated driver—whether himself or someone else.

Unfortunately, no matter how calmly and rationally you explain the conditions you are placing on your teen, he may see these restrictions as unreasonable. If he protests your limitations, stand your ground. And if you see unsafe driving patterns or habits that your adolescent refuses to correct, don't let him have the keys. Your first priority is not to win a popularity contest. It's to keep him (and others on the road) alive and well while he learns to operate an automobile safely and skillfully.

Financial Responsibility

Teaching adolescents how to manage money can be one of the greatest benefits parents provide for them before they leave home. Before you attempt to teach your teenager about money, however, determine how you are doing with your own finances. Do you set goals? Are you out of debt? Do you have long- and short-term savings? Have you begun investing in a college-education fund or your retirement? If so, you're definitely making wise decisions.

On the other hand, do you live from paycheck to paycheck? Do you have trouble keeping track of how much money is in your checking account? Is there always "too much month at the end of the money"? Are you an impulse buyer? Do you depend on your credit cards to make ends meet? If this is the case, before you start teaching your teenager how to manage money, you need to get your spending habits in order.

Whether you are a financial wizard or still struggling to balance your checkbook, the most important lesson your adolescent needs to learn about money is that *God owns it all.* God is the creator and ultimate owner of every resource, and He has entrusted you to be a wise steward of whatever He has loaned to you.

It is important to realize that children begin shaping their views about money at an early age. Unfortunately, many families deal with this important topic haphazardly, offering their children little specific guidance while presuming that they can learn the nuts and bolts of money management when they're older. But if you wait until your kids are ready to leave the nest before you begin to broach this subject, they may enter adulthood at a serious disadvantage when it comes to handling their finances wisely.

As a starting point, formulate coherent policies within your family for the following three issues. Keep in mind that there are several possible approaches and reasonable viewpoints for each issue.

Unpaid responsibilities. Each child over age five (some would say as young as three or four) should have certain jobs at home to do regularly without any specific pay. These might involve tasks related to his own possessions (e.g., cleaning up his room or helping with his laundry) as well as chores done for the good of the entire family (setting the table or feeding the dog). Obviously, the duration and complexity of the assignments should be appropriate for his age and capabilities, but well before adolescence arrives he should learn that it is usual and customary for everyone in the family to pitch in and work for the common good without expecting a reward every time.

Allowances. Parents and financial advisors alike hold all sorts of divergent opinions about this subject. Some feel that giving a child a

---

When You Pay Your Adolescent for Work

- *Be clear about what you want done, and what you are offering.* Also, be sure to let your teenager know if there is a time frame involved ("I need this done by four o'clock").
- *Make sure that your teen is capable of accomplishing the task.* If you tend to be a perfectionist, be careful that the standards you set for the work you want done aren't beyond his reach. On the other hand, don't make the mistake of lowering your expectations if he is in fact capable of performing the task.
- *When possible, give your child some "on-the-job training."* Your teenager may be more open to learn how to use tools properly, for example, if the job helps earn money to buy something she wants.

weekly allowance teaches her to expect a "free lunch," while others see it as part of a parent's appropriate expression of provision for her. (Parents normally don't charge their grade-school children monthly rent or leave a food bill in their lunch box, for example, yet no one sees this as contributing to an expectation of free room and board throughout life.)

If you choose to give a weekly or monthly allowance, you should state clearly any guidelines you might have for the money you provide. For example, is the entire amount meant to be "mad money" for fun activities, or do you want your child to allocate amounts for certain expenses (such as school lunches), savings, and giving? As your child enters adolescence, you would be wise to give her the responsibility of managing funds designated for expenses such as clothing.

Opportunities to earn money. Both you and your adolescent will benefit if he seeks opportunities to earn extra money in exchange for the satisfactory completion of a specific task (see sidebar below).

In addition to setting basic policies about money and work, consider implementing the following ideas regarding money management as you prepare him to earn a living and eventually disconnect from your financial supply line:

Teach adolescents to share their resources. As you provide money for your teenagers, and as they begin to earn more on their own,

continued

- *Pay only for jobs that are completed.* Remind your adolescents that *you* as a parent aren't paid a salary unless you go to work every day, work all day, and perform your duties completely.
- *Pay for quality work.* If your teenager didn't do his best, you're only penalizing him by paying for laziness. Teach him to strive to do a job right the first time.
- *Pay fairly within your budget, but don't overpay merely because you can afford it.* Even if you have a bountiful income, it doesn't make sense to pay your teenager fifty dollars for taking out the trash or doing the dishes. This only sets unrealistic expectations for the future. Pay according to the job description.
- *Reward extra effort.* If your adolescent goes out of her way to do an outstanding job, reward her both emotionally and financially.

teach them the rewards of giving to others. Talk to them about the importance of giving back to God (who, don't forget, owns everything) by contributing regularly to church and other ministries. Encourage them by your own example.

Teach adolescents to save. It's never too early to teach your child to save for the future, and during the preteen years she can begin to learn "the magic of compounding"—how money accumulates over time when left in an account that earns interest.

Teach your teenager the principles of budgeting.
This will be important whether his future income is modest or abundant. Beginning at sixteen or seventeen, your adolescent should be allowed to make most of his own financial decisions. You may choose to provide him with a monthly allowance to be budgeted among several items such as clothing, toiletries, and other personal supplies you used to buy. Help him set up a budget, but he must also be given the freedom to fail—and in the process learn valuable lessons. For example, if he blows his entire clothing budget in the first six months of the year, he will have to forgo desirable purchases later on. Allocating cash between basic necessities, entertainment, savings, and giving to church and other worthy causes is a concept most teens do not understand without some guidance. But if you teach your child budgeting principles now, he'll benefit for a lifetime.

Your adolescent should be given the opportunity to use and maintain her own checking account under your supervision. It is vitally important that you teach an older teenager how to balance a checkbook monthly. Many parents obtain a credit card (with a very modest spending limit) for an older child—perhaps in the senior year of high school—to train her to use it properly. Two warnings she must receive: (1) Never buy anything with a card that she would not have purchased with cash, and (2) pay off the total amount on the credit card each month without fail.

Teach your teenager to manage personal expenses wisely. Your adolescent, whether living at home or away at college, should begin to deal with the amazing ability of "miscellaneous expenses" to derail his budget. Teach him to use self-control in his spending through your example. Show him where to shop and help him learn to seek the best values for his limited supply of dollars.

Career Preparation

Children begin thinking about "what I want to be when I grow up" early in life, as they play with their friends and watch their parent(s) go off to work every day. An ideal time to start career preparation is during the preteen years. Take the time to expose your children to a variety of occupations. If your daughter is interested in medicine, for example, let her spend time talking to her physician about the demands and rewards of this profession. The same approach can be taken for virtually any type of career that might interest your child.

Guiding and equipping your adolescent with skills to be gainfully employed is a major responsibility, one that must begin before he leaves home. The following are some ideas that might help in this process.

Equip your adolescent to discover his or her strengths and weaknesses.
- Expose him to job opportunities that fit his personality.
- Don't project your expectations on your child. Not all childen follow in their parents' footsteps. If you're an accountant but your child has difficulty with math, don't push her into a career that would make her miserable. If you're an attorney but your son wants to be an artist, don't try to make him fit his artistic "square peg" temperament into the "round hole" demands of a legal career.
- Help your child discover her natural, God-given talents. During your child's formative years, she will excel in some areas and fail at others. Help her develop her strengths and identify possible career opportunities that might match them.

Equip your adolescent to think of vocation and career in spiritual terms.
- He is uniquely designed by God (Psalm 139:13-14).

- She has been given specific talents for a purpose (Romans 12:6-8).
- He must develop his God-given talents and strive for excellence (Proverbs 22:29).
- Work is a stage for her higher calling (Matthew 5:16).

Equip your adolescent to obtain guidance in the pursuit of education, training, and possible career fields.

You should be able to get some help in this area from the local school's professional guidance counselor.

- Identify your adolescent's likes and dislikes and expose him to fields he is interested in.
- Discover natural talents before college or vocational training. Work with your child (for example, by becoming involved with her in science class or in arts and crafts). Before spending thousands of dollars on college or vocational training, help your child find the path on which she is most likely to excel.
- Teach your child to pray for God's guidance and seek what He would have him do for a career.

Finally, consider seeking career-testing services that may help your older adolescent determine what career options fit her personality. These tests often help young adults hone in on their special talents, if they have not already done so, and they can also confirm whether a certain career choice is a logical path. Adolescents who are somewhat aimless might find that the test results point them in one or more specific directions. Others who are endowed with a number of definite interests might benefit from tests that help them focus on their areas of greatest strength. This might spare at least some from changing majors one or more times during college, which could prove both expensive and time-consuming.

Preparation for Marriage

One of your most important goals when passing the baton to your adolescent is to prepare him or her for marriage. If you have a strong and vibrant marriage, it is important to share the principles upon which you have built and maintained this relationship. But if your marriage is less than ideal or you have experienced a divorce, lessons you have learned the hard way can still benefit your teens, assuming that you are willing to be candid and transparent about your experience.

At a time when approximately 50 percent of marriages end in divorce and only 10 to 20 percent of the remaining marriages (5 to 10 percent of the total) are characterized by true satisfaction, parents face a formidable job educating their adolescents about selecting a husband or a wife for life. Recent studies show that partners with similar interests have a better chance of achieving a fulfilling marriage. Because we are a mobile society, young adults who have been reared in stable and loving homes often select partners with different backgrounds, customs, goals, interests, and beliefs. This does not mean that they cannot succeed in marriage, but in such cases both parties must enter the relationship with their eyes open and a willingness to work through their differences.

Early adolescence is a good time to begin discussing characteristics and traits to seek in a future wife or husband. You may want to give your teen a list of twenty or thirty of these qualities and have him rank in order the ones he thinks are the most important. Quite often, teens will discover that their mental image of a "dream partner"—very often a fantasy derived from movies and television shows—does not match with this ranking. It might be helpful to have your adolescent save this list (or make a copy) and review it annually.

Also early in adolescence—perhaps on a special birthday such as the thirteenth—encourage your child to begin praying for a future spouse. As parents, you should be doing the same if you haven't started already. Toward the end of high school, however, give your adolescent some books that explore the process of selecting a partner and building a strong marriage. One excellent book is Dr. James Dobson's *Love for a Lifetime.* Another is *Finding the Love of Your Life,* by psychologist Dr. Neil Warren, which lists the following ten principles of mate selection, along with seven deadly mate-selection errors:

Principle #1: Eliminate the seven deadly mate-selection errors.

1. Don't get married too quickly. Longer courtships produce consistently healthier marriages.
2. Don't get married too young. Wait to get married until you know yourself well, and until you know well the kind of person with whom you can be happy. This usually means that first marriages will not begin until the mid to late 20s.
3. Don't be too eager to get married, and don't let anyone else who is overly eager push you into marriage. Make sure your mind is clear and settled.
4. Don't try to please someone else with your choice. You are the one who will profit or suffer from your choice for a lifetime.
5. Don't marry someone until you know him or her in a lot of different ways. You can make a far more accurate prediction about how much you will enjoy being married to a person if your experience is broad.
6. Don't get married with unrealistic expectations. Marriage isn't a panacea; it requires an incredible amount of hard work. Don't allow yourself to expect too much from your marriage.
7. Don't marry anyone who has a personality or behavioral problem that you're not willing to live with forever. These problems don't vanish; in fact, they often get worse. "Miracle cures" are far easier to come by before you are married. If the problem can be cured, make sure it is cured before you are married.

Principle #2: Develop a high degree of conscious clarity about the person you wish to marry, and filter this image through your conscious mind until you are completely comfortable with it.

Principle #3: Make sure the person you marry is very similar to you.

Principle #4: Get married only if both you and the person you want to marry are emotionally healthy.

Principle #5: Make sure you are passionately attracted to the person you want to marry, but wait until you are married to express the full intensity of your passion.

Principle #6: Decide to get married only after you have experienced a deeper, more stable kind of love. Passion may fade, but this kind of deeper love endures.

Principle #7: Develop mastery in the area of verbal intimacy. The love between two people who know how to be intimate with each other will grow dramatically.

Principle #8: Learn how to resolve differences before you get married. This will keep the road to love free and clear.

Principle #9: Get married only when you are ready to be absolutely committed to your partner—no matter what—for a lifetime.

Principle #10: If your parents, relatives, and close friends support your contemplated marriage, celebrate with them! If they don't, listen carefully to them before you make your final decision.

Encourage your adolescent or young adult to obtain counseling before an official engagement is announced, even if he is certain that he has found the "love of his life." Offer to pay for counseling if it is not furnished by the church. Many inventories are available to help counselors uncover any potential problem areas. The *Prepare* inventory, for example, identifies both strengths and weaknesses of each potential spouse and can predict which marriages are likely to succeed and which are at higher risk for divorce.

Inform your child that, even when married, he or she will need to work on this relationship for a lifetime. If you have grown children who are married, volunteer to pay for them to attend a marriage enrichment weekend (such as the Family Life Conference 1-800-FL-TODAY). You might even offer to baby-sit their children, if needed. (By the way, you might consider attending such a conference yourself.)

Finally, *warn your child once more about becoming sexually involved before marriage.* Among other things, premarital sex might lead him to marry the wrong person and rob him of a satisfying lifelong marriage. Children of divorce might be tempted to cohabit prior to marriage in hopes of avoiding their parents' mistakes. But statistics indicate that cohabitors have an even greater chance of divorce (approaching 75 percent).

The most important thing you can do for your children to help them develop a healthy concept of marriage is to *allow them to see you loving, cherishing, and respecting your partner.* If you are not married, allow your children to spend time with one or more families in which a nurturing, respectful marital relationship is modeled.

When It's Time to Let Go

In reality, you have been slowly releasing your child since birth, and, if he or she marries in the future, you will once again have to release your now-grown child—this time to become one flesh with a spouse. But whatever the circumstances might be, there will come a time when you must pass the baton to your child. You, of course, will be a parent for life, but your role must change to that of a coach and friend, encouraging your grown child's progress—and perhaps, later on, watching your grandchildren take the baton to begin their lap.

But ready or not, shortly after your son or daughter graduates from high school, your formal job of parenting should be completed, and he or she will need to be released. *The fact that you are doing so should be specifically conveyed to your grown child,* either verbally or in writing or perhaps both. The advantage of a letter is that it allows you time to organize your thoughts, it conveys a sense of permanence, and it allows your young adult to reread this important letter in the future.

Whether expressed in spoken or written words, your message of release may be communicated to a young adult who has given you a great deal more joy than grief and about whose future you feel confident. Or you may have to express sorrow and honest concern about your grown child's future health, safety, and financial stability. (Such a letter might have been written by the father of the Prodigal Son as the son was leaving home.) Regardless of the circumstances, however, the release must be given.

The specific wording of this conversation and/or letter will be different for each parent, but (among other things) it should communicate the following:

- Your job is done.
- You acknowledge that you have not been a perfect parent.
- You hope and pray that she will forgive you for your failings.
- You will continue to pray for her.
- If one day God allows her to marry and have children of her own, you hope that she will build on the positive traits of her parents and grandparents, avoid your mistakes, and improve in areas where you were weak.
- Whatever the future holds for her, you will always love her.
- You hope that she will hold fast to, and teach to her own children, the values that you care about.
- She should hold fast to her faith or strongly consider beginning her relationship with God if she has not done so already.

A Final Thought: Looking Ahead

As you invest your time and energy into shaping the life of your adolescent, keep the ultimate goal, the prize at the end of this marathon called parenting, firmly in mind. Picture the baby you introduced to the world not too many years ago living as a responsible, self-sufficient, productive, and morally integrated adult. Imagine walking and talking together, swapping ideas and insights over a cup of coffee, enjoying a concert or a film (perhaps with your child paying for your ticket!), fighting back tears as he or she stands at the wedding altar, and ultimately, watching your child start a family.

In the midst of raging hormones and overdue homework assignments, this may seem like an impossible fantasy. But your child will indeed reach adulthood, and we anticipate that, through all of the sweat, tears, and laughter, you will emerge as friends and allies.

Few rewards in your life will be more satisfying.

Book Notes

1. A detailed review of this topic as it applies to all age-groups may be found in the *Focus on the Family Complete Book of Baby and Child Care* (Wheaton, Ill.: Tyndale House Publishers, Inc., 1997).
2. The use of disciplinary spanking is controversial within our culture, with some voices claiming that it teaches violence, perpetuates abuse, damages a child's dignity, and doesn't change behavior. But when utilized with appropriate guidelines, spanking can and should be neither abusive nor damaging to a child's physical or emotional well-being. With toddlers and preschoolers, a controlled swat on the behind may be appropriate to bring a confrontation to a timely conclusion. Guidelines for disciplinary spanking are described in detail in the *Focus on the Family Complete Book of Baby and Child Care* (Wheaton, Ill: Tyndale House Publishers, Inc., 1997), 306–308.
3. It should be noted that this number is skewed somewhat by those who marry and divorce more than once.
4. Family Research Council, "Divorce Reform," *The Whole Family Catalogue: 25 Policy Planks for a Pro-Family Future* (1996).
5. J. S. Wallerstein and S. Blakeslee, *Second Chances: Men, Women and Children a Decade after Divorce* (New York: Ticknor and Fields, 1989).
6. J. S. Wallerstein, J. M. Lewis, and S. Blakeslee. *The Unexpected Legacy of Divorce* (New York: Hyperion, 2000).
7. Centers for Disease Control and Prevention, "National and State-Specific Pregnancy Rates among Adolescents—United States, 1995-1997," *Morbidity and Mortality Weekly Report* (14 July 2000), 49.
8. Centers for Disease Control and Prevention, "CDC Surveillance Summaries," *Morbidity and Mortality Weekly Report* (8 December 2000), 49.
9. R. A. Maynard, (ed.). *Kids Having Kids: A Robin Hood Foundation Special Report on the Costs of Adolescent Childbearing* (New York: Robin Hood Foundation, 1996).
10. Ibid.
11. American Social Health Association, *Sexually Transmitted Diseases in America: How Many Cases and at What Cost?* (Menlo Park, Ca: Kaiser Family Foundation, 1998).
12. Centers for Disease Control and Prevention, Division of STD Prevention, "The challenge of STD prevention in the United States" (November 1996). Available at <http://www.cdc.gov>.
13. Centers for Disease Control and Prevention, "Sexually transmitted disease surveillance 1996."

14. For example, a study published in the *New England Journal of Medicine* in 1997 estimates that one in five Americans twelve years of age and over are infected with genital herpes. (D. Fleming et. al., "Herpes simplex virus type 2 in the United States, 1976-1994," *New England Journal of Medicine,* 337, no. 16 (October 1997) 1105–1111.)

15. The Alan Guttmacher Institute, "Sexually transmitted diseases in the United States," *Facts in Brief* (September 1993).

16. Thomas R. Eng and William T. Butler, *The Hidden Epidemic.*

17. Centers for Disease Control and Prevention, "HIV/AIDS Surveillance Report," 9, no. 2 (December 1997).

18. Substance Abuse and Mental Health Services Administration. Highlights of the 1999 National Household Survey on Drug Abuse. (See <http://www.samhsa.gov/oas/NHSDA/1999/Highlights.htm>).

19. U.S. Department of Health and Human Services, "Preliminary Estimates from the 1995 National Household Survey on Drug Abuse," Advance Report No. 18 (Public Health Service, GPO, August 1996).

20. National Highway Traffic Safety Administration, "1998 Youth Fatal Crash and Alcohol Facts." (See <http://www.nhtsa.dot.gov/people/injury/alcohol/Fatal1998Y/Index.htm>).

21. See American Academy of Pediatrics Web site: <http://www.aap.org> (2000).

22. L. D. Johnston, P. M. O'Malley, and J. G. Bachman. "The monitoring of the future national results on adolescent drug use: Overview of key findings, 1999." (NIH Publication No. 00-4690, 2000).

23. See American Academy of Pediatrics Web site: <http://www.aap.org> (2000).

24. L. D. Johnston et al., "The monitoring of the future national results on adolescent drug use."

25. Paul Meier, M.D., *Happiness Is a Choice for Teens* (Nashville: Thomas Nelson, 1997), 68.

26. While the term *ideal weight* is commonly used in many charts and other resources, it carries some negative baggage. First it implies that there is an exact weight that is "just right" for *everyone* at a given age and height. More important, it implies that anyone who doesn't achieve this standard is "less than ideal," an attitude that can contribute to disordered eating behaviors.

27. Ellyn Satter, *Child of Mine* (Bull Publishing, 1991).

28. National Highway Traffic Safety Administration, Department of Transportation, "Traffic Safety Facts 1998: Young People," HS 808 963.

29. Ibid.

30. National Highway Traffic Safety Administration, Department of Transportation. "Saving Teenage Lives: A Case for Graduated Driver Licensing." (See <http://www.nhtsa.dot.gov/people/injury/newdriver/SaveTeens/Index.html>).

31. National Highway Transportation Safety Administration, Department of Transportation, "Traffic Safety Facts 1997: Speeding." (See <http://www.nhtsa.dot. gov/search97cgi/s97 . . . cgi.exe>).

32. National Highway Transportation Safety Association, "1998 Youth Fatal Crash and Alcohol Facts." (See <http://www.nhtsa.dot.gov/people/injury/alcohol/Fatal1998Y/Index.htm>).
33. Morbidity and Mortality Weekly Report, Centers for Disease Control, "Youth Risk Behavior Surveillance—United States, 1999," 49, no. SS-5 (June 9, 2000).
34. Anita Smith, "Tips for parents on teen driving," *The Youth Connection*, 3, no. 2 (Institute for Youth Development, Mar/Apr 2000).
35. Centers for Disease Control, "Youth Risk Behavior Surveillance."

Sidebar Notes

1. National Sleep Foundation survey, "Sleep in America," 1999. See <http://www.sleepfoundation.org>.
2. A. Wolfson and M. Carskadon, "Sleep schedules and daytime functioning in adolescents," *Child Development,* 69 (1998), 875–887; cited in *Adolescent Sleep Needs and Patterns,* National Sleep Foundation (2000).
3. National Highway Traffic Safety Administration, "Crashes and fatalities related to driver drowsiness/fatigue," *Research Notes* (1994).
4. M. Carskadon et al., "Pubertal changes in daytime sleepiness," *Sleep,* 2 (1980), 453–460; cited in *Adolescent Sleep Needs and Patterns,* National Sleep Foundation (2000).
5. A. Wolfson and M. Carskadon, "Sleep schedules."
6. The Vegetarian Resource Group, "Vegetarian Resource Group conducts Roper poll on eating habits of youths," *Vegetarian Journal,* 11 no. 1 (1995).
7. K. Munoz, S. M. Krebs-Smith, R. Ballard-Barbash et al., "Food intakes of U.S. children and adolescents compared to recommendations," *Pediatrics,* 100 (1997), 323–329.

COMPLETE BOOK OF BABY AND CHILD CARE

This first-rate parenting manual gives guidance from some of today's most respected Christian physicians. Comprehensive in its scope from the early stages of pregnancy throughout adolescence, expert advice is offered enabling parents to create an environment that will meet the mental, physical, emotional, and spiritual needs of their children.

COMPLETE BOOK OF BABY AND CHILD CARE CALENDAR

Taken from the wisdom and sound advice given in the best-selling *Complete Book of Baby and Child Care*, this day-by-day calendar will encourage moms and dads in the challenges they face as parents. Scripture and inspirational quotes accompany practical guidance satisfying the requirements of parenting from prebirth through adolescence.

PARENTS' GUIDE TO THE SPIRITUAL GROWTH OF CHILDREN

Christian parents *want* to help their children grow in the Lord, but often the task seems daunting. Enter the solution—*Parents' Guide to the Spiritual Growth of Children*. Designed to meet the needs of parents new in their faith or reared in a Christian home, this book is a treasure chest of creative tools aiding parents in passing on their faith.

PARENTS' GUIDE TO THE SPIRITUAL MENTORING OF TEENS

No one said parenting teens was easy! But parents wanting to fulfill their God-given role of spiritual mentor to their teen will get a helping hand from this book. Contained within these powerful pages are family-tested tips for parents as they seek to build relationships with teens—relationships that will endure beyond the home and into adulthood, as well as practical helps for maximizing their Christian influence in the final stretch of their teen's years at home.